THE VODKA BIBLE

PAUL
KNORR

ENJOY!

THE VODKA BIBLE

WITHDRAWN

STERLING INNOVATION
An imprint of Sterling Publishing Co., Inc.

New York / London
www.sterlingpublishing.com

STERLING, the Sterling logo, STERLING INNOVATION,
and the Sterling Innovation logo are registered trademarks of
Sterling Publishing Co., Inc.

Library of Congress Cataloging-in-Publication Data Available

2 4 6 8 10 9 7 5 3 1

Published by Sterling Publishing Co., Inc.
387 Park Avenue South, New York, NY 10016

© 2010 by Paul Knorr

Distributed in Canada by Sterling Publishing
c/o Canadian Manda Group, 165 Dufferin Street
Toronto, Ontario, Canada M6K 3H6

Distributed in the United Kingdom by GMC Distribution Services
Castle Place, 166 High Street, Lewes, East Sussex, England BN7 1XU

Distributed in Australia by Capricorn Link (Australia) Pty. Ltd.
P.O. Box 704, Windsor, NSW 2756, Australia

Sterling ISBN 978-1-4027-6951-1

For information about custom editions, special sales, premium and corporate
purchases, please contact Sterling Special Sales Department at 800-805-5489
or specialsales@sterlingpublishing.com.

CONTENTS

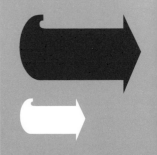

PART 1

"A GLASS FOR FOR THE BEER FOR THE TABL COMPANY!"

UNDERSTANDING VODKA

HE VODKA,
A MUG, AND
:, CHEERFUL

– RUSSIAN TOAST

INTRODUCTION

WHAT IS THE POINT OF A BOOK ABOUT VODKA? TO MOST PEOPLE, VODKA IS JUST THE SPIRIT THAT IS MIXED INTO THEIR MARTINI OR THEIR COSMOPOLITAN. THE MAJORITY OF THOSE WHO DRINK IT DON'T GIVE IT A SECOND THOUGHT; IT'S MEANT TO BE INVISIBLE. IT'S A WAY OF ADDING ALCOHOL TO WHATEVER YOU HAPPEN TO BE MIXING IT WITH. ➤➤ ➤➤ ➤➤ ➤➤ ➤➤ ➤➤ ➤➤ ➤➤

This is a misleading simplification of what vodka truly is and what truly good vodka tastes like. Vodka has a long and complex history. To this day there is still a dispute over whether it was invented in Russia or Poland, with a great amount of national pride at stake either way. Vodka was once the drink of kings, celebrated in the court of Tsar Ivan III. At the same time, it was a drink for the common man and had a profound effect on the society of the time.

The vodka most of us are used to, the Western style of vodka, prides itself on its purity. Our vodka has no smell or taste on its own and is therefore perfect for mixing with anything. If you go closer to vodka's roots in Poland and Russia, you will notice a distinctive flavor and feel to each brand. Polish vodka has a certain sweetness to it. Russian vodka, while less sweet, has more texture.

Vodka is a neutral spirit and can be made from beets or potatoes as easily as from grain. This makes vodka unlike other white spirits that use specific ingredients, such as rum, which is made from sugarcane, or tequila from agave. Vodka is also not aged, which makes it different from spirits like bourbon or whiskey. Because of this, producing great vodka represents the pinnacle of the distiller's art—the distiller has nothing to hide behind. If there were shortcuts taken during the distillation or during the filtration, they would be more clearly exposed in a bad vodka than they would be in a bad gin or a bad rum.

My point with this book is to show both the fun and the serious sides to vodka. Mixed drinks are what made vodka popular in the United States, and they continue to be innovative and exciting. However, even while vodka is typically masked by mixers, it is a drink that can stand on its own and can be appreciated in its own right. Before you add the vermouth or the cranberry juice, take a moment to stop and taste the vodka.

Vodka Production

The production of vodka begins with something—anything—that ferments. In general, vodka can be made from any vegetable matter that can be fermented, including grain, potatoes, beets, molasses, and grapes. The source material is mixed with water and yeast to create what is called a *wash*. The wash is allowed to ferment just as a beer or a wine ferments. Once the fermentation is complete, the wash has an alcohol content of around 15 percent. To make vodka, the alcohol must be distilled.

Distillation is the process of separating out just the alcohol from the fermented mash. Distilling is a process that dates back to at least 2000 BC, when perfume makers used it to concentrate the oils they used. In twelfth-century Europe, medicine was made from distilled alcohol. The technology was imported from the Middle East and India, where it had been known since at least the eighth century AD. Distilled alcohol as a recreational beverage (as opposed to a medicinal one) dates back to about the same time. Distillation relies on the fact that alcohol boils at 172°F (78°C) and water boils at 212°F (100°C). By heating a liquid that contains alcohol just enough, the alcohol will boil but the water will not. If you catch that vapor that is high in alcohol, cool it, and condense it, you have a distilled spirit. This makes it sound much easier than it actually is. Distillation is as much an art as it is a science.

There are two main ways of distilling vodka: with a pot still or a column still. The pot still is by far the oldest distilling method. Specially shaped clay pots have been found in Babylonia and Mesopotamia dating back to 2000 BC and were used in the production of perfume. Modern pot stills can hold several thousand gallons and are made of copper, which resists corrosion by the alcohol steam.

A pot still starts with a large vessel with a long neck pointing to the side at a downward angle. From there the vapors travel to a condenser, typically a hose or pipe bathed in cold water. Here the vapor cools and condenses into a liquid. The liquid, now high in alcohol, can be filtered and distilled or it can be distilled again to raise the alcohol concentration and to help eliminate some of the impurities. Pot stills are considered to be the best way to capture the flavors and character of the spirit being distilled. For vodka, this method is often touted as giving smoothness not found in vodka from column stills. The drawback to the pot still is the lack of control over what is being distilled out of the wash. The beginning of a batch (called the head) can have methanol, fusel oil, and other impurities. The final portion of the batch (called the tail), created as the temperature rises, contains much more water vapor. Usually the head and tail of each batch is discarded and only the middle, or the heart, of the spirit is kept.

A continuous still uses a different and more complex process. The continuous still was patented by an Irish inventor named Aeneas Coffey in 1831 for the distillation of whiskey. Versions of his device are the basis for most modern vodka distilling equipment. As the name implies, a continuous still does not have to work in batches like the pot still but instead runs continuously for long periods of time. A continuous still works by heating the wash in a tall narrow column and condensing it in another column through gradual cooling. The column where the wash is heated is called the analyzer and the column where the vapor is cooled is called the rectifier. In the analyzer, steam is used to heat the wash, which is slowly fed into the still through a pipe at the bottom of the column. The analyzer column is divided by plates that act as a series of small pot stills, one feeding into the next. The hot steam vaporizes the liquids in the wash and the vapors exit through a pipe at the top of the column. The solids and condensed steam drain out the bottom. The vapors then enter the bottom of the rectifier column. Inside this column is the pipe of cold wash that is being fed to the analyzer. As the vapor hits the cold pipe, it condenses, heating the wash and at the same time separating out the various parts of the vapor. The condensed vapor is allowed to drain out the bottom through perforated plates. Because the vapor is being cooled slowly from the bottom up, different compounds will condense at different levels in the column. By placing a catch plate, called the spirit plate, at just the right height in the rectifier column, the alcohol can be caught just as it condenses. This plate collects the alcohol so it can be siphoned off to be distilled again in a separate still. This process can be repeated as many times as the vodka distiller wants. The two major benefits of the continuous still are an increase in efficiency and an increase in the purity of the resulting spirit. Energy is saved by using the cold wash to condense the vapors. Also, by removing the unwanted impurities at the lower levels of the column, a cleaner, more pure alcohol is produced.

After the distillation is complete, the alcohol needs to be filtered to remove the impurities. This is a tricky step in the production of vodka. After distillation, even with the continuous still, there are chemicals in the alcohol called congeners. Congener is a catchall term for the by-products of fermentation and distillation. Congeners account for the flavor, smell, and color of the distilled spirit. For vodka, the goal is usually to filter out as many of the congeners as possible, including amyl alcohol, which smells like nail polish remover, and fusel oil, a thick greasy substance that is actually desirable in very small quantities because it improves the smoothness. Acetaldehyde, a cause of hangovers, is also removed as much as possible. Unfortunately, it cannot be removed completely through distillation and is a primary factor in separating the good vodkas from the bad. But don't think that the absence of acetaldehyde will prevent a hangover altogether— acetaldehyde is also produced when alcohol is broken down in the liver. Drinking too much too quickly will lead to a hangover-inducing buildup in the body.

Once the vodka has been distilled, it is at about 190 proof or 95 percent alcohol and 5 percent water. Before it is filtered, bottled, and sold, it needs to be brought down to around 80 proof or 40 percent alcohol and 60 percent water. More than half of that very expensive top-shelf vodka is water. Some brands of vodka use distilled water, but that tends to give the vodka a flat taste. Water that has a high mineral content can make the vodka appear cloudy or make it turn slightly yellow over time. The water that is added to the vodka is normally filtered and demineralized before being blended into the distilled alcohol sent on to be filtered.

There are many ways that vodka can be filtered using traditional methods such as river sand, peat, and cloth. The most common and the most effective filtration method is with activated charcoal, hardwood charcoal that has been heated to more than 1000°F, making it porous. Activated charcoal looks like a sponge under a microscope. The charcoal is arranged in a column with larger pebble-size pieces toward the bottom and the finer powder at the top. The vodka is then pumped in from the bottom and removed at the top using pressure to force it through the charcoal. It can be fed again into another column (or two or three) to be filtered even more. Smirnoff vodka is charcoal filtered under pressure for up to eight hours using seven tons of hardwood charcoal.

Styles of Vodka

Whether vodka originated in Poland or Russia is to this day an intense debate that will not be settled in these pages. However, there are distinct differences between the vodkas produced in Poland and those produced in Russia. Both the Polish and Russian vodkas are different from those produced in Western Europe and North America. Those who feel that vodkas are all the same should taste a sample of each of these styles side by side with no mixers and at room temperature. While they may all look the same, there are clear differences that emerge as they are compared. What accounts for the differences? As matters of national pride and local tastes, the Polish and Russian vodkas each developed a certain character that made them distinct from one another. A native Russian can tell by the taste alone if a vodka is not Russian. He or she would be able to tell if it was Polish, Scandinavian, or American. Not that this Russian would complain—it is vodka, after all.

In the Western style, which predominates in the rest of the world, the focus is on purity and creating a clean, crisp taste. The differences among the various Western-style vodkas will be expressed in the quality of the distillation and the filtration.

RUSSIAN VODKA

Russia's experience with vodka goes back more than four hundred years. The Russians have documented evidence that vodka was being distilled in a monastery in Moscow in the fifteenth century. Quintessentially Russian vodka such as Stolichnaya or Jewel of Russia will have a slightly sweet but not cloying taste and be exceptionally smooth. Almost all of the best Russian vodkas are distilled from wheat or rye. This tends to give them a slightly fruity taste and in some cases the sweetness of the rye can be clearly pronounced. Russian vodkas also tend to have more fusel oil in them which gives them a thicker taste. Bad Russian vodka can be almost greasy in the mouth, seeming more like vodka-flavored motor oil.

POLISH VODKA

Poland's history with vodka is just as long as Russia's. Poland also has the advantage of not having the gaps in production that Russia has had due to prohibition laws. Traditional Polish vodka is made mostly from rye, but there is a significant amount that is made from potatoes and sugar beet molasses. Good Polish vodka such as Potocki (distilled from rye) or Chopin (from potatoes) has a sweet, silky taste. The vodka made from rye tends to have a floral or fruity flavor whenever the character of the rye is allowed to express itself. Those made from potatoes tend to have a more pronounced alcohol taste or more of a burn to them. Many of the Polish vodkas are only minimally filtered, allowing the character of the distillate to come through.

WESTERN VODKA

The Western style is what most of us in the United States are familiar with. Western vodka prizes a neutral flavor and smell with little or no discernible taste other than the alcohol burn. A Western vodka can be distilled from just about anything, including corn, potatoes, molasses, wheat, rye, and grapes. Because of the more advanced distillation and filtration process that Western-style vodka goes through, it tends to not express the source material as much as Polish or Russian vodka would. That is not to say that Western vodkas have no character at all. There are many brands such as Tito's Handmade, L v, Finlandia, and Absolut that are consistently on "best of" lists. Līv (rhymes with five and short for Long Island Vodka) is close to my heart since it's made in Long Island, New York, less than 50 miles from where I live. Līv is made from potatoes that are grown locally and is distilled locally in a pot still. Many of the Western-style vodkas are not distilled by the same company that bottles them. In fact, more than 90 percent of the vodka produced in the United States is distilled by one of four bulk distillers. It is then shipped in tanker trucks or by rail to the manufacturer who then rectifies, or distills, it again for increased purity, dilutes it with water to the right proof, and then filters it with their own process. Brands that perform their own initial distillation like Līv or Tito's are an exception in the American market. In some other countries like Finland, Germany, and Sweden, the government owns the distilling process, providing the raw materials to private companies who then do additional rectification and filtering before bottling.

Flavored Vodkas

To American vodka drinkers, the trend toward flavored vodkas might seem like a new thing. That couldn't be further from the truth. Flavored vodka is as old as vodka itself, older even than the word *vodka*. Vodka started out as a medicinal drink that was infused with herbs, berries, and barks thought to have healing properties. The alcohol in the vodka helped to leech out the beneficial attributes of these plants to make a kind of alcoholic tea. Later, as vodka began to be a recreational drink rather than a medicine, various flavors were used to mask what was at the time a rather crude distillation process.

Poland and Russia have a long tradition of flavored vodkas. Originally, the only way to create flavored vodka was to create what is called an infusion. Creating an infusion is simple: combine vodka and your flavorings in a sealed container and let them sit in a cool dark place for a few days (or a few months). In vodka's early days, the local monastery, manor, or tavern would each have its own still for making vodka. For certain important guests there would be a special flavored vodka made right there using the best local ingredients, such as fresh fruit and berries and various herbs, spices, and secret ingredients. The secret recipes would be passed down from generation to generation. These recipes gave the vodka a complex and hopefully memorable taste that the visitor would tell others about.

That is not how today's flavored vodkas are produced. Today, flavored vodkas are produced on an industrial scale. There are many drawbacks to the use of natural ingredients in flavoring vodka. Fresh fruit contains things like pectin, oils, and acids that will make the vodka cloudy or will discolor it, turning the vodka brown over time. To combat this, most large-scale distillers resort to using essential oils and flavor concentrates when creating their formulas. Depending on the flavors that are used, some come across as seeming artificial or harsh while others can give a very nice natural flavor.

There are commercial distillers who do actually infuse their vodka with fresh fruit. For example, Skyy has recently come out with a line called Skyy Infusions, which is flavored with actual fruit. The process is proprietary and Skyy would not reveal just how much actual fruit is used, but the result is quite tasty. The label makes the claim "all natural" and we all know that means it must be good, right? The Skyy brand of vodka is the eighth best-selling spirit brand in the United States, selling millions of cases of vodka every year. There are other smaller craft distilleries that are also producing excellent-flavored vodka. For example, the Charbay distillery in California produces one of the only lines of vodka to use organically grown fruit. They use it to make Meyer lemon, blood orange, and pomegranate flavored vodkas all from certified organic fruit.

As flavored vodka continues to rise in popularity and in sales figures, the race is on to find the next big flavor. For a short period only a few years ago, the flavor of the moment was pomegranate. Now manufacturers are looking for more unique flavor profiles. The Charbay distillery that uses organically grown fruit also produces green tea–flavored vodka. Zubrowka Bison Grass vodka, a Polish potato vodka, is bottled with a blade of bison grass. Zubrowka is not exactly "cutting edge" since the vodka has been produced that way for more than three hundred years. Legend has it that the bison grass in eastern Poland is an aphrodisiac. Some other less common flavors include hemp seed, cactus, and the legendary bacon-flavored vodka. In a return to a centuries-old tradition, some establishments are creating their own vodka infusions and displaying them proudly behind the bar. They not only make an attractive display, they also provide the bartender with some exciting new flavors to offer.

HOW TO MAKE FLAVORED VODKA AT HOME

Making a vodka infusion at home is very simple. In a nutshell, you put some "stuff" in a jar, cover it with vodka, and let it sit. What exactly the "stuff" is will be up to you. Some easy flavors to start with are peach, lemon, and orange. These tend to make a very nice tasting infusion and also tend to keep their color longer. You can also experiment with more interesting flavors like jalapeño peppers or vanilla beans.

Add the fruit or other ingredients to a jar and cover with good quality vodka. You should make sure that the ingredients are completely covered, because any that are exposed to the air might turn brown and could start to rot, ruining the entire batch.

Make sure that the jar you are using is glass with no metal parts that will touch the vodka (a metal closure on the outside is okay). The metal might be corroded by the vodka or by the acidity in the fruit. Also make sure that the container is clean and large enough for the bottle of vodka and the other ingredients to allow for the flavorings to be completely covered by the vodka.

The alcohol in the vodka will preserve the fruit, but if you notice that your concoction is starting to turn brown or has an off smell, it should be discarded.

Vodka Drinking Traditions

With such a long history, it is little wonder that the countries that consume the most vodka, Russia and Poland, have their own traditions regarding the "proper" way to drink it. The foremost among these is to drink a *zakuvski*, which is Russian for something like "with hors d'oeuvres." This is probably the most sensible of the vodka-drinking guidelines. Drink your vodka in small amounts, frequently and with lots of food. Another tradition is to make a toast with each round of drinks. This has become a very popular tradition in other countries as well. Poland and Russia also have the tradition of drinking each glass *do dna* (Polish for "to the bottom"). Vodka is not to be sipped but to be knocked back and chased with a bite of *zakuvski* while your glass is being refilled.

Finally, the main tradition as far as Russians and Poles are concerned is, "Often, much, and for long." In other words, drink vodka often, drink a lot of it, and drink it over a long period of time, perhaps all night and into the next morning, if necessary.

HISTORY OF VODKA

1

RUSSIA

VS

POLAND

  CHEERS!

THE DEBATE BETWEEN POLAND AND RUSSIA AS TO WHO INVENTED VODKA HAS BEEN ONGOING FOR MANY YEARS. IT CAME TO A HEAD IN 1977 WHEN POLAND SUED RUSSIA IN THE WORLD TRADE COURT CLAIMING THAT VODKA WAS KNOWN WITHIN THE BORDERS OF WHAT IS NOW POLAND BEFORE IT WAS KNOWN WITHIN WHAT IS NOW RUSSIA. THE COURT DECLINED TO HEAR THE CASE AND THE ISSUE IS STILL FESTERING TO THIS DAY.

Who Invented Vodka?

The first written Polish reference to vodka comes from Polish literature that dates from 1405, but the year has not been confirmed. Russia has several confirmed documents that show that vodka was being distilled at a monastery within Moscow in 1440. The Polish potato vodka Zubrowka, which includes a blade of bison grass in each bottle, has been distilled since the 1500s. They claim that Polish nobility was adding bison grass to their vodka as early as the 1200s because of the grass's supposed aphrodisiacal qualities.

Other accounts of vodka in both Russia and Poland go back even further, with references to "bread wine" and *aqua vitae* (Latin for "water of life") dating to 950 AD. The answer to whether vodka is native to Poland or Russia may never be resolved. What everyone seems to agree on is that vodka as we know it today started in the general region where Poland, Russia, Lithuania, Belarus, and Ukraine all come together. It also began at a time when the exact boundaries between countries were not as clear as they are today.

RUSSIA

Early references to vodka refer to it as "bread wine" or "burnt wine." The *bread wine* label referred to the process of fermenting grain. *Burnt wine* is a reference to the distillation process. The name vodka doesn't appear until the 1600s. Vodka is a diminutive of *voda* or "water" in Russian. So, *vodka* roughly translates as "little water."

The technology of distillation was known in southern and western Europe as early as the 1100s and in the Middle East, China, and India long before that. The process of distillation was introduced to the region by foreign visitors, either traveling merchants or more likely by clergy and monks. The earliest documented distilleries were in monasteries.

Around the late 1400s, at the same time that monasteries were experimenting with distillation, Russian farmers were experimenting with seasonal crop rotation. The dramatic increase in crop yields led to a large grain surplus. For the first time, instead of worrying if there was enough grain to feed everyone, the Russian people could now think of ways to put the extra grain to other uses. When these two events combined, there was an explosion in the amount of vodka produced and in the amount of per capita consumption. In fact, one of the pieces of evidence used to help support the claim that vodka was invented in Russia is the obvious damage it did to society then. Chronicles from the time show villagers swinging between abstinence and wild drinking bouts that could last for days during festivals. It was around this time, in 1505, that Russia started exporting vodka to Sweden. About a century later, Polish vodka (then called *wodka*) was also being exported.

By the end of the 1400s, in part to combat the rash of drunkenness and in part to raise money through export and taxes, Tsar Ivan III introduced a monopoly on the production of all alcoholic beverages, especially vodka. In 1533, the tsar opened the first *kabak*. At the time, a kabak was the name of an official Russian tavern where vodka could be purchased and consumed. No food was sold at a kabak, which led to drunkenness all over again.

By 1716, owning distilleries had become the exclusive right of the nobility. Those rights were expanded to include taxation by Empress Elizabeth, Peter the Great's daughter, in 1751. The taxes collected on vodka became a chief source of income for the Russian government, accounting for up to 40 percent of the revenue collected. The tax revenues proved hard to resist and the government started to encourage the people to drink more vodka, provided it was Russian vodka. This made vodka the national drink of Russia by the 1860s and in 1863, the vodka production monopoly was repealed. When that happened, hundreds of companies sprang up producing vodka and the price dropped to the point where even some of the poorest citizens could afford to partake in the national drink.

In 1865, scientist Dimitri Mendeleev wrote his dissertation "On the Combinations of Water with Alcohol." College students haven't changed much in the past 150 years. This was, of course, before he went on to invent the periodic table of elements. For his thesis, Mendeleev experimented with different concentrations of alcohol and water and decided that the ideal ratio was 38.2 percent alcohol (or 76.4 proof). This was rounded up to 40 percent to make the calculation of the tax easier. Mendeleev determined that at that concentration the burn of the alcohol does not overpower the other more subtle flavors of the vodka. In 1896, this was made the national standard for vodka and yet another new state monopoly on vodka was created.

The state monopoly this time lasted until the Russian Revolution in 1917. When the Bolsheviks took over, they banned the distillation of vodka and the sale of all alcoholic beverages. Being drunk was considered the opposite of being a good Communist and led to the longest dry period for Russia. Although beer and wine were permitted in 1924 and small amounts of vodka were allowed in 1936, it wasn't until the end of World War II in 1945 that the Russians really tucked into their vodka again. In 1945, each Russian soldier started getting a three-ounce (100 gram) daily ration of vodka. Since by the end of the war almost every Russian male was in the military, vodka drinking once again became a national pastime and a patriotic activity.

The most recent attempt at breaking the state monopoly on vodka production was in June 1992 when President Boris Yeltsin issued the "Decree on the Abolition of the State Monopoly on Vodka." This once again flooded the country with cheap vodka just as it did in 1863. But this time, there was a rash of fake and low-quality vodka that killed several people and made many more sick. Only a year later, in June 1993, the state monopoly was restored.

POLAND

Poland's history with vodka at first follows the same path as its neighbor, Russia. Poland also claims it is the birthplace of vodka but has not completed the extensive research that Russia has. There are references to drinks similar to vodka in Polish literature dating back to the early 1400s, but there is no real evidence of its widespread consumption until King Jan Olbracht gave his people the right to distill and sell it. As usual, along with the right to sell vodka came the right of the nobility to tax it. The first tax decree on Polish vodka was recorded in 1564. During this time, vodka in Poland was known by the name *gorzalka*. Vodka (or *wodka* as it was known) was something different. Wodka was a low-alcohol spirit that was infused with herbs and used as a medicine both to be drunk and also to rub on the skin. By the 1700s, the two terms started to merge.

In the 1500s, vodka production started on a large scale, originating in Krakow but quickly outpaced by Poznan. The city of Poznan boasted forty-nine distilleries in 1580. By this time, Polish vodka was being exported to Austria, Germany, and even into Russia. By the end of the 1500s, Polish vodka was world renowned and competed directly with the Russian brands.

Poland did not have to contend with periods of prohibition as Russia did. From the 1670s, vodka had become a national drink, and drinking vodka had become a national pastime. Between the late 1600s and 1919, the production and consumption of vodka grew consistently. Poland was annexed in 1772 by Russia, Austria, and Prussia, but that did not slow down the vodka production. The largest distillery in Poland was built by Prussian troops in 1823. When Poland regained its independence after World War I in 1919, the Polish government created a monopoly on distillation. The government then controlled the production and sale of all alcoholic beverages. The monopoly lasted until the German invasion in 1939. After the Germans were forced out, the monopoly was broken up into separate distilleries. The distilleries are to this day government owned but are now run as independent companies. These companies have, since the 1990s, started to try to compete in the global market and are releasing premium and super-premium brands.

Vodka in the United States

The United States has a very short history with vodka. Vodka has been distilled in the United States since the 1930s, but it didn't really catch on until a single marketing campaign brought vodka to the attention of the American consumer.

In 1934, shortly after the repeal of prohibition, a man named Rudolph Kunett purchased the rights to sell vodka under the Smirnoff name from Vladimir Smirnoff. Kunett had been a grain supplier to Smirnoff in Russia. After the Bolshevik revolution, both men had fled the country. Kunett set up his distillery in Bethel, Connecticut, where there was a large Russian population. He was ahead of his time because the American consumers, outside of his Russian immigrant neighbors, didn't know what to do with vodka. At its peak, his plant produced less than six thousand cases a year under the Smirnoff brand. In 1939, Kunett sold his company to Heublein, a distributor of wines, spirits, and premixed cocktails, for fourteen thousand dollars and a continued position with the company.

John G. Martin, the owner of Heublein, kept the brand going at about the same production level that Kunett did up until his friend Jack Martin invented the

Moscow Mule cocktail. Jack Martin owned a ginger beer brewery as well as the popular Cock 'n Bull restaurant in Los Angeles. The cocktail consisted of lemon juice, vodka, and ginger beer. During the 1950s, this cocktail became very popular and spread across the United States. By the end of the 1950s, other vodka brands started to appear, with the second being Gordon's in a break from their gin brands.

By the 1960s, vodka had taken off. Fueled by a more laid-back moral atmosphere and by vodka's inherent ability to mix with almost anything, it was the perfect drink to meet the needs of the changing American tastes. By the 1970s, Smirnoff was selling more than six million cases of vodka a year. Today, Smirnoff is the number-one-selling spirit brand in the United States.

Today there are more than a hundred different American vodka brands. Vodka is the top-selling spirit category, with just under $867 million in sales, which is almost double the second-place American spirit, whiskey, with sales of $565 million. In fact, currently four of the top ten spirits in the United States are vodkas: Smirnoff, Absolut, Skyy, and Grey Goose.

The Vodka War

In 2006, what is now commonly referred to as the "Vodka War" started. At this time, Diageo Brands started marketing Ciroc, a vodka produced in France from wine grapes. Poland put forth a demand within the European Union (EU) that only spirits made exclusively from cereals, potatoes, and sugar beet molasses may be branded as vodka. This argument was supported by the other vodka-producing EU countries and by Germany. Their argument was that spirits distilled from grapes were already being labeled as brandy, eau-de-vie, and grappa, and that vodka produced from the grain had a certain prestige and quality. In a compromise, the EU parliament suggested that vodkas made from items other than cereals, potatoes, and molasses should say "Vodka produced from..." on the label. So far, it seems that the compromise will be approved, but the vote is still out.

In response to the compromise, a Polish member of the EU parliament, Ryszard Czarnecki, said, "Would the French like champagne to be distilled from plums, and would the British accept whiskey from apricots? That sounds like heresy. So please don't be surprised that we are refusing to recognize vodka made from waste."

If the demand succeeds, it will force brands like Ciroc to be rebranded as something other than vodka. If the compromise is approved, then Ciroc will need to add vodka produced from grapes to their label even though the bottle already proudly proclaims distilled from the finest french grapes.

Trends and New Directions

Up until 2007, the trend in vodka sales in the United States was toward the more expensive brands and away from the cheaper brands. At the same time, overall consumption was declining. This would indicate that until then, Americans were drinking less vodka, but the quality of the vodka they were drinking was better. With the recent economic collapse, a new trend is already starting to emerge. It seems that Americans are going back to the midtier-priced and economy-priced brands. It also is becoming apparent that Americans are going out less and are drinking at home instead of in bars and clubs. Vodka sales as a whole in the United States have risen by 4.8 percent from a year ago, but the market share has only risen by 0.7 percent. This is still better than all other categories of spirits, which have either declined in sales or not risen nearly as much. The exception to this is Irish whiskey, which saw sales rise almost 26 percent over. It's still too early to tell if this trend will continue or if we are right around the corner from another burst of innovation in the world of vodka.

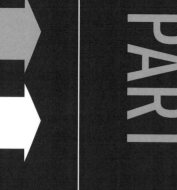

PART 2

"VODKA IS YOU SO POUND IT GULLET!"

TOOLS
AND TECHNIQUES

R ENEMY,
N THE

2

BARTENDING TOOLS

CHEERS!

HAVING THE RIGHT BARTENDING TOOLS IS ESSENTIAL TO MAKING THE PERFECT DRINK. THEY WILL ALLOW YOU TO MAKE YOUR DRINKS MORE EASILY—AND QUICKLY! ➤➤ ➤➤ ➤➤ ➤➤ ➤➤ ➤➤ ➤➤ ➤➤ ➤➤ ➤➤ ➤➤ ➤➤

Bar Mats

Also known as spill stops, these mats trap spillage and keep the bar neat. They are especially handy during messy tasks such as pouring shots. Don't forget to empty the mats and wash them after each use.

Bar Rags

Always keep at least two bar rags handy to wipe up spills and keep the bar clean.

Bar Spoon

A bar spoon is a small spoon with a very long handle. It has many uses behind the bar. It can be used for stirring cocktails, of course, but you can also pour a liqueur over the back of the spoon when layering it on top of another liqueur. You can also use it to scrape the bottom of the blender.

Blender

What bar would be complete without a blender for making fancy frozen drinks? A heavy-duty, multispeed blender is a good choice.

Boston Shaker

This is a less elegant, but easier, cheaper, and more reliable alternative to the martini shaker. It consists of a metal cup and a pint glass. Place ice and liquids in the cup, press the glass tightly over the cup to form a seal, shake, and serve. Since a Boston shaker does not have a strainer built in, you will need a separate strainer to hold back the ice as you poor.

Garnish Tray

A nice, neat, covered tray to hold your lemon slices, lime wedges, orange wheels, and cherries.

Ice Scoop

All commercial establishments require a designated scoop for use with ice, and it's wise to use an ice scoop at home as well. Ice is legally considered a food, so all the food-handling safety procedures apply. Do not use a glass to scoop the ice, or you run the risk of chipping the glass—imagine trying to find a glass chip in an ice bin! Also, keep your hands, used glassware, and any other potentially dirty object out of contact with the ice.

Jigger

A jigger is a measuring device that consists of two metal cups welded bottom to bottom. One of the cups is 1.5 ounces (45 ml) and the other is 1 ounce (30 ml). Some fancier jiggers have handles.

Knife

A good, sharp knife is essential for cutting fruit for garnish. A knife can also serve as a zester and peeler. It can also be used to cut wedges and slices or to make lemon zest or lime twists.

Liquor Pours or Spouts

A liquor pour is used to control the flow of liquor from the bottle. This helps to prevent spilling and splashing and also controls under- or over-pouring. Most pours flow at 1 ounce per second; with a little practice and a liquor pour, a bartender can accurately measure an ounce counting.

A "measured pour" has a built-in measurement, and stops the flow after that amount.

Shaker

Also called a "cocktail shaker" or "martini shaker," a shaker has three parts: the cup, the top, and the cap. Place ice in the cup followed by the liquids, press the top and the cap on tightly, and shake (away from the customer!). To serve, remove the cap and use the top as a strainer.

Strainer

A strainer fits over the top of a Boston shaker or any other glass and is used to strain the ice from a drink after it's been stirred or shaken.

BLEND
UNTIL
SMOOTH

SHAKE
WITH
ICE &
POUR

CHAPTER

3

BARTENDING
TECHNIQUES

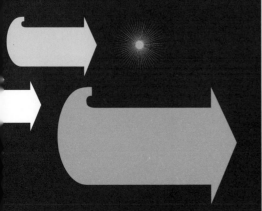

TRICKS!

FOLLOWING THESE BARTENDING TECHNIQUES FROM THE PROS WILL MAKE YOU THE HIT AT ANY FUNCTION. NOT ONLY WILL YOUR DRINKS COME ACROSS AS SOPHISTICATED AND WELL THOUGHT-OUT, BUT YOUR GUESTS WILL BE AMAZED AT YOUR BARTENDING SKILLS! ➥ ➥ ➥ ➥ ➥ ➥ ➥ ➥

Pour ingredients into glass neatly (do not chill).

Add all of the ingredients to the glass (typically a shot glass) straight from the bottle. Don't chill them if they're not already cold.

Layer in a shot glass.

Pour each of the ingredients into a shot glass or a pousse-café glass, keeping each ingredient in its own distinct layer. To achieve the layering effect, place a bar spoon upside down against the inner rim of the glass, just above the first ingredient. Gently pour the next ingredient over the back of the spoon to prevent the liquor from entering the glass too quickly and therefore mixing with the previous ingredient. For these types of drinks, the order is important; for best results, pour heavier ingredients first.

Layer over ice.

Fill the glass with ice and gently add each ingredient so they mix as little as possible.

Layer over ice. Drink through a straw.

Layer the drink over ice as described above, but finish by adding a straw. These types of drinks are meant to be consumed quickly, with the layers of the drink providing different flavors.

Shake with ice and strain.

Fill the cup of a cocktail or Boston shaker with ice, add the ingredients, and cover it with the lid. Shake it briskly until the outside begins to frost, then take the top lid off (for a cocktail shaker) or remove the pint glass and place the strainer over the cup (for a Boston shaker) and strain the drink into the glass, leaving the ice behind in the shaker. This method is commonly used to create a martini.

Shake with ice and strain over ice.

Follow instructions to shake with ice and strain just as described, but strain into a glass filled with ice.

Shake with ice and pour.

Follow instructions to shake with ice and strain, but remove the strainer and allow the ice to pour into the glass with the liquid.

Build over ice.

Fill a glass with ice and add the ingredients, allowing them to mix naturally.

Build over ice and stir.

Fill the glass with ice, add the ingredients, then stir the drink with a stir stick or a bar spoon.

Build in the glass with no ice.

Add the ingredients to the glass without ice. This is typically called for when the ingredients are already cold and should not be diluted with ice. Most champagne or beer-based drinks are created this way.

Build in a heatproof cup or mug.

Combine the ingredients in a heatproof container such as a coffee mug or Irish coffee cup in the order listed. This method is typically called for with hot drinks, such as an Irish coffee.

Stir gently with ice and strain.

Using a cocktail shaker or a Boston shaker, combine the ingredients and ice. Stir them gently with a bar spoon before straining the mixture into the appropriate glass. Do not shake.

Combine all ingredients in a blender. Blend until smooth.

Place all the ingredients in a blender without adding any ice. Blend everything until smooth. This is the method commonly used for drinks made with ice cream.

Combine all ingredients in a blender with ice. Blend until smooth.

Add ice to a blender and then add all the ingredients. Blend everything until smooth. This is the method commonly used for most frozen drinks.

Shake all but "X" with ice and strain into the glass. Top with "X".

In this case, "X" is typically club soda or tonic water, but it could also be ginger ale or even champagne. Shake all the ingredients with ice and strain them into a glass, then fill the glass the rest of the way with "X." Whether ice should be added to the glass before straining in the liquid depends on the type of drink; if ice would dilute the mixer (champagne, for example) then do not add it.

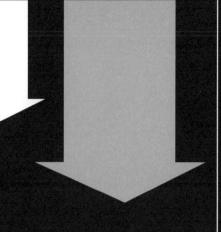

4

GLOSSARY
OF INGREDIENTS

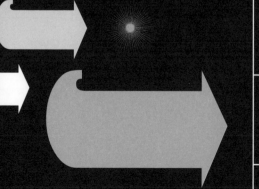

TRICKS!

THE FOLLOWING IS A DESCRIPTION OF SOME OF THE INGREDIENTS CALLED FOR IN THIS BOOK. SEVERAL INTERNET SOURCES WERE USED TO PRODUCE THESE DEFINITIONS, INCLUDING THE WIKIPEDIA FREE ENCYCLOPEDIA (WIKIPEDIA. ORG), THE INTERNET COCKTAIL DATABASE (COCKTAILDB.COM), AND VARIOUS PRODUCT AND COMPANY WEB SITES. ➡➡ ➡➡ ➡➡ ➡➡ ➡➡ ➡➡ ➡➡

Absinthe
A high-percent proof (50 to 75 percent alcohol by volume) anise-flavored spirit made from several herbs and flowers including the flowers and leaves of the *Artemisia absinthium*, also called wormwood. Sale of absinthe has been banned since 1915 in most of the world. The usual substitute for absinthe is Pernod®.

Advocaat
A creamy Dutch liqueur made from a blend of brandy, herb extracts, sugar, vanilla, and egg yolks. The drink started in the Dutch colonies in South America, where it was made from avocados; when the drink was brought north, egg yolks were used instead.

Agavero® Liqueur
A tequila-based liqueur made from a blend of tequila and damiana flower tea. The liqueur is very sweet with a strong agave flavor.

Alizé®
A French brand that offers several varieties of cognac and fruit juice blends. The original flavor of Alize® (Alize® Gold Passion) is a blend of French cognac and passion-fruit juice.

Amaretto
An Italian liqueur made from apricot kernels and seeds combined with almond extract steeped in brandy and sweetened with sugar syrup. Amaretto is Italian for "a little bitter."

Amaro Averna®
An Italian herbal liqueur based on a secret recipe created in Caltanissetta in 1854. The liqueur has a mild bitter flavor and is used as a digestive in Italy.

Amarula® Crème Liqueur
A crème liqueur made in South Africa from the fruit of the marula tree.

Amer Picon®

A bittersweet French aperitif made from herbs with a distinct orange flavor. Produced and sold in France, Amer Picon® is rarely exported and is difficult to find. Torani (Amer®) is the version sold in the United States.

Anisette

An Italian anise-flavored liqueur mainly consumed in France and Spain. It is sweeter than most anise-flavored liqueurs (such as pastis or Pernod®), and also has a lower alcohol content (typically 25 percent by volume, versus 40 percent in most others).

Aperol™

An Italian aperitif made by infusing neutral spirits with bitter orange, gentian, rhubarb, and an array of herbs and roots, using a secret recipe that has been unchanged since 1919. It has a sweet, bitter orange and herbs taste and a red-orange color.

Applejack

An alcoholic beverage produced from apples that originated during the American colonial period. It is made by concentrating hard cider, either by the traditional method of freeze distillation or by true evaporative distillation. The term "apple-jack" is derived from "jacking," an expression referring to freeze distillation.

Aquavit

A caraway-flavored liqueur from Scandinavia. The name comes from *aqua vitae*, Latin for "water of life."

Armagnac

A brandy similar to cognac that is produced in the Armagnac region of France. Armagnac differs from cognac in that it is distilled once instead of twice. The distillation also occurs at a lower temperature, allowing more of the character of the fruit to remain.

Bärenjäger®

A German neutral spirit-based liqueur that is sweetened and then flavored with honey. The word translates as "bear hunter."

Benedictine®

A brandy-based herbal liqueur produced in France. Benedictine® is believed to be the oldest liqueur continuously made, having first been developed by Dom Bernardo Vincelli in 1510 at the Benedictiner Abbey of Fécamp in Normandy. Every bottle of Benedictine carries the initials "D.O.M." which stand for Deo Optimo Maximo, or, "To God, most good, most great."

Bitters

Bitter-tasting herbal flavorings. Originally marketed as patent medicines, the few remaining varieties are principally used as a flavoring in food recipes or in cocktails.

ANGOSTURA® BITTERS

Angostura® was named for the town of Angostura in Venezuela. It contains no angostura bark, a medicinal bark named after the same town. Angostura® Bitters is the most widely distributed bar item in the world.

CURAÇAO

A liqueur flavored with the dried peels of larahas, bitter relatives of oranges grown on the island of Curaçao. The liqueur has an orange flavor and is packaged with coloring added. The most common color is blue, but it also is sold in green, orange, and red colors.

ORANGE BITTERS

Made from the rinds of unripe oranges.

PEYCHAUD'S® BITTERS

Is associated with New Orleans, Louisiana, and can be difficult to find elsewhere. It has a subtly sweeter taste than the Angostura® brand.

Bourbon

An American form of whiskey made from at least 51 percent corn, with the remainder being wheat or rye and malted barley. It is distilled to no more than 160 proof and aged in new, charred white-oak barrels for at least two years. It must be put into the barrels at no more than 125 U.S. proof.

Calvados

An apple brandy from the French region of Lower Normandy.

Campari®

A branded alcoholic beverage (20 to 24 percent alcohol by volume) introduced in Italy in 1860 by Gaspare Campari. It is a mild bitters-type aperitif, often combined with soda or orange juice or served in mixed drinks.

Chambord®

A French liqueur made from small black raspberries.

Champagne

A sparkling wine produced only in the Champagne region of France. Champagne is produced by adding sugar to bottled wine, allowing additional fermentation to occur in the bottle, which then produces carbon dioxide bubbles.

Chartreuse®

A famous French liqueur produced by the Carthusian monks, from a formula created in 1605 that contains 130 herbs and spices.

GREEN CHARTREUSE®

Fifty-five percent alcohol by volume and naturally green in color. The color chartreuse is named after the liqueur.

YELLOW CHARTREUSE®

Only forty percent alcohol by volume, it has a milder and sweeter flavor than the green.

Cherry Heering®

A proprietary Danish cherry liqueur with a brandy base. It has been produced since 1818 and sold under several different names, including Heering, Peter Heering, and Cherry Heering®.

Clamato®

A blend of tomato juice and clam broth that is sold by Motts.

Cognac

A type of brandy that is produced only in the Cognac region of western France and is universally recognized as the finest and most elegant liqueur in the world. Not a drop of any other wine or brandy is ever allowed to enter a bottle labeled cognac. The Cognac region is divided into six districts; the cognac of Grand Champagne is considered the best. Cognac is coded on the label by the following letters: V (very), S (superior), O (old), P (pale), E (extra or especial), F (fine), and X (extra). French law states that cognac with three stars must be aged at least one year to be rated VS, and four years to be rated VSOP (although seven to ten years is more common). By French law, the words extra, Napoleon, reserve, and vieille may not appear on the label unless the cognac has been aged at least five years.

Cointreau®

A fine, colorless, orange-flavored liqueur made from the dried skins of oranges grown on the island of Curaçao in the Dutch West Indies. The generic term for this type of liqueur is curaçao. If it is redistilled and clarified, it is called triple sec.

Courvoisier®

A type of cognac. Courvoisier® is famous for being the favorite drink of Napoleon.

Cream Soda

A vanilla-flavored carbonated soda.

Cream Sherry

A style of sweet sherry created by blending dry sherry with sweet wines. The result is a dark, rich wine with a soft, sweet finish.

Crème Liqueurs

Crème liqueurs are very sweet with a single flavor that dominates.

CRÈME DE ALMOND

Almond-flavored sweet liqueur.

CRÈME DE BANANA

Banana-flavored sweet liqueur.

CRÈME DE CACAO (DARK)

Chocolate-flavored sweet liqueur that is dark brown in color.

CRÈME DE CACAO (WHITE)

Colorless chocolate-flavored sweet liqueur.

CRÈME DE CASSIS

Black currant–flavored sweet liqueur.

CRÈME DE COCONUT

Coconut-flavored sweet liqueur.

CRÈME DE MENTHE (GREEN)

Mint-flavored sweet liqueur that is green in color.

CRÈME DE MENTHE (WHITE)

Colorless mint-flavored sweet liqueur.

CRÈME DE NOYAUX

Sweet liqueur made from fruit pits; has a bitter almond flavor.

CRÈME DE VIOLETTE (OR CRÈME YEVETTE)

Sweet liqueur made from and flavored with violets.

Crown Royal®

A brand of blended Canadian whiskey.

Drambuie®
A famous whiskey liqueur consisting of Highland malt Scotch whiskey, heather honey, and herbs.

Dubonnet®
A brand of quinquina, a sweetened fortified aperitif wine that contains quinine. It is produced in France and available in two varieties.

BLONDE
Lighter in color and less sweet.

ROUGE
Red in color and more sweet.

Everclear®
A brand of grain alcohol that is 95 percent alcohol by volume (190 proof).

Fernet® Branca
An extremely bitter Italian herbal aperitif or digestif made from cinchona bark, gentian root, rhubarb, calamus, angelica, myrrh, chamomile, and peppermint. It is often employed as a stomach settler and/or hangover remedy. It is classified as bitters.

Fire Water®
A brand of cinnamon-flavored liqueur that is bright red in color.

Frangelico®
An Italian brand of hazelnut-flavored liqueur packaged in a distinctive monk-shaped bottle.

Galliano®
A sweetish, golden Italian liqueur with an herby, spicy taste.

Gin
Gin begins as a neutral spirit. It is then redistilled with or filtered through juniper berries and botanicals such as coriander seeds, cassia bark, orange peels, fennel seeds, anise, caraway, angelica root, licorice, lemon peel, almonds, cinnamon bark, bergamot, and cocoa. It is this secondary process that imparts to each gin its particular taste.

DRY (OR LONDON DRY) GIN
Most of the gin now produced is London dry, which is light, dry, and perfect for making martinis and other mixed drinks.

PLYMOUTH GIN
A sweeter and more mild gin originally produced in Plymouth, England.

Ginger Beer
A type of fermented, carbonated beverage, flavored with ginger, lemon, and sugar. Ginger beer reached the height of its popularity in England in the 1900s. It is popular today in Bermuda and is part of the national drink of Bermuda, the "Dark and Stormy."

Godiva® Liqueur
A neutral spirit–based liqueur flavored with Godiva® brand Belgian chocolate and other flavors. There are currently four types: milk chocolate, original chocolate, white chocolate, and mocha.

Goldschläger®
A cinnamon-flavored liqueur produced in Switzerland that includes flakes of real gold in the bottle.

Gosling's Black Seal® Rum
An eighty-proof dark rum produced in Bermuda. Along with ginger beer, an essential part of Bermuda's national drink, the "Dark and Stormy."

Grain Alcohol
An unaged neutral spirit with a very high alcohol content (greater than 90 percent alcohol by volume, or 180 proof). Grain alcohol cannot be legally sold in many states in the United States.

Grand Marnier®
A French brand of aged, orange-flavored liqueur (triple sec) with a brandy base.

Grappa
An Italian brandy distilled from the pulpy mass of skins, pits, and stalks left in the wine press after the juice of the grapes has been extracted. Young grappa can be harsh, but it mellows with age.

Grenadine
A sweet syrup made from pomegranate juice, containing little or no alcohol.

Hard Apple Cider (or Hard Cider)
Fermented apple cider with an alcohol content similar to beer.

Hennessy®
A brand of cognac produced in France.

Hot Damn!® Cinnamon Schnapps

A brand of cinnamon-flavored liqueur with a strong cinnamon flavor and a red color.

Hypnotiq®

A French fruit liqueur made from vodka, cognac, and tropical fruit juices.

Irish Cream Liqueur

A mocha-flavored whiskey and double-cream liqueur, combining Irish whiskey, cream, coffee, chocolate, and other flavors.

Irish Mist®

A liqueur produced in Ireland, consisting of Irish whiskey flavored with heather honey.

Jack Daniel's®

A whiskey made in Tennessee that is perhaps the most famous whiskey made in America. The Jack Daniel's® distillery in Lynchburg, Tennessee, dates from 1875 and is the oldest registered distillery in the United States. Jack Daniel's® is made according to the sour-mash process, and by the "Lincoln County Process" of filtration through sugar maple charcoal before being aged in charred American oak casks.

Jägermeister®

A complex, aromatic liqueur containing 56 herbs, roots, and fruits that has been popular in Germany since its introduction in 1935. In Germany, it is frequently consumed warm as an aperitif or after-dinner drink. In the United States, it is widely popular as a chilled shooter.

KeKe Beach® Liqueur

A key lime–flavored cream liqueur with a hint of graham cracker flavor.

Kirschwasser

A clear brandy made from double distillation of the fermented juice of black cherries.

Kümmel

A sweet, colorless liqueur flavored with caraway seed, cumin, and fennel.

Licor 43® (Cuarenta y Tres)

A yellow-colored liqueur from Spain made from 43 ingredients including fruit juices, vanilla, and other aromatic herbs and spices.

Lillet®

An aperitif wine from the Bordeaux region of France. Lillet® is sold in both red and white.

Limoncello

An Italian liqueur made from lemons.

Malibu® Rum

A Jamaican coconut-flavored rum liqueur.

Mandarine Napoléon® Liqueur

A liqueur made from mandarin orange–flavored cognac.

Maraschino Liqueur

A very sweet, white, cherry liqueur made from the marasca cherry of Dalmatia, Yugoslavia. This liqueur is sometimes used in sours in place of sugar.

Melon Liqueur

A pale green liqueur that tastes of fresh muskmelon or cantaloupe. The most famous brand, Midori®, is Japanese in origin and produced by the Suntory Company in Mexico, France, and Japan.

Mescal

A Mexican distilled spirit made from the agave plant. Tequila is a mescal made only from the blue agave plant in the region around Tequila, Jalisco. Spirits labeled mescal are made from other agave plants and are not part of the tequila family.

Metaxa®

A strong, sharp-tasting, aromatic Greek brandy.

Nassau Royale®

A rum-based liqueur with a vanilla flavor.

Ouzo

An anise-flavored liqueur from Greece, usually served on the rocks. Ouzo can be used as a substitute for absinthe in many cases.

Parfait Amour

A cordial made of citrus juices, cinnamon, coriander, and brandy.

Passoã®

A passion fruit–flavored liqueur produced by Remy Cointreau.

Pastis

A semisweet anis-flavored liqueur produced to be a substitute for absinthe.

Peach Schnapps

A sweet peach-flavored liqueur.

Pernod®

A brand of pastis produced by the Pernod-Ricard company.

Pisang Ambon®

A Dutch liqueur green in color and flavored with banana.

Pisco

A brandy made in the wine-producing regions of South America. It is the most popular spirit in Chile and Peru.

Ponche Kuba®

A "ponche" is a homemade cream liqueur similar to eggnog that is popular in Caribbean and Latin American countries. Ponche Kuba® is a packaged form of this liqueur. It is made from a rum base with cream, eggs, and sugar added. It is flavored with a proprietary blend of spices.

Red Bull®

A carbonated soft drink with additives and extra caffeine that claims to reduce mental and physical fatigue.

Rock & Rye®

A blend of rye whiskey with rock candy and fruit juice.

Rum

A liquor made from fermented and distilled sugarcane juice or molasses. Rum has a wide range of flavors, from light and dry like a vodka to very dark and complex like a cognac.

AMBER RUM

Gold in color and sweeter than a light rum.

AÑEJO RUM

A rum that has been aged in wood for a period of time.

DARK RUM

Almost black in color, with a rich and complex flavor.

FLAVORED RUMS

Like vodka, rum is now available in a wide array of flavors. Some of the first flavored rums featured vanilla or lemon. Now almost any flavor can be found.

LIGHT RUM

Clear in color and dry in flavor.

RUM CREAM

Cream liqueurs made with a rum base, with cream and flavoring added. The flavors are typically tropical, such as banana, coconut, and pineapple.

SPICED RUM

The original flavored rum. Spiced rum consists of an amber rum with vanilla and cinnamon flavor added.

Rumple Minze®

A 100 proof (50 percent alcohol by volume) peppermint schnapps produced in Germany.

Safari®

A fruit liqueur flavored with mango, papaya, passion fruit, and lime.

Sake

A Japanese alcoholic beverage brewed from rice. It is commonly referred to as rice wine in the United States, but its method of production is more similar to that of a malt liquor.

Sambuca

An Italian liqueur flavored with anis and elderberry, produced in both clear ("white sambuca") and dark blue or purple ("black sambuca") versions.

Schnapps

A liqueur distilled from grains, roots, or fruits. Real schnapps has no sugar or flavoring added, as the flavor should originate from the base material. Many syrupy sweet fruit liqueurs are called schnapps; these are not true schnapps because they have both sugar and flavorings added.

Scotch

Scotch whiskey is whiskey that is produced in Scotland. In the United States, this whiskey is commonly referred to as Scotch. In Scotland, however, it is referred to simply as whiskey.

Sherry

A type of wine produced in Spain that is fortified with brandy.

Simple Syrup (or Sugar Syrup)

A combination of equal parts sugar and boiling water that, once cooled, is used as a sweetener in many mixed drinks.

Sloe Gin

A liqueur flavored with sloe berries and blackthorn fruit. It traditionally was made with a gin base with sugar added; most modern versions use a neutral spirit base and add flavorings later.

Sour Mix

A syrup made from a blend of sugar and lemon juice. A simple recipe is to mix equal parts of simple syrup and lemon juice.

Southern Comfort®

A liqueur with a neutral spirit base and peach and almond flavors.

Strega®

An Italian herbal liqueur with mint and fennel flavors. Saffron gives it a yellow color. In Italian, *strega* means witch.

Sweetened Lime Juice

As the name would imply, lime juice with sugar added.

T.Q. Hot®

A brand of tequila flavored with hot peppers.

Tabasco® Sauce

A brand of hot pepper sauce made from a blend of tabasco peppers, vinegar, and salt, aged in wood casks.

Tang®

An orange-flavored powdered drink mix brand owned by Kraft Foods. It was introduced in 1959 but became popular when NASA gave it to astronauts in the Gemini program in 1965.

Tequila

A type of mescal that is made only from the blue agave plant in the region surrounding Tequila, a town in the Mexican state of Jalisco. Tequila is made in many different styles, with the difference between them dependent on how long the distillate has been aged before being bottled.

AÑEJO
Tequila aged between 1 and 3 years.

GOLD ("ORO" OR "JOVEN ABOCADO")
Meaning "bottled when young," this is white tequila with coloring added.

REPOSADO ("RESTED")
Tequila aged at least 1 year.

SILVER ("PLATA" OR "BANCO")
This is clear, unaged tequila, with a very strong flavor.

Tequila Rose®
A brand of cream liqueur with a tequila base and a strawberry flavor.

Tia Maria®
A Jamaican rum flavored with spices.

Tonic Water
Carbonated water with quinine added. Originally used to prevent malaria, the amount of quinine in bottled tonic water today is only about half the dose given to patients.

Triple Sec
A highly popular flavoring agent in many drinks, triple sec is the best known form of curaçao, a liqueur made from the skins of the curaçao orange.

Vermouth
A fortified wine flavored with aromatic herbs and spices. There are three common varieties of vermouth.

DRY VERMOUTH
Clear or pale yellow in color and very dry in flavor.

SWEET VERMOUTH
Red in color and sweeter than dry vermouth.

WHITE VERMOUTH
Clear or pale yellow in color, but sweeter than dry vermouth.

Wasabi
A member of the cabbage family, its root is ground and used as a very potent Japanese spice.

Whiskey (or Whisky)
A beverage distilled from fermented grain and aged in oak casks. The location, grain, type of oak, and length of the aging all affect the flavor of the whiskey. Whiskey is spelled with an "e" in Ireland and the United States and without the "e" everywhere else. There are four major regions where whiskey is produced: Ireland, Scotland, Canada, and the United States. Each has a different style that imparts a distinctive flavor.

Wild Turkey®
A brand of Kentucky bourbon whiskey. It is available in both 80 proof and 101 proof versions.

Wine

An alcoholic beverage produced by the fermentation of fruit juice, typically grapes. The type of grape, where the grapes were grown, and the way the wine is stored as it ferments affect the taste and color.

Yukon Jack®

A Canadian liqueur made from a whiskey base and flavored with honey.

Zima®

A colorless alcoholic carbonated malt beverage. It is produced by the Coors company and was introduced in the United States in 1994. It was the first of the "clear malt" beverages that now include products like Smirnoff® Ice and Skyy® Blue. These types of beverages are commonly referred to as "clear beer" or "near beer."

PART

3

"WE GOT TOGE
FRIENDS TO H
LET'S DRINK
TOGETHER AS

DRINKS

HER AS

VE A DRINK.

O GETTING

RIENDS."

SHAKE
WITH
ICE &
STRAIN

CHAPTER

5

MARTINIS

THERE ARE THOSE WHO CLAIM THAT ANYTHING
OTHER THAN A COMBINATION OF GIN OR
VODKA AND VERMOUTH IS NOT AND NEVER
CAN BE A "MARTINI." FOR THE PURPOSES OF
THIS BOOK, A MARTINI IS ANY DRINK THAT HAS
"TINI" IN THE NAME. THIS IS A VERY BROAD
RANGE OF FLAVORS AND STYLES, AND COVERS
EVERYTHING FROM THE CLASSIC JAMES BOND
MARTINI TO THE QUESTIONABLE CHOCOLATE
BANANA MARTINI.

DRINK UP!

Absolute Martini

2½ parts Vodka
½ part Triple Sec

GLASS: COCKTAIL
Shake with ice and strain

Alizé Martini

2½ parts Alizé®
1 part Vodka

GLASS: COCKTAIL
Shake with ice and strain

Alterna-tini #1

2 parts Vodka
½ part Crème de Cacao (White)
¼ part Dry Vermouth
¼ part Sweet Vermouth

GLASS: COCKTAIL
Shake with ice and strain

Alterna-tini #2

½ part Vodka
½ part Red Curaçao
½ part Blue Curaçao
1 part Apple Juice

GLASS: COCKTAIL
Shake with ice and strain

Apollo XI Martini

2 parts Vodka
splash Vermouth
splash Tang®
fill with Gatorade®

GLASS: COCKTAIL
Shake with ice and strain. Serve in a cocktail glass rimmed with Tang® granules.

Apple Cintini

1½ parts Apple-Flavored Vodka
½ part Amaretto
1 part Sour Mix

GLASS: COCKTAIL
Shake with ice and strain

Apple Martini #1

1 part Vodka
1 part Sour Apple Schnapps
splash Lime Juice

{ GLASS: COCKTAIL

Shake with ice and strain

Apple Martini #2

3 parts Vodka
1 part Sour Apple Schnapps
splash Pineapple Juice
splash Sour Mix
splash Melon Liqueur

{ GLASS: COCKTAIL

Shake with ice and strain

Applepucker-tini

2 parts Sour Apple Schnapps
2 parts Vodka
fill with Mountain Dew®

{ GLASS: COLLINS

Build over ice and stir

Apple-tini

2 parts Vodka
1 part Apple Liqueur
splash Lime Juice

{ GLASS: COCKTAIL

Shake with ice and strain

Armada Martini

3 parts Vodka

{ GLASS: COCKTAIL

Shake with ice and strain

Austin Fashion Martini

1½ parts Vodka
½ part Dry Vermouth
splash Blue Curaçao

{ GLASS: COCKTAIL

Shake with ice and strain

B&T's Purple Martini

1 part Vodka
½ part Blue Curaçao
splash Cranberry Juice Cocktail
dash Vermouth

{ GLASS: COCKTAIL
Shake with ice and strain

Baby Face Martini

3 parts Raspberry-Flavored Vodka
½ part Dry Vermouth
¼ part Maraschino Liqueur

{ GLASS: COCKTAIL
Shake with ice and strain

Banana Martini

1 part Vodka
1 part Banana Liqueur

{ GLASS: HIGHBALL
Shake with ice and strain

Bellini-tini

2 parts Vodka
½ part Peach Schnapps
½ part Peach Puree
dash Bitters

{ GLASS: COCKTAIL
Shake with ice and strain

Berlin Martini

2 parts Vodka
1 part Peach Schnapps
splash Black Sambuca

{ GLASS: COCKTAIL
Shake with ice and strain

Berry-tini

3 parts Currant-Flavored Vodka
½ part Raspberry Liqueur

GLASS: COCKTAIL

Shake with ice and strain

Black and White Martini

3 parts Vanilla-Flavored Vodka
1 part Crème de Cacao (Dark)

GLASS: COCKTAIL

Shake with ice and strain

Black Forest Cake Martini

1½ parts Vodka
1 part Crème de Cacao (White)
splash Raspberry Liqueur

GLASS: COCKTAIL

Shake with ice and strain

Black Martini

1½ parts Vodka
1 part Raspberry Liqueur
1 part Blue Curaçao

GLASS: COCKTAIL

Shake with ice and strain

Blue Jaffa Martini

1 part Vodka
1 part Blue Curaçao
1 part Crème de Cacao (White)

GLASS: COCKTAIL

Shake with ice and strain

Blue on Blue Martini

3 parts Vodka
½ part Blue Curaçao

GLASS: COCKTAIL

Shake with ice and strain

Bond's Martini

3 parts Gin
1 part Vodka
½ part Vermouth

GLASS: COCKTAIL

Shake (don't stir) with ice and strain

California Martini

2 parts Vodka
1 part Red Wine
¼ part Dark Rum

GLASS: COCKTAIL

Shake with ice and strain

Campari® Martini

3 parts Vodka
1 part Campari®

GLASS: COCKTAIL

Shake with ice and strain

Caramel Apple Martini

2 parts Butterscotch Schnapps
2 parts Sour Apple Schnapps
1 part Vodka

GLASS: COCKTAIL

Shake with ice and strain

Caribbean Martini

1½ parts Vanilla-Flavored Vodka
¾ part Malibu® Rum
splash Pineapple Juice

GLASS: COCKTAIL

Shake with ice and strain

Chocolate Banana Martini

2 parts Vodka
1 part Crème de Cacao (White)
1 part 99-Proof Banana Liqueur

GLASS: COCKTAIL

Shake with ice and strain

Chocolate Lovers' Martini

1½ parts Irish Cream Liqueur
1½ parts Vodka
1½ parts Crème de Cacao (White)
1 tbsp. Chocolate Syrup

GLASS: COCKTAIL

Shake with ice and strain

Chocolate Martini #1

2 parts Vodka
½ part Crème de Cacao (White)

GLASS: COCKTAIL

Shake with ice and strain

Chocolate Martini #2

1½ parts Vanilla-Flavored Vodka
1 part Godiva® Liqueur

{ GLASS: COCKTAIL ∇

Shake with ice and strain

Chocolate Rasp Martini

1½ parts Raspberry Vodka
1 part Crème de Cacao (White)

{ GLASS: COCKTAIL ∇

Shake with ice and strain

Christmas Martini

2 parts Vodka
½ part Crème de Menthe (White)
½ part Dry Vermouth

{ GLASS: COCKTAIL ∇

Shake with ice and strain

Cool Yule Martini

3 parts Vodka
½ part Crème de Menthe (White)
½ part Dry Vermouth

{ GLASS: COCKTAIL ∇

Shake with ice and strain

Crantini #1

1½ parts Vodka
½ part Triple Sec
½ part Vermouth
2 parts Cranberry Juice Cocktail

{ GLASS: COCKTAIL ∇

Shake with ice and strain

Crantini #2

1 part Sweet Vodka
1 part Cointreau®
1 part Cranberry Juice Cocktail
splash Lime Juice

{ GLASS: COCKTAIL ∇

Shake with ice and strain

Dark Chocolate Martini

1 part Vodka
1 part Crème de Cacao (Dark)

{ GLASS: COCKTAIL ∇

Shake with ice and strain

Daydream Martini

2 parts Citrus-Flavored Vodka
1 part Orange Juice
½ part Triple Sec
dash Powdered Sugar

GLASS: COCKTAIL

Shake with ice and strain

Dirty Vodka Martini #1

2 parts Vodka
1 tbs Dry Vermouth
2 tbs Olive Brine
2 Olives

GLASS: COCKTAIL

Shake with ice and strain

Dirty Vodka Martini #2

2 parts Vodka
1 splash Olive Brine

GLASS: COCKTAIL

Shake with ice and strain

Double Fudge Martini

3 parts Vodka
½ part Crème de Cacao (Dark)
½ part Coffee Liqueur

GLASS: COCKTAIL

Shake with ice and strain

Euro-tini

1 part Vodka
½ part Triple Sec
1 part Orange Juice
¼ dash Sugar

GLASS: COCKTAIL

Shake with ice and strain

Extra Dry Vodka Martini

1½ parts Vodka
1 drop Vermouth

GLASS: COCKTAIL

Shake with ice and strain

Fire-tini Hunter

2 parts Pepper-Flavored Vodka
1 part Dry Vermouth

GLASS: COCKTAIL

Shake with ice and strain

French Martini

1 part Vodka
1 part Raspberry Liqueur
1 part Grand Marnier®
1 part Pineapple Juice
1 part Sour Mix

GLASS: COCKTAIL

Shake with ice and strain

Fuzzy Martini

2½ parts Vodka
1 part Peach Schnapps
splash Orange Juice

GLASS: COCKTAIL

Shake with ice and strain

Granny Smith Martini

1½ parts Vanilla-Flavored Vodka
½ part Sour Apple Schnapps
¼ part Melon Liqueur

GLASS: COCKTAIL

Shake with ice and strain

Green Apple Martini

1½ parts Sour Apple Schnapps
1½ parts Vodka
splash Vermouth

GLASS: COCKTAIL

Shake with ice and strain

Gumball Martini

2 parts Gin
1 part Vodka
½ part Southern Comfort®
¼ part Dry Vermouth

GLASS: COCKTAIL

Shake with ice and strain

Gumdrop Martini

1 part Citrus-Flavored Rum
½ part Vodka
¼ part Dry Vermouth
¼ part Southern Comfort®

GLASS: COCKTAIL
Shake with ice and strain

Honeydew Martini

2 parts Vodka
½ part Triple Sec
½ part Melon Liqueur

GLASS: COCKTAIL
Shake with ice and strain

Hot and Dirty Martini

2 parts Absolut® Peppar Vodka
½ part Dry Vermouth
½ part Olive Brine

GLASS: COCKTAIL
Shake with ice and strain

Hpnotiq® Martini

1 part Cherry-Flavored Vodka
2 parts Hpnotiq® Liqueur

GLASS: COCKTAIL
Shake with ice and strain

Irish Martini

2 parts Vodka
½ part Dry Vermouth
¼ part Whiskey

GLASS: COCKTAIL
Shake with ice and strain

Jack London Martini

3 parts Currant-Flavored Vodka
½ part Maraschino Liqueur

GLASS: COCKTAIL
Shake with ice and strain

James Bond Martini

1½ parts Gin
½ part Vodka
¼ part Lillet®
Lemon Twist

GLASS: COCKTAIL

Shake with ice and strain. The original order that Mr. Bond used was "Three measures Gordon's®, one of Vodka, half a measure of Kina Lillet®. Shake it very well until it's ice-cold, then add a large thin slice of Lemon Peel." (From Casino Royale by Ian Fleming, 1953.)

Jamie's Martini

2 parts Vodka
1 part Orange Juice
½ part Triple Sec
dash Powdered Sugar

GLASS: COCKTAIL

Shake with ice and strain

Kamitini

1 part Vodka
½ part Raspberry Liqueur
½ part Vanilla Liqueur
1 part Raspberry Juice
splash Fresh Lime Juice

GLASS: COCKTAIL

Shake with ice and strain

Leap Year Martini

3 parts Citrus-Flavored Vodka
½ part Sweet Vermouth

GLASS: COCKTAIL

Shake with ice and strain

Lemon Splash Martini

1½ parts Vodka
½ part Triple Sec
½ part Amaretto

GLASS: COCKTAIL

Shake with ice and strain

Long Kiss Goodnight

1 part Vodka
1 part Vanilla-Flavored Vodka
1 part Crème de Cacao (White)

GLASS: COCKTAIL

Shake with ice and strain

Low Tide Martini

3 parts Vodka
½ part Dry Vermouth
½ part Oyster Juice

GLASS: COCKTAIL
Shake with ice and strain

Main Beach Martini

1½ parts Orange Vodka
½ part Crème de Cacao (White)

GLASS: HIGHBALL
Shake with ice and strain over ice

Mama's Martini

2 parts Vanilla-Flavored Vodka
½ part Apricot Brandy

GLASS: COCKTAIL
Shake with ice and strain

Mangotini

1½ parts Vodka
½ part Sour Apple Schnapps
1 part Mango Nectar
splash Vermouth

GLASS: COCKTAIL
Shake with ice and strain

Martini Colorado

½ part Gin
½ part Vodka
1½ parts Vermouth
2 dashes Angostura® Bitters
dash salt

GLASS: COCKTAIL
Shake with ice and strain.
Garnish with two olives

Ma-tini

1 part Vodka
½ part Blackberry Liqueur
½ part Cointreau®
1 part Lemonade

GLASS: COCKTAIL
Shake with ice and strain

Mellow Martini

1½ parts Vodka
¾ part Crème de Banana
splash Lychee Liqueur
2 parts Pineapple Juice

{ GLASS: COCKTAIL

Shake with ice and strain

Melon Martini

2½ parts Vodka
½ part Melon Liqueur

{ GLASS: COCKTAIL

Shake with ice and strain

Milky Way® Martini

1 part Vanilla-Flavored Vodka
1 part Chocolate Liqueur
1 part Irish Cream Liqueur

{ GLASS: COCKTAIL

Shake with ice and strain

Mint-tini

2 parts Vodka
1 part Crème de Menthe (White)
½ part Dry Vermouth

{ GLASS: COCKTAIL

Shake with ice and strain

Mocha Blanca Martini

1 part Vodka
1 part Chocolate Liqueur
1 part Coffee Liqueur

{ GLASS: COCKTAIL

Shake with ice and strain

Mocha Martini

2½ parts Vodka
½ part Coffee Liqueur
1 part Crème de Cacao (White)

{ GLASS: COCKTAIL

Shake with ice and strain

Monk's Martini

1 part Vodka
1 part Crème de Menthe (White)
1 part Crème de Banana
1 part Irish Cream Liqueur

GLASS: COCKTAIL

Shake with ice and strain

Mortini

2 parts Vodka
splash Amaretto
splash Grenadine

GLASS: COCKTAIL

Shake with ice and strain

Mozart Martini

1 part Crème de Cacao (Dark)
1 part Chocolate Liqueur
2 parts Cream
splash Vodka

GLASS: COCKTAIL

Shake with ice and strain

Neopolitan Martini

1 part Vanilla-Flavored Vodka
1 part Orange-Flavored Vodka
½ part Grand Marnier®
½ part Parfait Amour
splash Lime Juice

GLASS: COCKTAIL

Shake with ice and strain

New Orleans Martini

2 parts Vanilla-Flavored Vodka
½ part Dry Vermouth
½ part Pernod®

GLASS: COCKTAIL

Shake with ice and strain

Nutty Martini

3 parts Vodka
½ part Frangelico®

GLASS: COCKTAIL

Shake with ice and strain

Old Country Martini

1 part Vodka
1 part Kirschwasser
1 part Madeira

GLASS: COCKTAIL

Shake with ice and strain

Olorosa Martini

2 parts Sherry
½ part Vodka

GLASS: COCKTAIL

Shake with ice and strain

Orange Martini

3 parts Vodka
1 part Triple Sec
dash Orange Bitters

GLASS: COCKTAIL

Shake with ice and strain

Orangetini

1½ parts Orange-Flavored Vodka
1½ parts Triple Sec

GLASS: COCKTAIL

Shake with ice and strain

Oyster Martini

3 parts Vodka
1 part Dry Vermouth

GLASS: COCKTAIL

*Shake with ice and strain.
Garnish with an oyster*

Peach Blossom Martini

2 parts Peach-Flavored Vodka
½ part Maraschino Liqueur

GLASS: COCKTAIL

Shake with ice and strain

Peppar Bayou Martini

1½ parts Absolut® Peppar Vodka
¼ part Dry Vermouth

GLASS: COCKTAIL

Shake with ice and strain

Pineapple Martini

1 part Orange-Flavored Vodka
1 part Pineapple-Flavored Rum
1 part Pineapple Juice

GLASS: COCKTAIL

Shake with ice and strain

Pontberry Martini

2 parts Vodka
½ part Blackberry Liqueur

GLASS: COCKTAIL

Shake with ice and strain

Pretty Martini

2 parts Vodka
½ part Dry Vermouth
½ part Amaretto

GLASS: COCKTAIL

Shake with ice and strain

Prospector Martini

1½ parts Vanilla-Flavored Vodka
¾ part Goldschläger®
½ part Butterscotch Schnapps
splash Vanilla Extract

GLASS: COCKTAIL

Shake with ice and strain

Really Dry Vodka Martini

3 parts Vodka
Dry Vermouth
2 Olives

GLASS: COCKTAIL

*Place 2 olives in a chilled glass.
Pour Vodka in a shaker with ice.
Hold an open bottle of Vermouth,
lean over the shaker and whisper
"Vermouth." Strain the Vodka into
the glass.*

Red Dog Martini

2 parts Vodka
½ part Port
½ part Grenadine

GLASS: COCKTAIL

Shake with ice and strain

Red Vodka-tini

2 parts Vodka
1 part Sweet Vermouth
splash Crème de Cassis

GLASS: COCKTAIL
Shake with ice and strain

Redhead Martini

2½ parts Vodka
½ part Strawberry Syrup

GLASS: COCKTAIL
Shake with ice and strain

Rontini

1 part Vodka
fill with Mountain Dew®

GLASS: HIGHBALL
Build over ice and stir

Russian Peachtini

1½ parts Vodka
splash Peach Schnapps

GLASS: COCKTAIL
Shake with ice and strain

Salt and Pepper Martini

2 parts Absolut® Peppar Vodka
splash Dry Vermouth

GLASS: COCKTAIL
*Shake with ice and strain. Serve in a
cocktail glass with a salted rim.*

Smoked Martini

1 part Scotch
1 part Vodka

GLASS: COCKTAIL
Shake with ice and strain

South Beach Martini

1 part Orange-Flavored Vodka
1 part Citrus-Flavored Vodka
½ part Cointreau®
½ part Lime Juice

GLASS: COCKTAIL
Shake with ice and strain

Soviet Martini

2 parts Currant-Flavored Vodka
½ part Dry Vermouth
½ part Dry Sherry

Springtime Martini

2 parts Vodka
1 part Lillet®

Strawberry Blonde Martini

2 parts Strawberry-Flavored Vodka
1 part Lillet®

Sweet and Spicy Martini

2 parts Vodka
½ part Sweet Vermouth
½ part Triple Sec

Tini Rita

1¼ parts Vodka
¼ part Cointreau®
¼ part Grand Marnier®
splash Lime Juice
splash Sour Mix

Toffee Martini

1 part Frangelico®
1 part Vanilla Liqueur
1 part Vodka

Transylvanian Martini

1½ parts Vodka
1½ parts Passion Fruit Liqueur

Truffle Martini

3 parts Strawberry-Flavored Vodka
½ part Crème de Cacao (Dark)

{ GLASS: COCKTAIL Y
Shake with ice and strain

Ultimate Arctic Martini

2 parts Vodka
½ part Dry Vermouth
½ part Lemon Juice

{ GLASS: COCKTAIL Y
Shake with ice and strain

Violet Martini

2 parts Citrus-Flavored Vodka
½ part Parfait Amour
¼ part Raspberry Syrup

{ GLASS: COCKTAIL Y
Shake with ice and strain

Waikiki Martini

2 parts Pineapple-Flavored Vodka
½ part Dry Vermouth
½ part Lillet®

{ GLASS: COCKTAIL Y
Shake with ice and strain

Zippy Martini

2 parts Vodka
½ part Dry Vermouth
splash Tabasco® Sauce

{ GLASS: COCKTAIL Y
Shake with ice and strain

Zorbatini

1½ parts Vodka
1 part Ouzo

{ GLASS: COCKTAIL Y
Shake with ice and strain

Z-Tini

½ part Vodka
½ part Irish Cream Liqueur
½ part Strawberry Liqueur
1 part Raspberry Liqueur
1 part Cream

{ GLASS: COCKTAIL Y
Shake with ice and strain

TASTY TASTY TASTY TASTY TASTY TASTY TASTY

SHAKE
WITH
ICE &
STRAIN

CHAPTER

6

WHAT MAKES A COCKTAIL DIFFERENT FROM A
MARTINI? WHAT MAKES IT DIFFERENT FROM
A RUN-OF-THE-MILL MIXED DRINK? HERE, A
COCKTAIL IS A MIXED DRINK THAT IS SHAKEN
OR STIRRED WITH ICE AND STRAINED IN A
COCKTAIL GLASS. ADDITIONALLY, NONE OF THE
DRINKS END WITH "TINI."

DRINK UP!

1 Randini

2 parts Cranberry Juice Cocktail
3 parts Vodka
1 Lime Wedge
1 part Triple Sec

GLASS: COCKTAIL

Shake with ice and strain

1-900-Fuk-Meup

2 parts Currant-Flavored Vodka
1 part Grand Marnier®
1 part Raspberry Liqueur
1 part Melon Liqueur
1 part Coconut-Flavored Rum
1 part Amaretto
2 parts Cranberry Juice Cocktail
1 part Pineapple Juice

GLASS: COCKTAIL

Shake with ice and strain

21 Joc

1 part Vodka
½ part Triple Sec
½ part Strawberry Liqueur
splash Lime Juice

GLASS: COCKTAIL

Shake with ice and strain

2lips

⅔ part Vodka
½ part Parfait Amour
splash Crème de Cassis
splash Lime Juice
splash Cranberry Juice Cocktail

GLASS: COCKTAIL

Shake with ice and strain

420 Kicker

2 parts Absolut® Peppar Vodka
1 part Peppermint Schnapps
1 part Sour Mix

GLASS: COCKTAIL

Shake with ice and strain

44 Special

1 part Cranberry-Flavored Vodka
1 part Vodka
1 part Peach Schnapps
2½ parts Grape Juice
2½ parts Pineapple Juice

GLASS: COCKTAIL

Shake with ice and strain

4th of July

1½ parts Vodka
½ part Blue Curaçao
½ part Triple Sec
½ part Sour Mix

GLASS: COCKTAIL

Shake with ice and strain.
Top with splash of grenadine.

'57 Chevy

1 part Southern Comfort®
1 part Gin
1 part Vodka
splash Orange Juice
splash Pineapple Juice
splash Grenadine

GLASS: COCKTAIL

Shake with ice and strain

8th Birthday

¾ part Raspberry Liqueur
¼ part Crème de Cacao (Dark)
1 part Vodka
1 part Milk

GLASS: COCKTAIL

Shake with ice and strain

9 1/2 Weeks

2 parts Citrus-Flavored Vodka
½ part Triple Sec
1 part Orange Juice
splash Strawberry Liqueur

GLASS: COCKTAIL

Shake with ice and strain

Abbey in the Hills

²/₃ part Vodka
½ part Crème de Cacao (White)
½ part Irish Cream Liqueur
½ part Frangelico®

{ GLASS: COCKTAIL

Shake with ice and strain

Abe's Tropical Night in Hell

2 parts Vodka
2 parts Banana Liqueur
2 parts Godiva® Liqueur
1 part Grenadine

{ GLASS: COCKTAIL

Shake with ice and strain

Absolut® Evergreen

²/₃ part Absolut® Citrus-Flavored Vodka
¹/₃ part Pisang Ambon® Liqueur
splash Lemon Juice

{ GLASS: COCKTAIL

Mix with ice and strain

Absolut® Northern Style

1 part Absolut® Vodka
splash Apple Brandy
½ part Cream
fill with White Wine

{ GLASS: COCKTAIL

Shake with ice and strain

Absolut® Pissy

2 parts Vodka
1 part Lime Juice
2 parts Pineapple Juice

{ GLASS: COCKTAIL

Shake with ice and strain

Accidental Tourist

1½ parts Gin
1 part Vanilla-Flavored Vodka
½ part Apple Brandy
½ part Passion Fruit Liqueur

{ GLASS: COCKTAIL

Shake with ice and strain

Admirals Only

½ part Citrus-Flavored Vodka
⅔ part Amaretto
⅔ part Grand Marnier®
1½ parts Cranberry Juice Cocktail

GLASS: COCKTAIL

Shake with ice and strain

Afterburner

1 part Vodka
½ part Triple Sec
1 splash Grapefruit Juice

GLASS: COCKTAIL

Shake with ice and strain

Aftermath

2 parts Vodka
1 part Mandarine Napoléon® Liqueur
4 parts Grapefruit Juice

GLASS: COCKTAIL

Shake with ice and strain

Ahh

1 part Vodka
1 part Parfait Amour
1 part Fruit Juice

GLASS: COCKTAIL

Shake with ice and strain

Aladdin Sane

1 part Citrus-Flavored Vodka
½ part Lime
½ part Cointreau®
2 parts Fruit Punch

GLASS: COCKTAIL

Shake with ice and strain

Aleluia

1 part Vodka
½ part Peach Schnapps
½ part Apricot Brandy
1 part Orange Juice

GLASS: COCKTAIL

Shake with ice and strain

Alley Shooter

1 part Irish Cream Liqueur
1 part Coffee Liqueur
1 part Frangelico®
1 part Amaretto
1 part Vodka

GLASS: COCKTAIL

Shake with ice and strain

Almond Colada

3 parts Amaretto
¼ cup Crème de Coconut
1½ parts Vodka
1 part Chocolate Syrup

GLASS: COCKTAIL

Shake with ice and strain

Almondini

1 part Vodka
1 part Amaretto

GLASS: COCKTAIL

Shake with ice and strain

Ambrosia

2 parts Vodka
½ part Melon Liqueur
¼ part Orange Bitters

GLASS: COCKTAIL

Shake with ice and strain

Amethyst

1 part Parfait Amour
½ part Raspberry Liqueur
½ part Vanilla-Flavored Vodka

GLASS: COCKTAIL

Shake with ice and strain

Amore Me Amore

1 part Blackberry Liqueur
1 part Currant-Flavored Vodka
½ part Frangelico®
½ part Lemon Juice
2 parts Raspberry-Flavored Seltzer

GLASS: COCKTAIL

Shake with ice and strain

Año

²⁄₃ part Raspberry Liqueur
²⁄₃ part Vodka
²⁄₃ part Dry Vermouth

> GLASS: COCKTAIL ☖
> *Shake with ice and strain*

Apple Judy

½ part Grand Marnier®
½ part Vodka
3 parts Apple Juice

> GLASS: COCKTAIL ☖
> *Shake with ice and strain*

April Rain

2 parts Dry Vodka
½ part Lime Cordial
½ part Vermouth

> GLASS: COCKTAIL ☖
> *Shake with ice and strain*

Aprishot

2 parts Vodka
½ part Apricot Brandy
1 part Pineapple Juice

> GLASS: COCKTAIL ☖
> *Shake with ice and strain*

Aqueduct

1½ parts Vodka
¾ part Amaretto
¾ part Triple Sec
½ part Fresh Lime Juice

> GLASS: COCKTAIL ☖
> *Shake with ice and strain*

Ariete

1 part Vodka
1 part Dry Vermouth
½ part Dry Sherry
splash Peach Schnapps
splash Blue Curaçao

> GLASS: COCKTAIL ☖
> *Shake with ice and strain*

Armon

1 part Vodka
½ part Coffee Liqueur
splash Crème de Menthe (White)
splash Blue Curaçao

GLASS: COCKTAIL
Shake with ice and strain

Asphalt Jungle

1 part Vodka
½ part Irish Cream Liqueur
½ part Lime Juice

GLASS: COCKTAIL
Shake with ice and strain

Atlantis

1½ parts Citrus-Flavored Vodka
½ part Blue Curaçao
⅔ part Passion Fruit Juice
⅔ part Grapefruit Juice

GLASS: COCKTAIL
Shake with ice and strain

Azulejo

1 part Vodka
½ part Parfait Amour
½ part Triple Sec
splash Pineapple Juice
dash Bitters

GLASS: COCKTAIL
Shake with ice and strain

Ballet Russe Cocktail

2 parts Vodka
½ part Crème de Cassis
4 splashes Lime Juice

GLASS: COCKTAIL
Shake with ice and strain

Banana Split

½ part Vodka
1½ parts Crème de Banana
1 part Crème de Cacao (White)
1 part Light Cream

GLASS: COCKTAIL
Shake with ice and strain

Bananarama

½ part Vodka
1 part Crème de Banana
½ part Triple Sec
1 part Light Cream

GLASS: COCKTAIL

Shake with ice and strain

Bank Holiday

1 part Orange-Flavored Vodka
1 part Crème de Cacao (White)
1 part Blackberry Liqueur

GLASS: COCKTAIL

Shake with ice and strain

Barbazul

⅔ part Triple Sec
⅔ part Currant-Flavored Vodka
1½ parts Grapefruit Juice
splash Lime Juice
splash Blue Curaçao

GLASS: COCKTAIL

Shake with ice and strain

Bare Cheeks

1 part Vodka
1 part Apple Juice
splash Grenadine
splash Lemon Juice

GLASS: COCKTAIL

Shake with ice and strain

Bartender's Delight

1 part Dry Vermouth
1 part Gordon's® Orange Vodka
1 part Dry Sherry

GLASS: COCKTAIL

Shake with ice and strain

Bastardly

½ part Vodka
½ part Blackberry Liqueur
splash Vanilla Liqueur
splash Amaretto

GLASS: COCKTAIL

Shake with ice and strain

Bavarian Cherry

½ part Kirschwasser
½ part Citrus-Flavored Vodka
¼ part Crème de Cassis
1 Egg White

GLASS: COCKTAIL
Shake with ice and strain

Beach Blanket Bop

½ part Vodka
½ part Coconut-Flavored Liqueur
½ part Melon Liqueur
½ part Blackberry Liqueur
1 part Pineapple Juice
½ part Cranberry Juice Cocktail

GLASS: COCKTAIL
Shake with ice and strain

Beauty Gump

½ part Blue Curaçao
½ part Peach Schnapps
½ part Orange-Flavored Vodka
splash Sour Mix

GLASS: COCKTAIL
Shake with ice and strain

Before Midnight

½ part Vodka
½ part Orange Juice
½ part Gin
splash Apricot Brandy

GLASS: COCKTAIL
Shake with ice and strain

Belching Dragon

1 part Pepper-Flavored Vodka
1 part Cinnamon Schnapps
1 part Vanilla Liqueur

GLASS: COCKTAIL
Shake with ice and strain

Belmont Stakes

1½ parts Vodka
¾ part Rum
½ part Fresh Lime Juice
½ part Strawberry
¼ part Grenadine

GLASS: COCKTAIL

Shake with ice and strain

Berry Deauville

1 part Vodka
½ part Blackberry Liqueur
½ part Raspberry Liqueur
½ part Peach Schnapps
1½ parts Pineapple Juice

GLASS: COCKTAIL

Shake with ice and strain

Berry Festival

1 part Vodka
1 part Crème de Cacao (White)
½ part Blackberry Liqueur
1 part Cream

GLASS: COCKTAIL

Shake with ice and strain

Berry Patch

1 part Currant-Flavored Vodka
¼ part Fresh Lime Juice
¼ part Blackberry

GLASS: COCKTAIL

Shake with ice and strain

Better than Ever

1 part Vodka
½ part Triple Sec
½ part Fresh Lime Juice
½ part Pear Liqueur
½ part Raspberry Syrup

GLASS: COCKTAIL

Shake with ice and strain

Beware of the Currant

1½ parts Blue Curaçao
½ part Raspberry Liqueur
1 part Currant-Flavored Vodka
1 part Pineapple Juice

{ GLASS: COCKTAIL
Shake with ice and strain

Bibe '77

1 part Vodka
1 part Sweet Vermouth
1 part Dry Vermouth
½ part Apricot Brandy
splash Amaretto
splash Grenadine

{ GLASS: COCKTAIL
Shake with ice and strain

Bikini

1 part Light Rum
2 parts Vodka
½ part Milk
1 dash Sugar
½ part Lemon Juice
Lemon Twist

{ GLASS: COCKTAIL
Shake with ice and strain

Bikini Top

1½ parts Vanilla-Flavored Vodka
1 part Blackberry Liqueur
⅔ part Crème de Cacao (White)

{ GLASS: COCKTAIL
Shake with ice and strain

Black and Blue

2 parts Black Death® Vodka
1 part Blue Curaçao
1 part Cranberry Juice Cocktail

{ GLASS: COCKTAIL
Shake with ice and strain

Black Bite

1 part Vodka
1 part Blackberry Liqueur
1 part Grapefruit Juice

GLASS: COCKTAIL

Shake with ice and strain

Black Cherry

1 part Vodka
1 part Southern Comfort®
1 part Amaretto
1 part Melon Liqueur
1 part Cranberry Juice Cocktail

GLASS: COCKTAIL

Shake with ice and strain

Black Friday

1 part Gin
1 part Black Vodka
1 part Grapefruit Juice
1 part Fresh Lime Juice

GLASS: COCKTAIL

Shake with ice and strain

Black Metal

½ part Vodka
½ part Blue Curaçao
½ part Crème de Cassis
½ part Lime Cordial

GLASS: COCKTAIL

Shake with ice and strain

Bledsko Jezero

1 part Vodka
1 part Sweet Vermouth
1 part Maraschino Liqueur
splash Blue Curaçao

GLASS: COCKTAIL

Shake with ice and strain

Blind Melon

1 part Melon Liqueur
½ part Vodka
½ part Light Rum
½ part Triple Sec

GLASS: COCKTAIL

Shake with ice and strain

Blood Shot

1 part Whiskey
1 part Vodka
1 part Apricot Brandy
1 part Sweet Vermouth
2 dashes Bitters

GLASS: COCKTAIL

Shake with ice and strain

Blood Transfusion

1 part Orange Liqueur
2 parts Citrus-Flavored Vodka
3 parts Orange Juice
splash Lime Cordial

GLASS: COCKTAIL

Shake with ice and strain

Bloody Lip

1 part Cherry Brandy
½ part Vodka
½ part Maraschino Liqueur

GLASS: COCKTAIL

Shake with ice and strain

Blue and Gold

1 part Vodka
½ part Blueberry Schnapps
½ part Pineapple Juice

GLASS: COCKTAIL

Shake with ice and strain

Blue Buddha

2 parts Vodka
splash Blue Curaçao
splash Sake
splash Grapefruit Juice
½ part Lemon Juice
½ part Lime Juice
splash Simple Syrup

GLASS: COCKTAIL

Shake with ice and strain

Blue Chili

2 parts Blue Curaçao
1 part Vodka
½ part Gin
½ part Light Rum

GLASS: COCKTAIL

Shake with ice and strain

Blue Cosmopolitan

2 parts Citrus-Flavored Vodka
1 part Blue Curaçao
½ part Grapefruit Juice
½ part Simple Syrup

GLASS: COCKTAIL

Shake with ice and strain

Blue Danube

½ part Vodka
½ part Blue Curaçao
½ part Triple Sec
½ part Crème de Banana
splash Cream

GLASS: COCKTAIL

Shake with ice and strain

Blue Light Special

¾ part Sour Apple Schnapps
¼ part Vodka
¼ part Blue Curaçao
splash Pineapple Juice

GLASS: COCKTAIL

Shake with ice and strain

Blue Marine

1½ parts Vodka
1 part Butterscotch Schnapps
1 part Blue Curaçao
splash Lemonade

GLASS: COCKTAIL
Shake with ice and strain

Blue Monday

1 part Vodka
1 part Triple Sec
1 part Blue Curaçao

GLASS: COCKTAIL
Shake with ice and strain

Blue Morning

2 parts Vodka
1 part Blue Curaçao
1 part Peach Schnapps

GLASS: COCKTAIL
Shake with ice and strain

Blue Panther

2 parts Vodka
1 part Dry Vermouth
1 part Orange Juice
1 Egg White
½ part Crème de Cassis

GLASS: COCKTAIL
Shake with ice and strain

Blue Shark

1 part Silver Tequila
1 part Vodka
splash Blue Curaçao

GLASS: COCKTAIL
Shake with ice and strain

Blue Temptation

1 part Vodka
1 part Blue Curaçao
1 part Pisang Ambon® Liqueur
½ part Crème de Banana
2 parts Cream

GLASS: COCKTAIL
Shake with ice and strain

Blushing Mellow

1 part Vodka
½ part Strawberry Liqueur
½ part Grenadine
1½ parts Cream

GLASS: COCKTAIL

Shake with ice and strain

Bobbit

1 part Vodka
1 part Gin
½ part Peach Schnapps
½ part Campari®

GLASS: COCKTAIL

Shake with ice and strain

Boca Chico Banana

½ part Vodka
½ part Pisang Ambon® Liqueur
½ part Coconut-Flavored Liqueur
splash Passion Fruit Nectar
1 part Guava Juice

GLASS: COCKTAIL

Shake with ice and strain

Bold Gold Monkey

1 part Gold Rum
1 part Vodka
4 parts Orange Juice
splash Grenadine

GLASS: COCKTAIL

Shake with ice and strain

Bolo Blast

½ part Coconut-Flavored Liqueur
½ part Raspberry Liqueur
½ part Crème de Banana
½ part Blackberry Liqueur
½ part Orange-Flavored Vodka

GLASS: COCKTAIL

Shake with ice and strain

Bolshoi Punch

1 part Vodka
½ part Light Rum
¼ part Crème de Cassis
½ part Lemon Juice
2 splashes Simple Syrup

GLASS: COCKTAIL

Shake with ice and strain

Bombar Cocktail

1½ parts Blue Curaçao
1 part Orange-Flavored Vodka
1 part Coconut-Flavored Rum

GLASS: COCKTAIL

Shake with ice and strain

Bon Lis

⅔ part Vodka
⅔ part Passion Fruit Liqueur
2 parts Pear Juice
splash Lemon Juice

GLASS: COCKTAIL

Shake with ice and strain

Bongo

1 part Citrus-Flavored Vodka
1 part Lychee Liqueur
1 part Pisang Ambon® Liqueur
1 part Fresh Lime Juice

GLASS: COCKTAIL

Shake with ice and strain

Brazilian Night

1 part Blue Curaçao
1 part Vodka
1 part Coconut-Flavored Liqueur

GLASS: COCKTAIL

Shake with ice and strain

Brisas del Paraíso

1 part Dry Gin
1 part Vodka
1 part Parfait Amour
splash Lemon Juice

GLASS: COCKTAIL

Shake with ice and strain

Broadside

1 part Dark Rum
½ part Vodka
½ part Cherry Brandy
½ part Frangelico®
2 splashes Grenadine

GLASS: COCKTAIL

Shake with ice and strain

A Brood Bloodbath

2 parts Vodka
1 part Cherry Juice
1 Cherry
splash Orange Juice

GLASS: COCKTAIL

Shake with ice and strain

Buca Alma

1½ parts Vodka
1½ parts Sambuca
1 part Amaretto

GLASS: COCKTAIL

Shake with ice and strain

Burning North Pole Breeze

1 part Pepper-Flavored Vodka
1 part Peppermint Liqueur
1 part Crème de Menthe (White)

GLASS: COCKTAIL

Shake with ice and strain

Butterfly

1 part Vodka
1 part Crème de Banana
1 part Pineapple Juice
1 part Blackberry Brandy

GLASS: COCKTAIL

Shake with ice and strain

Cactus Jack

1 part Vodka
½ part Blue Curaçao
1½ parts Pineapple Juice
1½ parts Orange Juice

GLASS: COCKTAIL

Shake with ice and strain

Candy from Strangers

1½ parts Vodka
½ part Triple Sec
½ part Amaretto
½ part Dry Vermouth

{ GLASS: COCKTAIL ⍥

Shake with ice and strain

Cappuccino Cocktail

1 part Vodka
1 part Coffee-Flavored Brandy
1 part Light Cream

{ GLASS: COCKTAIL ⍥

Shake with ice and strain

Catholic Coronation

1 part Vodka
½ part Amaretto
½ part Butterscotch Schnapps
½ part Frangelico®
½ part Milk

{ GLASS: COCKTAIL ⍥

Shake with ice and strain

Chantilly Lace

1½ parts Vanilla Liqueur
1½ parts Maraschino Liqueur
½ part Vodka
splash Chocolate Syrup

{ GLASS: COCKTAIL ⍥

Shake with ice and strain

Charging Rhino

1½ parts Vodka
½ part Dry Vermouth
½ part Campari®

{ GLASS: COCKTAIL ⍥

Shake with ice and strain

Cheesecake

1 part Vanilla-Flavored Vodka
½ part Triple Sec
½ part Sour Mix
1 part Cream
splash Crème de Cacao (White)

GLASS: COCKTAIL
Shake with ice and strain

Chellengae

1 part Vodka
1 part Grand Marnier®
½ part Lime Juice

GLASS: COCKTAIL
Shake with ice and strain

Cherry Berry

1 part Vodka
1 part Raspberry Liqueur
½ part Cherry Brandy
½ part Blackberry Juice
splash Lime Juice

GLASS: COCKTAIL
Shake with ice and strain

Cherry Kid

1 part Cherry-Flavored Vodka
1 part Amaretto
1 part Cranberry Juice Cocktail

GLASS: COCKTAIL
Shake with ice and strain

Cherry Ripe

1½ parts Vodka
½ part Cherry Brandy
½ part Brandy

GLASS: COCKTAIL
Shake with ice and strain

The Child Prodigy

1½ parts Orange Vodka
½ part Vanilla Liqueur
½ part Coconut-Flavored Liqueur
⅔ part Mango Juice
⅔ part Cream

{ GLASS: COCKTAIL

Shake with ice and strain

Chocolate Chip

1½ parts Vodka
1½ parts Frangelico®

{ GLASS: COCKTAIL

Shake with ice and strain

Chocolate Screwdriver

2 parts Vodka
1 part Crème de Cacao (White)
fill with Orange Juice

{ GLASS: COCKTAIL

Shake with ice and strain

Chop-Nut

¾ part Vodka
1 part Crème de Banana
1 part Coconut Liqueur
½ part Orange Juice

{ GLASS: COCKTAIL

Shake with ice and strain

Cinammon Twist

1 part Vodka
1 part Triple Sec
splash Lemon-Lime Soda

{ GLASS: COCKTAIL

Shake Vodka and Triple Sec with ice and strain. Top with a splash of Lemon-Lime Soda and garnish with Cinnamon Candies.

Classy Sanctuary

1 part Vodka
1 part Melon Liqueur
1 part Sour Mix
splash Passion Fruit Liqueur

GLASS: COCKTAIL

Shake with ice and strain

Climax

½ part Vodka
½ part Amaretto
½ part Crème de Cacao (White)
½ part Triple Sec
½ part Crème de Banana
1 part Light Cream

GLASS: COCKTAIL

Shake with ice and strain

Coco Candy Cane

1 part Vodka
1 part Crème de Cacao (White)
1 part Peppermint Schnapps

GLASS: COCKTAIL

Shake with ice and strain

Coco Poco

1 part Vodka
1 part Coconut-Flavored Liqueur
1 part Tia Maria®

GLASS: COCKTAIL

Shake with ice and strain

Cold Plunge

1 part Vodka
½ part Triple Sec
½ part Apricot Brandy
splash Crème de Banana

GLASS: COCKTAIL

Shake with ice and strain

Collection

1 part Vodka
1 part Citrus-Flavored Vodka
½ part Blackberry Liqueur
1 part Fresh Lime Juice

GLASS: COCKTAIL

Shake with ice and strain

Compel to Work

1 part Citrus-Flavored Vodka
½ part Orange Liqueur
1 part Grapefruit Juice
½ part Lemon Juice

GLASS: COCKTAIL

Shake with ice and strain

Concrete Jungle

2 parts Vodka
½ part Apricot Brandy
½ part Banana Juice

GLASS: COCKTAIL

Shake with ice and strain

Contradiction

1 part Vodka
½ part Melon Liqueur
½ part Coffee Liqueur
1 part Cream

GLASS: COCKTAIL

Shake with ice and strain

Cool Summer Breeze

1 part Passion Fruit Liqueur
1 part Vodka
1 part Cranberry Juice Cocktail
1 part Pear Juice

GLASS: COCKTAIL

Shake with ice and strain

Cosmo Katie

2 parts Currant-Flavored Vodka
1 part Grand Marnier®
splash Lime Juice
splash Cranberry Juice Cocktail

GLASS: COCKTAIL

Shake with ice and strain

Cosmopolitan

1¼ parts Citrus-Flavored Vodka
¼ part Lime Juice
¼ part Triple Sec
splash Cranberry Juice Cocktail

GLASS: COCKTAIL

Shake with ice and strain

Cossack Charge

1½ parts Vodka
½ part Cognac
½ part Cherry Brandy

GLASS: COCKTAIL

Shake with ice and strain

Cranberry Blast

1½ parts Peach Schnapps
½ part Dark Rum
½ part Vodka
½ part Scotch
½ part Orange Juice
2 parts Cranberry Juice Cocktail
splash Lemon Juice

GLASS: COCKTAIL

Shake with ice and strain

Cranberry Kami

1½ parts Vodka
½ part Triple Sec
½ part Lime Juice
½ part Cranberry Juice Cocktail

GLASS: COCKTAIL

Shake with ice and strain

Cranmint

¾ part Raspberry Liqueur
½ part Crème de Menthe (White)
½ part Citrus-Flavored Vodka

GLASS: COCKTAIL

Shake with ice and strain

Crantango Bay

½ part Citrus-Flavored Vodka
1 part Blackberry Liqueur
2 parts Cranberry Juice Cocktail

GLASS: COCKTAIL

Shake with ice and strain

Crash Landing

1½ parts Vodka
2 splashes Grenadine
1 splash Lime Juice
1 splash Lemon Juice
1 dash Sugar

GLASS: COCKTAIL

Shake with ice and strain

Crazy Calypso

1 part Peach Schnapps
1 part Orange-Flavored Vodka
splash Sour Mix

GLASS: COCKTAIL

Shake with ice and strain

Crazy Fin

2 parts Vodka
1 part Dry Sherry
1 part Cointreau®
½ part Lemon Juice

GLASS: COCKTAIL

Shake with ice and strain

Crista Solar

1 part Vodka
1 part Dry Vermouth
1 part Triple Sec
1 part White Port
dash Bitters

GLASS: COCKTAIL

Shake with ice and strain

Cristal Blue

1½ parts Vodka
1 part Parfait Amour
1 part Dry Sherry
dash Bitters

GLASS: COCKTAIL
Shake with ice and strain

Current Event

1 part Orange Liqueur
2 parts Currant-Flavored Vodka
splash Cranberry Juice Cocktail

GLASS: COCKTAIL
Shake with ice and strain

Czarina

1 part Vodka
¾ part Apricot Brandy
½ part Dry Vermouth
½ part Sweet Vermouth

GLASS: COCKTAIL
Shake with ice and strain

Dancin'

1 part Vodka
1 part Dry Vermouth
1 part Whiskey
splash Triple Sec
splash Cherry Brandy

GLASS: COCKTAIL
Shake with ice and strain

Daring Apricot

2 parts Vodka
½ part Triple Sec
½ part Apricot Brandy
½ part Fresh Lime Juice

GLASS: COCKTAIL
Shake with ice and strain

Dawdle in the Snow

1½ parts Vodka
½ part Triple Sec
1½ parts Pear Juice
1 part Cream

{ GLASS: COCKTAIL ▼
Shake with ice and strain

Deanne

1 part Vodka
½ part Sweet Vermouth
½ part Triple Sec
Lemon Twist

{ GLASS: COCKTAIL ▼
Shake with ice and strain

Decadence

1 part Vanilla-Flavored Vodka
1 part Coffee Liqueur
1 part White Chocolate Liqueur
1 part Cherry Cola
1 part Chocolate Milk

{ GLASS: COCKTAIL ▼
Shake with ice and strain

Desire

1 part Crème de Cacao (Dark)
1 part Coffee Liqueur
½ part Vodka

{ GLASS: COCKTAIL ▼
Shake with ice and strain

Diabolique

1 part Vodka
splash Crème de Cassis
2 parts Pineapple Juice

{ GLASS: COCKTAIL ▼
Shake with ice and strain

Doctor's Orders

1 part Vodka
1 part Amaretto
splash Kiwi Schnapps
½ part Lime Juice

GLASS: COCKTAIL
Shake with ice and strain

Doggy Style

1 part Vodka
splash Coffee-Flavored Brandy
splash Cream

GLASS: COCKTAIL
Shake with ice and strain

Dolphin Fin

1 part Vodka
½ part Sweet Vermouth
1 part Orange Juice
¼ part Lemon Juice
2 splashes Grenadine

GLASS: COCKTAIL
Shake with ice and strain

Don't Shoot the Bartender

½ part Amaretto
½ part Sloe Gin
½ part Triple Sec
½ part Vanilla-Flavored Vodka

GLASS: COCKTAIL
Shake with ice and strain

Dorothy's Orgasm

⅔ part Vodka
splash Butterscotch Schnapps
splash Coffee Liqueur
½ part Cream

GLASS: COCKTAIL
Shake with ice and strain

Double Trouble

⅔ part Vodka
splash Amaretto
½ part Melon Liqueur
½ part Cranberry Juice Cocktail
½ part Orange Juice

GLASS: COCKTAIL
Shake with ice and strain

Dovjenko

1½ parts Vodka
splash Cherry Brandy
½ part Chartreuse®
½ part Grapefruit Juice

GLASS: COCKTAIL
Shake with ice and strain

Down Under

1 part Vodka
2 splashes Brandy
2 splashes Triple Sec
2 splashes Crème de Cassis

GLASS: COCKTAIL
Shake with ice and strain

Dr. Livingstone

1½ parts Vodka
1 part Kiwi Schnapps
½ part Crème de Banana

GLASS: COCKTAIL
Shake with ice and strain

Dragon Fire

1 part Pepper-Flavored Vodka
1 part Crème de Menthe (Green)

GLASS: COCKTAIL
Shake with ice and strain

Dry Ice

⅔ part Blackberry Liqueur
⅔ part Citrus-Flavored Vodka
splash Blue Curaçao
splash Lemon Juice

GLASS: COCKTAIL
Shake with ice and strain

Dune Buggy

1½ parts Vodka
¾ part Cherry Brandy
½ part Lime Juice
dash Powdered Sugar

GLASS: COCKTAIL

Shake with ice and strain

East Wing

3 parts Vodka
1 part Cherry Brandy
½ part Campari®

GLASS: COCKTAIL

Shake with ice and strain

Eden Eve

1 part Raspberry Liqueur
1 part Vodka
⅔ part Pineapple Juice
⅔ part Cranberry Juice Cocktail

GLASS: COCKTAIL

Shake with ice and strain

Ekatherina Andreevna

2 parts Vodka
1 part Orange Juice

GLASS: COCKTAIL

Shake with ice and strain

Elysium

1 part Peach Schnapps
1 part Vodka
1½ parts Orange Juice
1½ parts Pineapple Juice

GLASS: COCKTAIL

Shake with ice and strain

Eva

1 part Vodka
1 part Crème de Menthe (Green)
1 part Simple Syrup

GLASS: COCKTAIL

Shake with ice and strain

Evening Delight

2 parts Irish Cream Liqueur
1 part Vodka

{ GLASS: COCKTAIL   Y
Shake with ice and strain

Fade to Black

1 part Coffee Liqueur
1 part Vodka
½ part Crème de Menthe (White)

{ GLASS: COCKTAIL   Y
Shake with ice and strain

Fairy Queen

1 part Vodka
½ part Cream
½ part Coffee Liqueur

{ GLASS: COCKTAIL   Y
Shake with ice and strain

Farinelli

1½ parts Vodka
½ part Dry Vermouth
½ part Campari®
splash Amaretto

{ GLASS: COCKTAIL   Y
Shake with ice and strain

Fig Newton

½ part Vodka
½ part Grand Marnier®
¼ part Crème de Almond
splash Orange Juice
splash Lemon Juice

{ GLASS: COCKTAIL   Y
Shake with ice and strain

Fire and Ice

1½ parts Pepper-Flavored Vodka
2 splashes Dry Vermouth

{ GLASS: COCKTAIL   Y
Shake with ice and strain

Fire Island Sunrise

1 part Rum
1 part Vodka
½ part Orange Juice
½ part Lemonade
splash Cranberry Juice Cocktail

GLASS: COCKTAIL

Shake with ice and strain

Firehammer

1½ parts Vodka
½ part Amaretto
½ part Triple Sec
splash Lemon Juice

GLASS: COCKTAIL

Shake with ice and strain

Fish Lips

1½ parts Vodka
½ part Kirschwasser
½ part Triple Sec
½ part Grapefruit Juice

GLASS: COCKTAIL

Shake with ice and strain

Flame of Love

1½ parts Vodka
½ part Dry Sherry

GLASS: COCKTAIL

Shake with ice and strain

Flipside Beach Bomber

1 part Vodka
½ part Triple Sec
½ part Grapefruit Juice
½ part Orange Juice
½ part Apricot Brandy

GLASS: COCKTAIL

Shake with ice and strain

Florida Beach Breeze

1 part Vodka
½ part Crème de Cacao (White)
½ part Crème de Banana
1 part Orange Juice

{ GLASS: COCKTAIL
Shake with ice and strain

Flying Grasshopper

1 part Vodka
1 part Crème de Menthe (Green)
1 part Crème de Cacao (White)

{ GLASS: COCKTAIL
Shake with ice and strain

Flying Horse

1½ parts Vodka
1 part Cream
1 part Cherry Brandy

{ GLASS: COCKTAIL
Shake with ice and strain

Fog at Bowling Green

1 part Peppermint Liqueur
1 part Vodka
1 part Cream

{ GLASS: COCKTAIL
Shake with ice and strain

Foggy Afternoon

1 part Vodka
½ part Apricot Brandy
½ part Triple Sec
splash Crème de Banana
splash Lemon Juice
1 Maraschino Cherry

{ GLASS: COCKTAIL
Shake with ice and strain

Formal Wear

1 part Vodka
1 part Blackberry Liqueur
⅔ part Cranberry Juice Cocktail
⅔ part Orange Juice

GLASS: COCKTAIL

Shake with ice and strain

The Four-Hundred Blows

1 part Vodka
⅔ part Lime Juice
½ part Simple Syrup

GLASS: COCKTAIL

Shake with ice and strain

Free Fly

1½ parts Vodka
½ part Parfait Amour
¼ part Triple Sec
¼ part Sweet Vermouth
splash Kiwi Juice

GLASS: COCKTAIL

Shake with ice and strain

French Cosmopolitan

1 part Citrus-Flavored Vodka
½ part Grand Marnier®
½ part Sour Mix
½ part Cranberry Juice Cocktail
¼ part Lime Juice
splash Grenadine

GLASS: COCKTAIL

*Shake all but Grenadine with ice
and strain into the glass. Place
a few drops of Grenadine in the
center of the drink.*

Friendly Alien

1½ parts Vodka
½ part Coconut-Flavored Liqueur
½ part Mango Schnapps
½ part Lemon Juice
1 part Pineapple Juice

GLASS: COCKTAIL

Shake with ice and strain

Frightleberry Murzenquest

1 part Vodka
½ part Galliano®
½ part Triple Sec
½ part Lime Juice
splash Maraschino Liqueur
dash Bitters

GLASS: COCKTAIL

Shake with ice and strain

Frog's Tongue

1½ parts Vodka
½ part Scotch

GLASS: COCKTAIL

Shake with ice and strain

Fuck Me to Death

½ part Brandy
½ part Scotch
½ part Vodka
½ part Coconut-Flavored Liqueur

GLASS: COCKTAIL

Shake with ice and strain

Fuschia

1 part Peach Schnapps
1½ parts Vodka
splash Passion Fruit Juice

GLASS: COCKTAIL

Shake with ice and strain

Galactic Trader

1 part Vodka
splash Apricot Brandy
½ part Blue Curaçao
½ part Lime Juice

GLASS: COCKTAIL

Shake with ice and strain

Galway Gray

1½ parts Vodka
1 part Crème de Cacao (White)
1 part Cointreau®
½ part Lime Juice
splash Cream

GLASS: COCKTAIL

Shake with ice and strain

Geneva Convention

2 parts Vodka
½ part Goldschläger®
½ part Grain Alcohol

GLASS: COCKTAIL

Shake with ice and strain

Geneva Summit

1 part Southern Comfort®
1 part Vodka
½ part Orange Juice
½ part Lime Juice
splash Peppermint Schnapps
splash Lemon-Lime Soda

GLASS: COCKTAIL

Shake with ice and strain

Ghostbuster

1 part Vodka
½ part Irish Cream Liqueur
½ part Coffee Liqueur

GLASS: COCKTAIL

Shake with ice and strain

Gimme Some

½ part Coconut-Flavored Liqueur
1 part Vanilla-Flavored Vodka
1 part Chocolate Liqueur
splash Sweet Vermouth

GLASS: COCKTAIL

Shake with ice and strain

Glacier Mint

1½ parts Vodka
½ part Lemon-Flavored Vodka
½ part Crème de Menthe (Green)

GLASS: COCKTAIL

Shake with ice and strain

Gladness

1½ parts Vodka
½ part Green Chartreuse®
splash Triple Sec

GLASS: COCKTAIL

Shake with ice and strain

Glaucoma

1 part Vodka
1 part Rum
1 part Gin
½ part Coffee Liqueur
splash Lemon Juice
dash Sugar

GLASS: COCKTAIL

Shake with ice and strain

Gnome Depot

⅔ part Melon Liqueur
2 parts Orange-Flavored Vodka
splash Dry Vermouth

GLASS: COCKTAIL

Shake with ice and strain

Godfather Dada

2 parts Amaretto
2 parts Grand Marnier®
3 parts Ketel One® Vodka
Orange Twist

GLASS: COCKTAIL

Shake with ice and strain

Golden Flute

½ part Blue Curaçao
splash Peach Schnapps
2 parts Vodka
splash Campari®

GLASS: COCKTAIL

Shake with ice and strain

Goldilocks's Cosmo

2 parts Vodka
¼ part Lime Juice
¼ part Triple Sec
splash White Cranberry Juice

GLASS: COCKTAIL

Shake with ice and strain

Grape Ape

1 part Vodka
½ part Crème de Cacao (White)
1 part Grape Juice (Red)

GLASS: COCKTAIL

Shake with ice and strain

Green Hope

1½ parts Vodka
½ part Blue Curaçao
½ part Crème de Banana

GLASS: COCKTAIL

Shake with ice and strain

Green Kryptonite

2 parts Vodka
splash Lime Juice
1 part Melon Liqueur

GLASS: COCKTAIL

Shake with ice and strain

Guapasipati

1½ parts Vodka
½ part Dry Vermouth
¼ part Crème de Banana
splash Orange Juice
splash Grenadine

GLASS: COCKTAIL

Shake with ice and strain

Gun Barrel

½ part Currant-Flavored Vodka
½ part Triple Sec
splash Cranberry Juice Cocktail

GLASS: COCKTAIL

Shake with ice and strain

Harvey Wallpaper Hanger

2 parts Vodka
1 part Galliano®

GLASS: COCKTAIL

Shake with ice and strain

Headlights

1 part Vodka
½ part Chartreuse®
2 splashes Galliano®
2 splashes Blue Curaçao
splash Lemon Juice

GLASS: COCKTAIL

Shake with ice and strain

Hello Nurse

1½ parts Vodka
½ part Amaretto
½ part Coconut Cream
½ part Light Cream

GLASS: COCKTAIL

Shake with ice and strain

Hep Cat

3 parts Currant-Flavored Vodka
½ part Dry Vermouth
splash Sweet Vermouth

GLASS: COCKTAIL

Shake with ice and strain

Her Name in Lights

1 part Vodka
½ part Chartreuse®
2 splashes Galliano®
2 splashes Blue Curaçao
½ part Lemon Juice
1 Maraschino Cherry

GLASS: COCKTAIL

Shake with ice and strain

High Fashion

2 parts Vodka
1 part Scotch
1 part Triple Sec

GLASS: COCKTAIL

Shake with ice and strain

Hippo in a Tutu

2 parts Currant-Flavored Vodka
½ part Raspberry Liqueur
½ part Blue Curaçao

GLASS: COCKTAIL

Shake with ice and strain

Hollywood Shooter

3 parts Vodka
1 part Pineapple Juice

GLASS: COCKTAIL

Shake with ice and strain

Holy Grail

1 part Vodka
1 part Campari®
½ part Apricot Brandy
1½ parts Orange Juice
1 Egg White

GLASS: COCKTAIL

Shake with ice and strain

Honolulu Hammer

1½ parts Vodka
½ part Amaretto
splash Pineapple Juice
splash Grenadine

GLASS: COCKTAIL

Shake with ice and strain

Hoochie Mama

1½ parts Vodka
1 part Crème de Menthe (White)
½ part Chocolate Syrup

GLASS: COCKTAIL
Shake with ice and strain

Hornet Stinger

1 part Vodka
½ part Melon Liqueur
dash Powdered Sugar
splash Lime Juice

GLASS: COCKTAIL
Shake with ice and strain

Hot Lava

1¼ parts Pepper-Flavored Vodka
¼ part Amaretto

GLASS: COCKTAIL
Shake with ice and strain

Hurlyburly

1¼ parts Citrus-Flavored Vodka
½ part Cointreau®
½ part Orange Juice
½ part Cranberry Juice Cocktail
1 part Sour Mix

GLASS: COCKTAIL
Shake with ice and strain

I Love Lucy

1 part Vodka
½ part Fresh Lime Juice
¼ part Parfait Amour
¼ part Triple Sec

GLASS: COCKTAIL
Shake with ice and strain

Ice Crystals

1½ parts Vodka
½ part Lemon-Flavored Vodka
½ part Crème de Menthe (Green)

GLASS: COCKTAIL
Shake with ice and strain

Iguana

½ part Vodka
½ part Tequila
¼ part Coffee-Flavored Vodka
1½ parts Sour Mix
½ Lime Slice

GLASS: COCKTAIL

Shake with ice and strain

In a Nutshell

1 part Amaretto
½ part Vanilla-Flavored Vodka
½ part Frangelico®
2 parts Cream

GLASS: COCKTAIL

Shake with ice and strain

International Cocktail

1½ parts Cognac
1 part Triple Sec
1 part Anisette
½ part Vodka

GLASS: COCKTAIL

Shake with ice and strain

Island Nation

½ part Triple Sec
½ part Vodka
½ part Peppermint Liqueur
1½ parts Pineapple Juice

GLASS: COCKTAIL

Shake with ice and strain

It's Now or Never

1 part Vodka
splash Apricot Brandy
splash Campari®
splash Limoncello

GLASS: COCKTAIL

Shake with ice and strain

Jamaican Green Sunrise

1½ parts Light Rum
1 part Orange Juice
½ part Blue Curaçao
½ part Pineapple-Flavored Vodka

GLASS: COCKTAIL

Shake with ice and strain

Jamaican Russian Handshake

2 parts Vodka
½ part Grenadine
⅔ part Spiced Rum
⅔ part Lemon Juice

GLASS: COCKTAIL

Shake with ice and strain

Jamaican Tennis Beads

1 part Vodka
1 part Coconut-Flavored Rum
1 part Raspberry Liqueur
1 part Crème de Banana
1 part Pineapple Juice
1 part Half and Half

GLASS: COCKTAIL

Shake with ice and strain

Jerusalem Love Cream

1½ parts Guava Juice
1½ parts Vanilla-Flavored Vodka
½ part Lychee Syrup

GLASS: COCKTAIL

Shake with ice and strain

Josie & the Pussycats

1 part Cranberry-Flavored Vodka
1 part Triple Sec
½ part Currant-Flavored Vodka
½ part Citrus-Flavored Vodka
dash Angostura® Bitters

GLASS: COCKTAIL

Shake with ice and strain

Joy Jumper

1½ parts Vodka
2 splashes Kümmel
splash Lime Juice
splash Lemon Juice
dash Sugar
1 Lemon Twist

GLASS: COCKTAIL
Shake with ice and strain

Kabut

1½ parts Vanilla Liqueur
1 part Blue Curaçao
½ part Vodka

GLASS: COCKTAIL
Shake with ice and strain

Kahlodster

1 part Coffee Liqueur
1 part Vodka
1 part Jägermeister®

GLASS: COCKTAIL
Shake with ice and strain

Kangaroo

1½ parts Vodka
¾ part Dry Vermouth

GLASS: COCKTAIL
Shake with ice and strain

Kashmir

1 part Vodka
1 part Crème de Cacao (White)
2 splashes Grenadine
2 splashes Lemon Juice

GLASS: COCKTAIL
Shake with ice and strain

Kempinsky Fizz

2 parts Vodka
1 part Crème de Cassis

GLASS: COCKTAIL
Shake with ice and strain

Kharamazov

1 part Coffee Liqueur
1 part Vodka
1 part Blue Curaçao
splash Orange Juice

GLASS: COCKTAIL
Shake with ice and strain

Killer Whale

1½ parts Blue Curaçao
splash Orange-Flavored Vodka
1 part Orange Juice
splash Pineapple Juice
dash Sugar

GLASS: COCKTAIL
Shake with ice and strain

Kilt Club

⅔ part Citrus-Flavored Vodka
1 part Kiwi Schnapps
1 part Drambuie®
½ part Pineapple Juice

GLASS: COCKTAIL
Shake with ice and strain

Kinky Cherry

½ part Vodka
2 parts Cherry Brandy
½ part Jim Beam®
½ part Sweet Vermouth
½ part Lemon Juice

GLASS: COCKTAIL
Shake with ice and strain

Kuala Lumpur

1½ parts Vodka
⅔ part Pisang Ambon® Liqueur
1 part Coconut-Flavored Liqueur
fill with Orange Juice
splash Cream

GLASS: COCKTAIL
Shake with ice and strain

La Carré

1½ parts Vodka
2 splashes Dry Vermouth
2 splashes Kümmel

GLASS: COCKTAIL

Shake with ice and strain

La Manga

1 part Vodka
1 part Apricot Brandy
1 part Licor 43®
splash Grenadine

GLASS: COCKTAIL

Shake with ice and strain

Ladies' Night

1 part Vodka
½ part Peach Schnapps
½ part Triple Sec
½ part Lemon Juice

GLASS: COCKTAIL

Shake with ice and strain

Lady Man

½ part Peach Schnapps
1 part Vodka
splash Grenadine
splash Lemon Juice
splash Papaya Juice

GLASS: COCKTAIL

Shake with ice and strain

Laguna Cocktail

2 parts Brandy
¼ part Vodka
¼ part Vermouth
splash Campari®
dash Bitters

GLASS: COCKTAIL

Shake with ice and strain

Lemon Lance

1 part Vanilla Liqueur
1 part Limoncello
splash Citrus-Flavored Vodka
splash Bacardi® Limón Rum

GLASS: COCKTAIL
Shake with ice and strain

Licorice Stick

1 part Black Sambuca
1 part Vodka
½ part Crème de Cacao (White)

GLASS: COCKTAIL
Shake with ice and strain

Light Saber

½ part Vodka
½ part 151-Proof Rum
1 part Crème de Banana
½ part Triple Sec
½ part Vanilla Liqueur

GLASS: COCKTAIL
Shake with ice and strain

Lightning

1 part Blue Curaçao
1 part Citrus-Flavored Vodka
splash Crème de Cassis
splash Lime Juice

GLASS: COCKTAIL
Shake with ice and strain

Lime Light

2 parts Vodka
½ part Melon Liqueur
½ part Grapefruit Juice

GLASS: COCKTAIL
Shake with ice and strain

The Limey

2½ parts Vodka
½ part Blue Curaçao
½ part Lime Juice

GLASS: COCKTAIL
Shake with ice and strain

Liquid Gold

1 part Vodka
½ part Galliano®
½ part Crème de Cacao (White)
1 part Cream

{ GLASS: COCKTAIL

Shake with ice and strain

Love Boat

1 part Vodka
1 part Coconut Cream
1 part Pineapple Juice
splash Blue Curaçao

{ GLASS: COCKTAIL

Shake with ice and strain

The Love Doctor

2 parts Vodka
1 part Crème de Cacao (White)
½ part Raspberry Liqueur

{ GLASS: COCKTAIL

Shake with ice and strain

Love Heart

1 part Vodka
½ part Orange Juice
½ part Passion Fruit
splash Peach Schnapps

{ GLASS: COCKTAIL

Shake with ice and strain

LPR
(Liquid Pants Remover)

1 part Dark Rum
1 part Vodka
1 part Tequila
1 part Southern Comfort®
1 part Amaretto

{ GLASS: COCKTAIL

Shake with ice and strain

Lylyblue

1 part Vodka
1 part Fresh Lime Juice
1 part Lychee Liqueur
splash Blue Curaçao

GLASS: COCKTAIL
Shake with ice and strain

Macaroon

2 parts Vodka
½ part Amaretto
½ part Crème de Cacao (Dark)

GLASS: COCKTAIL
Shake with ice and strain

Machintoch

1 part Vodka
½ part Blackberry Liqueur
½ part Apple Brandy
2 parts Cream

GLASS: COCKTAIL
Shake with ice and strain

Major Tom

1½ parts Vodka
½ part Triple Sec
½ part Kirschwasser
½ part Grapefruit Juice

GLASS: COCKTAIL
Shake with ice and strain

Mama Mia

1½ parts Vodka
1 part Amaretto
½ part Cream

GLASS: COCKTAIL
Shake with ice and strain

Mandarin Dream

2 parts Orange-Flavored Vodka
splash Orange Juice
splash Cranberry Juice Cocktail

GLASS: COCKTAIL
Shake with ice and strain

Mandarin Metropolitan

1½ parts Orange-Flavored Vodka
1 part Cranberry Juice Cocktail
½ part Sweetened Lime Juice

GLASS: COCKTAIL

Shake with ice and strain

Medical Solution

1½ parts Vodka
½ part Parfait Amour
1 part Cream

GLASS: COCKTAIL

Shake with ice and strain

Melon Heaven

1 part Vodka
1 part Melon Liqueur
½ part Triple Sec
½ part Lime Juice

GLASS: COCKTAIL

Shake with ice and strain

Melrose Beauty

1 part Vodka
½ part Raspberry Liqueur
½ part Cranberry Juice Cocktail
splash Pineapple Juice
splash Lemon Juice
splash Lime Juice

GLASS: COCKTAIL

Shake with ice and strain

Merchant Prince

⅔ part Vodka
1 part Cherry Brandy
⅔ part Drambuie®
⅔ part Vanilla Liqueur

GLASS: COCKTAIL

Shake with ice and strain

Meteorite

1½ parts Vodka
½ part Triple Sec
½ part Cherry Brandy
⅔ part Dry Vermouth

GLASS: COCKTAIL
Shake with ice and strain

Midnight Delight

1½ parts Vodka
1 part Crème de Cacao (White)
1 part Chocolate Mint Liqueur

GLASS: COCKTAIL
Shake with ice and strain

Midnight Sun

2 parts Vodka
1 part Cointreau®
1 part Apricot Brandy
1 part Grenadine
½ part Lemon Juice

GLASS: COCKTAIL
Shake with ice and strain

Mintzerac

⅔ part Vodka
1 part Peppermint Liqueur
½ part Melon Liqueur
½ part Lime Juice

GLASS: COCKTAIL
Shake with ice and strain

Mother Russia

1½ parts Vodka
½ part Maraschino Liqueur
½ part Coconut-Flavored Rum
1 part Cream
½ part Egg White

GLASS: COCKTAIL
Shake with ice and strain

Mounds Bar Cocktail

1½ parts Chocolate-Flavored Vodka
1½ parts Coconut-Flavored Rum

GLASS: COCKTAIL
Shake with ice and strain

Mousse Cherry

1 part Vodka
1 part Grapefruit Juice
½ part Cherry Brandy

GLASS: COCKTAIL
Shake with ice and strain

Multi-Colored Smurf®

½ part Blueberry Schnapps
½ part Apricot Brandy
½ part Vodka
½ part Mango Nectar
1 part Orange Juice

GLASS: COCKTAIL
Shake with ice and strain

Naked Pear

½ part Apple-Flavored Vodka
½ part Melon Liqueur
½ part Triple Sec
1 part Pineapple Juice
splash Sour Mix

GLASS: COCKTAIL
Shake with ice and strain

Nasty

1¼ parts Vodka
¾ part Coffee Liqueur
¾ part Wild Turkey® Bourbon
¾ part Crème de Cacao (Dark)
½ part Cream

GLASS: COCKTAIL
Shake with ice and strain

Neopolitan Cocktail

1½ parts Cranberry-Flavored Vodka
½ part Cointreau®
splash Raspberry Liqueur
splash Lime Juice

GLASS: COCKTAIL
Shake with ice and strain

Neptune's Pond

1½ parts Vodka
1½ parts Dubonnet® Blonde

GLASS: COCKTAIL

Shake with ice and strain

New York Lemonade

1 part Citrus-Flavored Vodka
½ part Grand Marnier®
½ part Lemon Juice
1 part Club Soda

GLASS: COCKTAIL

Stir gently with ice and strain

Ninotchka Cocktail

1½ parts Vodka
½ part Crème de Cacao (White)
½ part Lemon Juice

GLASS: COCKTAIL

Shake with ice and strain

Nitro Cocktail

1½ parts Vodka
¾ part Scotch
1 part Cranberry Juice Cocktail
1 part Orange Juice

GLASS: COLLINS

Build over ice and stir

Oakland Cocktail

1 part Vodka
1 part Dry Vermouth
1 part Orange Juice

GLASS: COCKTAIL

Shake with ice and strain

Obsession

1 part Vodka
½ part Passion Fruit Liqueur
½ part Pisang Ambon® Liqueur
1 part Orange Juice

GLASS: COCKTAIL

Shake with ice and strain

Off-White

1 part Vodka
1 part Amaretto
1 part Coconut-Flavored Liqueur
1 part Vanilla Liqueur

{ GLASS: COCKTAIL
Shake with ice and strain

Old Car

1 part Vodka
½ part Apricot Brandy
½ part Triple Sec
¼ part Grapefruit Juice

{ GLASS: COCKTAIL
Shake with ice and strain

Oompa Loompa

½ part Vodka
½ part Chocolate Mint Liqueur
½ part Banana Liqueur
1½ parts Light Cream

{ GLASS: COCKTAIL
Shake with ice and strain

Opal

1½ parts Vodka
1 part Crème de Banana
splash Campari®
splash Grenadine

{ GLASS: COCKTAIL
Shake with ice and strain

Opium

1 part Vodka
1 part Amaretto
1 part Peach Schnapps

{ GLASS: COCKTAIL
Shake with ice and strain

Orange Kamikaze

1½ parts Vodka
½ part Triple Sec
½ part Orange Juice

{ GLASS: COCKTAIL
Shake with ice and strain

Orange Lion

1 part Orange-Flavored Vodka
1 part Peach Schnapps
1 part Orange Juice

GLASS: COCKTAIL
Shake with ice and strain

Orcabessa

1 part Peach Schnapps
splash Vodka
splash Orange Juice
splash Sour Mix

GLASS: COCKTAIL
Shake with ice and strain

Osaka Dry

3 parts Vodka
½ part Sake

GLASS: COCKTAIL
Shake with ice and strain

Ostwind Cocktail

1 part Vodka
1 part Dry Vermouth
1 part Sweet Vermouth
½ part Rum

GLASS: COCKTAIL
Shake with ice and strain

Pacific Fleet

½ part Peach Schnapps
½ part Kiwi Schnapps
½ part Vodka
½ part Light Rum
1 part Cranberry Juice Cocktail

GLASS: COCKTAIL
Shake with ice and strain

Pagoda

1 part Vodka
1 part Mandarine Napoléon® Liqueur
1 part Pineapple Juice

GLASS: COCKTAIL
Shake with ice and strain

Parrotti

1 part Vodka
½ part Apricot Brandy
splash Lychee Liqueur
splash Grenadine
splash Lime Juice

GLASS: COCKTAIL
Shake with ice and strain

Peachtree Square

1 part Vodka
1 part Peach Schnapps
½ part Crème de Cacao (White)
½ part Cream

GLASS: COCKTAIL
Shake with ice and strain

Peagreen

1 part Vodka
1 part Peppermint Liqueur
1 part Cream

GLASS: COCKTAIL
Shake with ice and strain

Peanut Butter Cup

½ part Vodka
½ part Frangelico®
½ part Crème de Cacao (White)
2 parts Light Cream

GLASS: COCKTAIL
Shake with ice and strain

Pear Drop

1½ parts Citrus-Flavored Vodka
1½ parts Lychee Liqueur

GLASS: COCKTAIL
Shake with ice and strain

Pedi Cocktail

2 parts Vodka
splash Triple Sec
⅔ part Campari®

GLASS: COCKTAIL
Shake with ice and strain

Pepper Perfect

½ part Vanilla Liqueur
½ part Pepper-Flavored Vodka
½ part Lemon-Lime Soda
1 part Cranberry Juice Cocktail

GLASS: COCKTAIL
Shake with ice and strain

Persian Delight

1 part Vodka
½ part Crème de Cacao (White)
½ part Lychee Liqueur
¼ part Maraschino Liqueur
¼ part Sweetened Lime Juice

GLASS: COCKTAIL
Shake with ice and strain

Petticoat

1 part Vanilla-Flavored Vodka
½ part Crème de Cacao (White)
½ part Chocolate Liqueur
1 part Cream
splash Galliano®

GLASS: COCKTAIL
Shake with ice and strain

Pimp Cocktail

2 parts Vodka
1 part Blue Curaçao
1 part Peach Schnapps
fill with Orange Juice

GLASS: COCKTAIL
Build over ice and stir

Pink Fluid

1½ parts Vodka
½ part Crème de Cacao (White)
½ part Strawberry Syrup

GLASS: COCKTAIL
Shake with ice and strain

Pink Mink

1 part Vodka
1 part Rum
1 part Strawberry Liqueur

{ GLASS: COCKTAIL

Shake with ice and strain

Pink Panther

1 part Amaretto
½ part Vodka
splash Grenadine
2 parts Light Cream

{ GLASS: COCKTAIL

Shake with ice and strain

Pink Teddy

1 part Vodka
1 part Passion Fruit Liqueur
½ part Lychee Liqueur
½ part Cream
splash Grenadine

{ GLASS: COCKTAIL

Shake with ice and strain

Piranha

1½ parts Vodka
1½ parts Crème de Cacao (Dark)

{ GLASS: COCKTAIL

Shake with ice and strain

Polynesian Cocktail

1½ parts Vodka
¾ part Cherry Brandy
½ part Lime Juice
dash Powdered Sugar

{ GLASS: COCKTAIL

Shake with ice and strain

Ponche Orinoco

1 part Light Rum
½ part Apricot Brandy
¼ part Vodka
¼ part Orange Juice
splash Grenadine
dash Bitters

{ GLASS: COCKTAIL
Shake with ice and strain

Potemkin

3 parts Vodka
splash Benedictine®

{ GLASS: COCKTAIL
Shake with ice and strain

Potpourri

1½ parts Vodka
½ part Cherry Brandy
½ part Brandy

{ GLASS: COCKTAIL
Shake with ice and strain

Psycho Therapy

1 part Vodka
1 part Rémy Martin® VSOP
1 part Scotch

{ GLASS: COCKTAIL
Shake with ice and strain

Pulsar

1 part Blue Curaçao
½ part Crème de Cassis
splash Vodka
splash Lime Juice

{ GLASS: COCKTAIL
Shake with ice and strain

Purple Mask

1 part Vodka
½ part Crème de Cacao (White)
1 part Grape Juice (Red)

{ GLASS: COCKTAIL
Shake with ice and strain

Pursuit Plane

1½ parts Vodka
⅔ part Vanilla Liqueur
⅔ part Butterscotch Schnapps

GLASS: COCKTAIL
Shake with ice and strain

Quicksand

1 part Vodka
⅔ part Coffee Liqueur
splash Vanilla Liqueur

GLASS: COCKTAIL
Shake with ice and strain

Quiet Sunday

1 part Vodka
1 part Orange Juice
½ part Amaretto
½ part Grenadine

GLASS: COCKTAIL
Shake with ice and strain

Radioactivity

1 part Vodka
½ part Lychee Liqueur
½ part Pisang Ambon® Liqueur
1 part Lemon Juice

GLASS: COCKTAIL
Shake with ice and strain

Ramasi

½ part Vodka
½ part Triple Sec
½ part Amaretto
1 part Sour Mix
½ part Pineapple Juice

GLASS: COCKTAIL
Shake with ice and strain

Randini

2 parts Cranberry Juice Cocktail
3 parts Gin
1 Lime Wedge
1 part Triple Sec
1 part Vodka

GLASS: COCKTAIL

Shake with ice and strain

Raquel

1 part Vodka
½ part Blue Curaçao
½ part Parfait Amour
½ part Cherry Brandy
splash Cream

GLASS: COCKTAIL

Shake with ice and strain

Rasp Royale

1 part Vodka
½ part Raspberry Liqueur
½ part Coffee Liqueur
½ part Irish Cream Liqueur

GLASS: COCKTAIL

Shake with ice and strain

Razzberi Kazi

1 part Raspberry-Flavored Vodka
1 part Triple Sec
1 part Sour Mix
½ part Grenadine

GLASS: COCKTAIL

Shake with ice and strain

Razzmopolitan

1½ parts Vodka
¾ part Raspberry Liqueur
½ part Fresh Lime Juice
splash Cranberry Juice Cocktail

GLASS: COCKTAIL

Shake with ice and strain

Recession Depression

1½ parts Citrus-Flavored Vodka
½ part Triple Sec
½ part Lemon Juice
2 splashes Sweetened Lime Juice

GLASS: COCKTAIL

Shake with ice and strain

Red Apple

1 part Vodka
1 part Apple Juice
2 splashes Lemon Juice
splash Grenadine

GLASS: COCKTAIL

Shake with ice and strain

Red Panties

1½ parts Vodka
1 part Peach Schnapps
splash Grenadine
1 part Orange Juice

GLASS: COCKTAIL

Shake with ice and strain

Red Russian

1 part Vodka
½ part Crème de Cacao (White)
1 part Cranberry Juice Cocktail

GLASS: COCKTAIL

Shake with ice and strain

Red Sonja

1 part Vodka
1 part Raspberry Liqueur
1 part Cranberry Juice Cocktail

GLASS: COCKTAIL

Shake with ice and strain

Redcoat

1½ parts Light Rum
½ part Vodka
½ part Apricot Brandy
½ part Lime Juice
splash Grenadine

GLASS: COCKTAIL

Shake with ice and strain

Risky Business

1½ parts Vodka
splash Raspberry Liqueur
splash Lime Juice
splash Blackberry Juice

GLASS: COCKTAIL

Shake with ice and strain

Roberta

1 part Vodka
1 part Dry Vermouth
1 part Cherry Brandy
splash Crème de Banana
splash Campari®

GLASS: COCKTAIL

Shake with ice and strain

Rococo

1 part Cherry Vodka
½ part Triple Sec
1 part Orange Juice

GLASS: COCKTAIL

Shake with ice and strain

Rolling Thunder

1½ parts Light Rum
½ part Vodka
½ part Apricot Brandy
¼ part Lime Juice
¼ part Grenadine

GLASS: COCKTAIL

Shake with ice and strain

Rose of Warsaw

1½ parts Polish Vodka
1 part Cherry Liqueur
½ part Cointreau®
dash Bitters

GLASS: COCKTAIL

Shake with ice and strain

Royal Passion

1½ parts Vodka
¾ part Raspberry Liqueur
½ part Passion Fruit Juice

GLASS: COCKTAIL
Shake with ice and strain

Rushkin

1 part Vodka
1 part Raspberry Liqueur
½ part Blackberry Liqueur
½ part Lime Juice
½ part Sour Mix

GLASS: COCKTAIL
Shake with ice and strain

Russian Armpit

½ part Orange-Flavored Vodka
½ part Citrus-Flavored Vodka
1 part Crème de Banana
1 part Mango Juice

GLASS: COCKTAIL
Shake with ice and strain

Russian Cocktail

1 part Vodka
1 part Gin
1 part Crème de Cacao (White)

GLASS: COCKTAIL
Shake with ice and strain

Russian Haze

1 part Vodka
½ part Frangelico®
½ part Irish Cream Liqueur

GLASS: COCKTAIL
Shake with ice and strain

Russian Peach

1 part Vodka
½ part Peach Schnapps
½ part Crème de Cassis
1 part Orange Juice

GLASS: COCKTAIL
Shake with ice and strain

Russian Smooth Side

1 part Vodka
½ part Orange Liqueur
½ part Mandarine Napoléon® Liqueur
½ part Lemon Juice
1 part Orange Juice

GLASS: COCKTAIL

Shake with ice and strain

Russian Twilight

1 part Vodka
1 part Crème de Cacao (White)
1 part Cream

GLASS: COCKTAIL

Shake with ice and strain

Russin' About

1½ parts Vodka
½ part Irish Cream Liqueur
½ part Tia Maria®
¼ part Frangelico®

GLASS: COCKTAIL

Shake with ice and strain

Sail Away

1 part Vodka
½ part Peach Liqueur
½ part Melon Liqueur
1 part Fresh Lime Juice

GLASS: COCKTAIL

Shake with ice and strain

Sake Cocktail

1 part Melon Liqueur
1 part Sake
1 part Citrus-Flavored Vodka

GLASS: COCKTAIL

Shake with ice and strain

Sake to Me

2 parts Orange-Flavored Vodka
½ part Blue Curaçao
splash Sake

GLASS: COCKTAIL

Shake with ice and strain

Salem

1 part Vodka
1 part Crème de Menthe (Green)
½ part Dry Vermouth
½ part Triple Sec

GLASS: COCKTAIL

Shake with ice and strain

Sangria

2 parts Orange-Flavored Vodka
½ part Red Wine
splash Cherry Brandy
½ part Orange Juice
splash Lemon Juice
splash Lime Juice

GLASS: COCKTAIL

Shake with ice and strain

Saratoga Party

1½ parts Vodka
splash Grenadine
dash Angostura® Bitters
splash Club Soda

GLASS: COCKTAIL

Shake with ice and strain

Save the Planet

1 part Vodka
1 part Melon Liqueur
½ part Blue Curaçao
2 splashes Green Chartreuse®

GLASS: COCKTAIL

Shake with ice and strain

Sayonara

1 part Vodka
½ part Dry Vermouth
¼ part Triple Sec
¼ part Apricot Brandy
splash Papaya Juice

GLASS: COCKTAIL

Shake with ice and strain

Scanex

2 parts Vodka
1 part Cranberry Liqueur
1 part Lemon Juice
1 part Grenadine
1 part Sugar

GLASS: COCKTAIL

Shake with ice and strain

Scarlet Lady

1½ parts Vodka
¼ part Coffee Liqueur
¼ part Cherry Brandy

GLASS: COCKTAIL

Shake with ice and strain

Scarlett Fever

1½ parts Citrus-Flavored Vodka
½ part Amaretto
1 part Cranberry Juice Cocktail

GLASS: COCKTAIL

Shake with ice and strain

Screaming Banana Banshee

½ part Banana Liqueur
½ part Vodka
½ part Crème de Cacao (White)
1½ parts Cream

GLASS: COCKTAIL

Shake with ice and strain

Screaming Orgasm

1 part Vodka
1 part Amaretto
1 part Crème de Cacao (White)
1 part Triple Sec
2 parts Cream

GLASS: COCKTAIL

Shake with ice and strain

Screaming Viking

2 parts Vodka
1 part Dry Vermouth
1 part Lime Juice

GLASS: COCKTAIL

Shake with ice and strain

Scuttle for Liberty

1½ parts Vodka
½ part Lychee Liqueur
⅔ part Pineapple Juice
⅔ part Mango Juice
⅔ part Lemon Juice

GLASS: COCKTAIL

Shake with ice and strain

Seaweed

1½ parts Pineapple-Flavored Vodka
1½ parts Melon Liqueur
¼ part Strawberry Liqueur
¼ part Pineapple Juice

GLASS: COCKTAIL

Shake with ice and strain

Seether

1½ parts Vodka
½ part Cherry Brandy
1 part Orange Juice
dash Orange Bitters

GLASS: COCKTAIL

Shake with ice and strain

Seventh Heaven Cocktail

1½ parts Vodka
2 splashes Grapefruit Juice
2 splashes Maraschino Cherry Juice

GLASS: COCKTAIL

Shake with ice and strain

Sex Apple

2 parts Vodka
splash Goldschläger®
½ part Apple Liqueur
1 part Apple Juice

GLASS: COCKTAIL

Shake with ice and strain

Shark's Breath

½ part Vodka
½ part Gin
½ part Light Rum
½ part Blue Curaçao
¼ part Fresh Lime Juice

GLASS: COCKTAIL
Shake with ice and strain

Shiver

1 part Vodka
1 part Crème de Banana
½ part Parfait Amour

GLASS: COCKTAIL
Shake with ice and strain

Short Girl

½ part Vodka
¼ part Coconut-Flavored Rum
¼ part Peach Schnapps
1 part Orange Juice
1 part Pineapple Juice
splash Cranberry Juice Cocktail

GLASS: COCKTAIL
Shake with ice and strain

Showbiz

1 part Vodka
1 part Grapefruit Juice
1 part Crème de Cassis

GLASS: COCKTAIL
Shake with ice and strain

Siberian Surprise

1 part Vodka
1 part Peach Schnapps
½ part Coconut-Flavored Liqueur
½ part Sour Mix

GLASS: COCKTAIL
Shake with ice and strain

Sintra

1 part Melon Liqueur
²⁄₃ part Orange-Flavored Vodka
1 part Cream

GLASS: COCKTAIL
Shake with ice and strain

Sister Moonshine

1 part Vodka
1 part Dry Vermouth
½ part Apricot Brandy
½ part Grapefruit Juice

GLASS: COCKTAIL
Shake with ice and strain

Skippy Cosmo

1 part Vodka
½ part Cointreau®
¼ part Grenadine

GLASS: COCKTAIL
Shake with ice and strain

Sleepwalker

1½ parts Orange-Flavored Vodka
½ part Blue Curaçao
½ part Chocolate Liqueur
1 part Cream

GLASS: COCKTAIL
Shake with ice and strain

Smooth Grand

²⁄₃ part Vodka
²⁄₃ part Amaretto
²⁄₃ part Root Beer Schnapps
1 part Cream

GLASS: COCKTAIL
Shake with ice and strain

Sogno d'autunno

1½ parts Vodka
½ part Crème de Banana
½ part Dark Rum
splash Blue Curaçao
splash Lime Juice

GLASS: COCKTAIL
Shake with ice and strain

Soul Bossa Nova

1 part Vodka
½ part Crème de Cacao (White)
splash Grenadine

GLASS: COCKTAIL
Shake with ice and strain

Sound of Silence

1½ parts Vodka
½ part Lychee Liqueur
½ part Lemon Juice
½ part Simple Syrup
splash Orange Juice

GLASS: COCKTAIL
Shake with ice and strain

Sour Apple Cosmopolitan

½ part Sour Apple–Flavored Schnapps
1½ parts Vodka
1 part Cranberry Juice Cocktail
splash Lime Juice

GLASS: COCKTAIL
Shake with ice and strain

South Beach Cosmopolitan

2 parts Citrus-Flavored Vodka
½ part Raspberry Liqueur
½ part Cranberry Juice Cocktail

GLASS: COCKTAIL
Shake with ice and strain

Southern Life

½ part Vodka
½ part Kiwi Schnapps
½ part Southern Comfort®
½ part Cranberry Juice Cocktail
1 part Orange Juice

GLASS: COCKTAIL
Shake with ice and strain

Southwest One

1 part Vodka
1 part Orange Juice
1 part Campari®

GLASS: COCKTAIL
Shake with ice and strain

Spellbinder

2 parts Citrus-Flavored Vodka
⅔ part Melon Liqueur
splash Blue Curaçao

GLASS: COCKTAIL
Shake with ice and strain

Spin Cycle

1 part Gin
1 part Orange-Flavored Vodka
½ part Blue Curaçao
½ part Mandarine Napoléon® Liqueur

GLASS: COCKTAIL
Shake with ice and strain

Spy's Dream

splash Melon Liqueur
1 part Currant-Flavored Vodka
1 part Bacardi® Limón Rum
splash Lime Cordial

GLASS: COCKTAIL
Shake with ice and strain

Srap Shrinker

1 part Cranberry-Flavored Vodka
½ part Raspberry Liqueur
splash Orange Liqueur
½ part Lemon Juice
⅔ part Grapefruit Juice

GLASS: COCKTAIL
Shake with ice and strain

Ssimo Suprize

1 part Citrus-Flavored Vodka
1 part Melon Liqueur
½ part Kiwi Schnapps
½ part Lemon Syrup

GLASS: COCKTAIL
Shake with ice and strain

St. Vincent

1 part Vodka
1 part Apricot Brandy
1 part Licor 43®
splash Grenadine

{ GLASS: COCKTAIL Y

Shake with ice and strain

Star Legend

1 part Vodka
¼ part Apricot Brandy
¼ part Campari®
¼ part Raspberry Liqueur
½ part Orange Juice
splash Blue Curaçao

{ GLASS: COCKTAIL Y

Shake with ice and strain

Star of Love

1 part Vodka
1 part Crème de Cacao (Dark)
splash Frangelico®
1 part Cream

{ GLASS: COCKTAIL Y

Shake with ice and strain

Star System

1½ parts Peach Schnapps
½ part Vanilla-Flavored Vodka
1 part Orange Juice
1 part Cream

{ GLASS: COCKTAIL Y

Shake with ice and strain

Sterlitamak

1½ parts Cherry Brandy
1½ parts Vodka
splash Dubonnet® Blonde
splash Lemon Juice

{ GLASS: COCKTAIL Y

Shake with ice and strain

Strawberry Girl

1 part Vodka
1 part Strawberry Liqueur
1 part Crème de Cacao (White)

GLASS: COCKTAIL

Shake with ice and strain

Strawsmopolitan

2 parts Strawberry-Flavored Vodka
1 part Cointreau®
splash Lime Juice
splash Cranberry Juice Cocktail

GLASS: COCKTAIL

Shake with ice and strain

Strike!

½ part Triple Sec
⅔ part Vodka
⅔ part Passoã®

GLASS: COCKTAIL

Shake with ice and strain

Stupid Cupid

2 parts Citrus-Flavored Vodka
½ part Sloe Gin
splash Sour Mix

GLASS: COCKTAIL

Shake with ice and strain

Summer Night Dream

2 parts Vodka
1 part Kirschwasser

GLASS: COCKTAIL

Shake with ice and strain

Sun Ray

1 part Maraschino Liqueur
1 part Amaretto
splash Citrus-Flavored Vodka

GLASS: COCKTAIL

Shake with ice and strain

Sunset Beach

1 part Vodka
1 part Melon Liqueur
1 part Coconut-Flavored Liqueur
1 part Apricot Juice

{ GLASS: COCKTAIL
Shake with ice and strain

Super Hero Respite

2/3 part Vodka
½ part Crème de Cacao (White)
½ part Raspberry Liqueur
1 part Milk

{ GLASS: COCKTAIL
Shake with ice and strain

Surf Rider

1 part Vodka
1 part Sweet Vermouth
½ part Lemon Juice
splash Grenadine
splash Orange Juice

{ GLASS: COCKTAIL
Shake with ice and strain

Swamp Water

1 part Vodka
1 part Blue Curaçao
1 part Galliano®

{ GLASS: COCKTAIL
Shake with ice and strain

Swedish Lady

1 part Vodka
½ part Strawberry Liqueur
1 part Simple Syrup
½ part Cream

{ GLASS: COCKTAIL
Shake with ice and strain

Sweet Dream Cocktail

1½ parts Vodka
½ part Coconut Cream
1 part Orange Juice
½ part Powdered Sugar
splash Coconut Liqueur

{ GLASS: COCKTAIL

Shake with ice and strain

Sweet Maria

1 part Vodka
1 part Amaretto
1 part Light Cream

{ GLASS: COCKTAIL

Shake with ice and strain

A Sweet Peach

2 parts Vanilla-Flavored Vodka
1 part Peach Schnapps
½ part Sour Mix
½ part Orange Juice

{ GLASS: COCKTAIL

Shake with ice and strain

Swiss Miss

1 part Vodka
1 part Crème de Cacao (White)
½ part Butterscotch Schnapps
½ part Frangelico®

{ GLASS: COCKTAIL

Shake with ice and strain

Tantric

2 parts Vodka
1 part Passion Fruit Liqueur
splash Cranberry Juice Cocktail
splash Pineapple Juice

{ GLASS: COCKTAIL

Shake with ice and strain

Tap Dance

1 part Vodka
½ part Amaretto
½ part Peach Schnapps
1 part Orange Juice

GLASS: COCKTAIL

Shake with ice and strain

Tasty Trinidad

1 part Citrus-Flavored Vodka
1 part Blue Curaçao
½ part Sour mix
½ part Orange Juice

GLASS: COCKTAIL

Shake with ice and strain

Tattoo You

1 part Peach Schnapps
1 part Cranberry-Flavored Vodka
1 part Orange Juice

GLASS: COCKTAIL

Shake with ice and strain

Tattooed Love Goddess

1 part Vodka
1 part Vanilla Liqueur
1 part Chocolate Liqueur
splash Cream

GLASS: COCKTAIL

Shake with ice and strain

Teenage Lobotomy

1½ parts Jim Beam®
1½ parts Vodka
splash Blue Curaçao

GLASS: COCKTAIL

Shake with ice and strain

Tenderness

⅔ part Vodka
½ part Passoã®
splash Grand Marnier®
splash Crème de Cassis
splash Lemon Juice

GLASS: COCKTAIL

Shake with ice and strain

Three Count

1 part Vodka
½ part Cherry Brandy
¼ part Crème de Banana
2 splashes Campari®

GLASS: COCKTAIL

Shake with ice and strain

Three Mile Island

¾ part Vodka
¾ part Midori®
¼ part Lime Juice
2 parts Apple Juice

GLASS: COCKTAIL

Shake with ice and strain

Thug Heaven

2 parts Alizé®
2 parts Vodka

GLASS: COCKTAIL

Shake with ice and strain

Tikini

1 part Vodka
½ part Raspberry Liqueur
½ part Blue Curaçao
splash Cranberry Juice Cocktail
splash Pear Juice
splash Lime Juice

GLASS: COCKTAIL

Shake with ice and strain

Titanic

1½ parts Vodka
½ part Dry Vermouth
½ part Galliano®
½ part Blue Curaçao

GLASS: COCKTAIL

Shake with ice and strain

Titi Pink

⅔ part Passion Fruit Liqueur
2 parts Vanilla-Flavored Vodka
splash Cranberry Juice Cocktail
splash Orange Juice

GLASS: COCKTAIL
Shake with ice and strain

Tokyo Cosmo

1½ parts Vodka
1½ parts Sake
¼ part Pineapple Juice

GLASS: COCKTAIL
Shake with ice and strain

Topps

1 part Crème de Banana
1 part Maraschino Liqueur
1 part Melon Liqueur
1 part Vodka
1 part Sour Mix
1 part Orange Juice

GLASS: COCKTAIL
Shake with ice and strain

Toronto Orgy

1 part Vodka
½ part Coffee Liqueur
½ part Irish Cream Liqueur
½ part Grand Marnier®

GLASS: COCKTAIL
Shake with ice and strain

Tovarich

1½ parts Vodka
¾ part Kümmel
2 splashes Lime Juice

GLASS: COCKTAIL
Shake with ice and strain

Train Stopper

1 part Vodka
1 part Blackberry Liqueur
splash Crème de Cassis
splash Simple Syrup
½ part Lemon Juice

GLASS: COCKTAIL

Shake with ice and strain

Tranquility Cove

1 part Vodka
1 part Peach Schnapps
⅔ part Cranberry Juice Cocktail
⅔ part Orange Juice

GLASS: COCKTAIL

Shake with ice and strain

Traveling Trocadero

⅔ part Citrus-Flavored Vodka
1 part Peppermint Liqueur
½ part Pineapple Juice
splash Lime Juice

GLASS: COCKTAIL

Shake with ice and strain

Tresserhorn

1 part Blue Curaçao
1 part Orange-Flavored Vodka
1 part Absinthe
1 part Sour Mix

GLASS: COCKTAIL

Shake with ice and strain

Trick Pony

1½ parts Vodka
splash Crème de Cassis
splash Amaretto

GLASS: COCKTAIL

Shake with ice and strain

Tropical Gaze

1 part Vodka
1 part Melon Liqueur
²/₃ part Cranberry Juice Cocktail
²/₃ part Pineapple Juice

{ GLASS: COCKTAIL

Shake with ice and strain

Twenny

1 part Vodka
1 part Coffee Liqueur
1 part Triple Sec
splash Apricot Brandy

{ GLASS: COCKTAIL

Shake with ice and strain

Twizzler®

2 parts Vodka
1 part Strawberry Liqueur
splash Grenadine

{ GLASS: COCKTAIL

Shake with ice and strain

Ultra Violet

2 parts Vodka
½ part Parfait Amour

{ GLASS: COCKTAIL

Shake with ice and strain

Uranus

1½ parts Vodka
½ part Pisang Ambon® Liqueur
½ part Passion Fruit Liqueur

{ GLASS: COCKTAIL

Shake with ice and strain

Valize

1 part Alizé®
1 part Vodka

{ GLASS: COCKTAIL

Shake with ice and strain

Valkyrie

1½ parts Vodka
splash Peppermint Liqueur
½ part Jägermeister®
1 part Cream

GLASS: COCKTAIL
Shake with ice and strain

Vampire

1 part Vodka
1 part Raspberry Liqueur
½ part Sweetened Lime Juice
½ part Cranberry Juice Cocktail

GLASS: COCKTAIL
Shake with ice and strain

Vanilla 43

¾ part Licor 43®
1¼ part Vanilla-Flavored Vodka
1 part Pineapple Juice

GLASS: COCKTAIL
Shake with ice and strain

Vanishing Cream

1 part Crème de Cacao (White)
1 part Chocolate Liqueur
1 part Cream
splash Vodka

GLASS: COCKTAIL
Shake with ice and strain

Velvet Elvis

2 parts Vodka
splash Amaretto
splash Chocolate Liqueur
½ part Pear Liqueur

GLASS: COCKTAIL
Shake with ice and strain

Veruska

1 part Vodka
½ part Campari®
¼ part Crème de Banana
splash Sweetened Lime Juice

GLASS: COCKTAIL
Shake with ice and strain

Vicious Kiss

3 parts Citrus-Flavored Vodka
2 splashes Maraschino Cherry Juice
2 splashes Lime Juice

GLASS: COCKTAIL

Stir gently with ice and strain

Violetta Comfort

1 part Vodka
1 part Parfait Amour
1 part Southern Comfort®
splash Fresh Lime Juice

GLASS: COCKTAIL

Shake with ice and strain

Virgin's Blood

2 parts Vodka
1 part Red Curaçao
1 part Strawberry

GLASS: COCKTAIL

Stir gently with ice and strain

Vodka Gibson

2 parts Vodka
½ part Dry Vermouth

GLASS: COCKTAIL

Shake with ice and strain.
Garnish with a pearl onion.

Vodka Grasshopper

1 part Vodka
1 part Crème de Menthe (Green)
1 part Crème de Cacao (White)

GLASS: COCKTAIL

Shake with ice and strain

Vodka Stinger

1½ parts Vodka
1½ parts Crème de Menthe (White)

GLASS: COCKTAIL

Shake with ice and strain

Volga

1 part Vodka
1 part Pineapple Juice
1 part Orange Juice
splash Grenadine

GLASS: COCKTAIL

Shake with ice and strain

Voodoo Cocktail

1 part Peach Schnapps
1 part Vodka
1 part Cream

GLASS: COCKTAIL

Shake with ice and strain

Vorhees Special

1 part Vodka
1 part Coconut-Flavored Rum
1 part Sambuca
1 part Orange Juice
splash Banana Liqueur
splash Tabasco® Sauce

GLASS: COCKTAIL

Shake with ice and strain

Warsaw Cocktail

1½ parts Vodka
½ part Dry Vermouth
½ part Blackberry Brandy
splash Lemon Juice

GLASS: COCKTAIL

Shake with ice and strain

Watchdog

1½ parts Citrus-Flavored Vodka
splash Maraschino Liqueur
1 part Lemon Juice

GLASS: COCKTAIL

Shake with ice and strain

Wembeldorf

1 part Vodka
1 part Apricot Brandy
½ part Lime Juice
½ part Sour Mix
½ part Pineapple Juice

GLASS: COCKTAIL

Stir gently with ice and strain

White House

1 part Coconut-Flavored Liqueur
1 part Chocolate Liqueur
1 part Cream
splash Vodka

GLASS: COCKTAIL

Stir gently with ice and strain

White Spider

1½ parts Vodka
½ part Crème de Menthe (White)

GLASS: COCKTAIL

Stir gently with ice and strain

Whore

1 part Vodka
1 part Triple Sec
½ part Lemon Juice

GLASS: COCKTAIL

Stir gently with ice and strain

Wicked Tasty Treat

2 parts Cinnamon-Flavored Vodka
1 part Amaretto
1 part Coffee Liqueur
1 part Irish Cream Liqueur
1 part Cream

GLASS: COCKTAIL

Stir gently with ice and strain

Wild Cherry

1 part Vodka
1 part Crème de Cacao (White)
½ part Coffee
½ part Frangelico®

GLASS: COCKTAIL

Stir gently with ice and strain

Witch of Venice

1½ parts Vodka
½ part Strega®
2 splashes Crème de Banana
1 part Orange Juice

GLASS: COCKTAIL

Shake with ice and strain

Wong Tong Cocktail

1 part Vodka
½ part Gin
½ part Dry Vermouth
1 part Lemonade

GLASS: COCKTAIL

Shake with ice and strain

Works of God

1 part Vodka
1 part Strawberry Liqueur
1 part Cream

GLASS: COCKTAIL

Shake with ice and strain

Yokohama Cocktail

1 part Gin
1 part Vodka
1 part Grenadine
1 part Orange Juice

GLASS: COCKTAIL

Shake with ice and strain

Yuma

1 part Vodka
1 part Triple Sec
½ part Apricot Brandy
½ part Cognac

GLASS: COCKTAIL

Shake with ice and strain

Zabriski Point

1 part Vodka
splash Vanilla Liqueur
splash Apple Brandy
1½ parts Apple Juice

GLASS: COCKTAIL

Shake with ice and strain

Zephyr

1 part Vodka
1 part Blue Curaçao
½ part Parfait Amour
splash Lemon Juice

GLASS: COCKTAIL

Stir gently with ice and strain

Zero

1½ parts Blue Curaçao
1 part Crème de Cacao (White)
1 part Vodka

GLASS: COCKTAIL

Stir gently with ice and strain

CHAPTER

SHAKE
WITH
ICE &
STRAIN

7

SHOTS & SHOOTERS

SERVED IN SMALL GLASSES AND CONSUMED IN A SINGLE GULP, SHOTS ARE MUCH EASIER TO DEFINE THAN MARTINIS OR COCKTAILS. IN THIS BOOK, THE BROAD CATEGORY OF "SHOTS" HAS BEEN REFINED EVER SO SLIGHTLY TO "SHOTS AND SHOOTERS" IN THIS CHAPTER, AND TO "LAYERED SHOTS" IN THE FOLLOWING CHAPTER.

DRINK UP!

40 Skit and a Bent Jant

1 part Blue Curaçao
1 part Jägermeister®
1 part Citrus-Flavored Vodka
1 part Peach Schnapps
1 part Cranberry Juice Cocktail
1 part Pineapple Juice
splash Lime Juice

GLASS: SHOT

Shake with ice and strain

8 Ball

4 parts Coconut-Flavored Rum
4 parts Peach Schnapps
4 parts Raspberry Liqueur
4 parts Vodka
splash Lemon-Lime Soda
1½ parts Cranberry Juice Cocktail
1½ parts Sour Mix
splash Grenadine

GLASS: SHOT

Shake with ice and strain

Absohot

½ part Absolut® Peppar Vodka
splash Hot Sauce
1 Beer

GLASS: SHOT

Mix Vodka and Hot Sauce in a shot glass. Serve with beer chaser.

Absolut® Antifreeze

1 part Melon Liqueur
2 parts Absolut® Citron Vodka
2 parts Lemon-Lime Soda

GLASS: SHOT

Shake with ice and strain

Absolut® Asshole

2 parts Absolut® Vodka
1 part Sour Apple Schnapps

GLASS: SHOT

Shake with ice and strain

Absolut® Hunter

2 parts Absolut® Vodka
1 part Jägermeister®

{ GLASS: SHOT

Shake with ice and strain

Absolut® Passion

2 parts Absolut® Vodka
1 part Passion Fruit Juice

{ GLASS: SHOT

Shake with ice and strain

Absolut® Pepparmint

1 part Absolut® Peppar Vodka
splash Peppermint Schnapps

{ GLASS: SHOT

Shake with ice and strain

Absolut® Testa Rossa

1 part Absolut® Vodka
½ part Campari®

{ GLASS: SHOT

Shake with ice and strain

Absolutely Fruity

1 part Vodka
1 part 99-proof Banana Liqueur
1 part Watermelon Schnapps

{ GLASS: SHOT

Shake with ice and strain

Absolutely Screwed

1 part Orange-Flavored Vodka
1 part Orange Juice

{ GLASS: SHOT

Shake with ice and strain

Adios, Motherfucker

1 part Vodka
1 part Gin
1 part Rum
1 part Tequila
1 part Triple Sec
2 parts Sour Mix
splash Cola
splash Blue Curaçao

GLASS: SHOT

Shake with ice and strain

Note: Because this recipe includes many ingredients, it's easier to make in volume, about 6 shots.

Adult Lit

1 part Dry Gin
1 part Vodka
1 part Triple Sec
1 part Light Rum

GLASS: SHOT

Shake with ice and strain

After Eight® Shooter

1 part Crème de Cacao (White)
1 part Crème de Menthe (White)
1 part Vodka

GLASS: SHOT

Shake with ice and strain

Afterburner #2

1 part Pepper-Flavored Vodka
1 part Coffee
1 part Goldschläger®

GLASS: SHOT

Pour ingredients into glass neatly (do not chill)

Alien Secretion

1 part Vodka
1 part Melon Liqueur
1 part Coconut-Flavored Rum
1 part Pineapple Juice

GLASS: SHOT

Shake with ice and strain

Amaretto Chill

1 part Vodka
1 part Amaretto
1 part Lemonade
1 part Pineapple Juice

GLASS: SHOT

Shake with ice and strain

Amaretto Kamikaze

1 part Vodka
1 part Amaretto
fill with Sour Mix

GLASS: SHOT

Shake with ice and strain

Amaretto Lemondrop

1 part Vodka
1 part Amaretto
fill with Lemonade

GLASS: SHOT

Build over ice and stir

Amaretto Sourball

1 part Vodka
1 part Amaretto
1 part Lemonade
1 part Orange Juice

GLASS: SHOT

Shake with ice and strain

Amaretto Sweet Tart

1 part Vodka
1 part Amaretto
1 part Cherry Juice
1 part Wild Berry Schnapps
fill with Lemonade

GLASS: SHOT

Shake with ice and strain

Anti Freeze

1 part Crème de Menthe (Green)
1 part Vodka

GLASS: SHOT

Pour ingredients into glass neatly (do not chill)

Apple Fucker

1 part Sour Apple Schnapps
1 part Vodka

GLASS: SHOT

Shake with ice and strain

Apple Kamikaze

1 part Vodka
1 part Sour Apple Schnapps
splash Sour Mix

GLASS: SHOT

Shake with ice and strain

Apple Lemondrop

1 part Vodka
1 part Sour Apple Schnapps
splash Lemonade

GLASS: SHOT

Shake with ice and strain

Arizona Antifreeze

1 part Vodka
1 part Melon Liqueur
1 part Sour Mix

GLASS: SHOT

Shake with ice and strain

Arizona Twister

1 part Vodka
1 part Coconut-Flavored Rum
1 part Tequila
splash Orange Juice
splash Pineapple Juice
splash Crème de Coconut
splash Grenadine

GLASS: SHOT

Shake with ice and strain

*Note: Because this recipe includes many ingredients, it's easier to make in volume, about 6 shots.

Astronaut Shooter

1 part Vodka (chilled)
1 Lemon Wedge
dash Sugar
dash Instant Coffee Granules

GLASS: SHOT

Coat the lemon with sugar on one side and instant coffee on the other, suck lemon and drink the chilled vodka

The Atomic Shot

1 part Tequila Silver
1 part Goldschläger®
1 part Absolut® Peppar Vodka
splash Club Soda

GLASS: SHOT

Shake with ice and strain

Back Shot

1 part Vodka
1 part Raspberry Liqueur
2 parts Sour Mix

GLASS: SHOT

Shake with ice and strain

Banana Boomer Shooter

1 part Vodka
1 part Crème de Banana

GLASS: SHOT

Shake with ice and strain

Banana Cream Pie

1 part Banana Liqueur
1 part Crème de Cacao (White)
1 part Vodka
1 part Half and Half

GLASS: SHOT

Shake with ice and strain

Banana Popsicle® Shooter

1 part Vodka
1 part Crème de Banana
1 part Orange Juice

GLASS: SHOT

Shake with ice and strain

Banana Split Shooter

1 part Banana Liqueur
1 part Vodka

{ GLASS: SHOT

Shake with ice and strain

Banana Sweet Tart

1 part Vodka
1 part Banana Liqueur
1 part Cherry Juice
fill with Lemonade

{ GLASS: SHOT

Shake with ice and strain

Barbie® Shot

1 part Coconut-Flavored Rum
1 part Vodka
1 part Cranberry Juice Cocktail
1 part Orange Juice

{ GLASS: SHOT

Shake with ice and strain

Barfing Sensations

1 part Blackberry Liqueur
1 part Peach Schnapps
1 part Vodka
1 part Apple Brandy
1 part Raspberry Liqueur

{ GLASS: SHOT

Shake with ice and strain

**Note: Because this recipe
includes many ingredients,
it's easier to make in volume,
about 6 shots.*

Bearded Boy

1 part Southern Comfort®
1 part Vodka
1 part Water
splash Grain Alcohol

{ GLASS: SHOT

Shake with ice and strain

Beaver Dam

1 part Vodka
1 part Peach Schnapps
1 part Gatorade®

{ GLASS: SHOT

Shake with ice and strain

Beowulf

1 part Blue Curaçao
1 part Vodka

GLASS: SHOT

Shake with ice and strain

The Berry Kix®

2 parts Currant-Flavored Vodka
1 part Sour Mix

GLASS: SHOT

Shake with ice and strain

Big Baller

2 parts Vodka
1 part Gin
1 part Triple Sec
splash Lemon Juice

GLASS: SHOT

Shake with ice and strain

The Big V

1 part Vodka
1 part Crème de Cacao (White)
1 part Blue Curaçao
1 part Sour Mix

GLASS: SHOT

Shake with ice and strain

Bite of the Iguana

1 part Tequila
1 part Triple Sec
½ part Vodka
2 parts Orange Juice
2 parts Sour Mix

GLASS: SHOT

Shake with ice and strain

Black and Blue Shark

2 parts Jack Daniel's®
1 part Gold Tequila
1 part Vodka
1 part Blue Curaçao

GLASS: SHOT

Shake with ice and strain

Black Death

3 parts Vodka
1 part Soy Sauce

GLASS: SHOT

Shake with ice and strain

Black Orgasm

1 part Vodka
1 part Sloe Gin
1 part Blue Curaçao
1 part Peach Schnapps

GLASS: SHOT

Shake with ice and strain

Black Pepper

1 part Pepper-Flavored Vodka
splash Blackberry Brandy

GLASS: SHOT

Shake with ice and strain

Blackberry Sourball

1 part Vodka
1 part Blackberry Liqueur
splash Lemonade
splash Orange Juice

GLASS: SHOT

Shake with ice and strain

Bleedin' Hell

1 part Vodka
1 part Strawberry Liqueur
1 part Lemonade

GLASS: SHOT

Shake with ice and strain

Bliss

1 part Vanilla Liqueur
1 part Vanilla-Flavored Vodka
1 part Vanilla Cola
splash Honey

GLASS: SHOT

Shake with ice and strain

Blue Ghost

1 part Banana Liqueur
1 part Blue Curaçao
1 part Coconut-Flavored Rum
1 part Vodka
1 part Crème de Cacao (White)
1 part Light Rum
1 part Triple Sec
4 parts Cream

GLASS: SHOT

Shake with ice and strain
**Note: Because this recipe
includes many ingredients,
it's easier to make in volume,
about 6 shots.*

Blue Meanie

1 part Blue Curaçao
1 part Vodka
1 part Sour Mix

GLASS: SHOT

Shake with ice and strain

Blue Polarbear

1 part Vodka
1 part Avalanche® Peppermint Schnapps

GLASS: SHOT

Shake with ice and strain

Blue Razzberry Kamikaze

2 parts Raspberry Vodka
1 part Blue Curaçao
splash Lime Cordial

GLASS: SHOT

Shake with ice and strain

Blue Slammer

1 part Blue Curaçao
1 part Sambuca
1 part Vodka
splash Lemon Juice

GLASS: SHOT

*Pour ingredients into glass
neatly (do not chill)*

Blue Spruce

1 part Maple Syrup
1 part Vodka

GLASS: SHOT

*Pour ingredients into glass
neatly (do not chill)*

Body Shot

1 part Vodka
dash Sugar
1 Lemon Wedge

GLASS: SHOT

With a partner, lick his or her neck, then pour the Sugar onto the moistened shot. Place the wedge of Lemon in his or her mouth with the skin pointed inward. Lick the Sugar from his or her neck, shoot the Vodka, then suck the Lemon from his or her mouth (while gently holding back of the neck).

A Bomb

1 part Vodka
1 part Coffee
½ part Cold Coffee

GLASS: SHOT

Shake with ice and strain

Bonnie's Berry's

1 part Vodka
1 part Amaretto
1 part Raspberry Liqueur

GLASS: SHOT

Shake with ice and strain

Boom Box

1 part Vodka
1 part White Wine
1 part Hot Coffee

GLASS: SHOT

Pour ingredients into glass neatly (do not chill)

Border Conflict Shooter

2 parts Vodka
2 parts Crème de Menthe (White)
1 part Grenadine

GLASS: SHOT

Shake with ice and strain

Braindead

1 part Vodka
1 part Sour Mix
1 part Triple Sec

GLASS: SHOT

Shake with ice and strain

Braveheart

1 part Vodka
splash Blue Curaçao

GLASS: SHOT

Shake with ice and strain

Breath Freshener

1 part Vodka
2 parts Peppermint Schnapps

GLASS: SHOT

Shake with ice and strain

Bruised Heart

1 part Vodka
1 part Raspberry Liqueur
1 part Peach Schnapps
1 part Cranberry Juice Cocktail

GLASS: SHOT

Shake with ice and strain

Bubble Gum

1 part Melon Liqueur
1 part Vodka
1 part Crème de Banana
1 part Orange Juice

GLASS: SHOT

Shake with ice and strain

Chariot of Fire

1 part Vodka
1 part Sambuca

GLASS: SHOT

Shake with ice and strain

Cherry Bomb #1

1 part Vodka
1 part Crème de Cacao (White)
1 part Grenadine

GLASS: SHOT

Shake with ice and strain

Cherry Bomb #2

2 parts Vodka
1 part Goldschläger®
1 part Light Rum
1 Maraschino Cherry

GLASS: SHOT

Shake with ice and strain

Chiquita

1 part Vodka
2 parts Crème de Banana
1 part Milk

GLASS: SHOT

Shake with ice and strain

Chocolate Cake

1 part Frangelico®
1 part Vodka
1 Lemon Wedge
dash Sugar

GLASS: SHOT

*Shake Frangelico® and Vodka
with ice and strain into a
shot glass. Moisten hand and
sprinkle Sugar onto it, drink the
shot, lick the Sugar, and suck
the Lemon.*

Chocolate Valentine

1 part Vanilla-Flavored Vodka
1 part Crème de Cacao (Dark)
1 part Cherry Juice
splash Cream
splash Club Soda

GLASS: SHOT

Shake with ice and strain
**Note: Because this recipe
includes many ingredients,
it's easier to make in volume,
about 6 shots.*

Citron My Face

2 parts Citrus-Flavored Vodka
1 part Grand Marnier®
1 part Sour Mix

GLASS: SHOT

Shake with ice and strain

Citron Sour

1 part Citrus-Flavored Vodka
1 part Lime Juice

GLASS: SHOT

Shake with ice and strain

Cocaine

1 part Vodka
1 part Raspberry Liqueur
1 part Grapefruit Juice

GLASS: SHOT

Shake with ice and strain

Cordless Screwdriver

1 part Vodka
1 Orange Wedge
dash Sugar

GLASS: SHOT

Shake the Vodka with ice and strain into a shot glass. Dip the Orange Wedge in the Sugar, drink the shot, and suck on the Orange.

Cough Syrup

1 part Vodka
1 part Blue Curaçao
1 part Crème de Menthe (White)

GLASS: SHOT

Shake with ice and strain

Cranapple Blast

1 part Sour Apple Schnapps
1 part Cranberry Juice Cocktail
1 part Vodka

GLASS: SHOT

Shake with ice and strain

Crimson Tide

1 part Vodka
1 part Coconut-Flavored Rum
1 part Raspberry Liqueur
1 part Southern Comfort®
1 part 151-Proof Rum
1 part Cranberry Juice Cocktail
1 part Lemon-Lime Soda

GLASS: SHOT

Shake with ice and strain
Note: Because this recipe includes many ingredients, it's easier to make in volume, about 6 shots.

Cruz Azul

1 part 151-Proof Rum
1 part Citrus-Flavored Rum
1 part Citrus-Flavored Vodka
1 part Rumple Minze®
1 part Blue Curaçao

GLASS: SHOT

Shake with ice and strain
*Note: Because this recipe includes many ingredients, it's easier to make in volume, about 6 shots.

Cucaracha

1 part Vodka
1 part Coffee Liqueur
1 part Tequila

GLASS: SHOT

Shake with ice and strain

Cum in a Pond

1 part Blue Curaçao
1 part Vodka
splash Irish Cream Liqueur

GLASS: SHOT

Shake all but Irish Cream with ice and strain into the glass. Place a few drops of Irish Cream in the center of the drink.

D-Day

1 part 151-Proof Rum
1 part Citrus-Flavored Vodka
1 part Crème de Banana
1 part Raspberry Liqueur
1 part Orange Juice

GLASS: SHOT

Shake with ice and strain
*Note: Because this recipe includes many ingredients, it's easier to make in volume, about 6 shots.

Death from Within

1 part Spiced Rum
1 part Dark Rum
1 part Vodka

GLASS: SHOT

Shake with ice and strain

Detox

1 part Peach Schnapps
1 part Vodka
1 part Cranberry Juice Cocktail

GLASS: SHOT

Shake with ice and strain

Dirty Diaper

1 part Vodka
1 part Amaretto
1 part Southern Comfort®
1 part Melon Liqueur
1 part Raspberry Liqueur
1 part Orange Juice

GLASS: SHOT

Shake with ice and strain
*Note: Because this recipe includes many ingredients, it's easier to make in volume, about 6 shots.

Dirty Rotten Scoundrel

1 part Vodka
1 part Melon Liqueur

GLASS: SHOT

Shake with ice and strain

Down the Street

1 part Vodka
1 part Grand Marnier®
1 part Raspberry Liqueur
1 part Orange Juice

GLASS: SHOT

Shake with ice and strain

Downinone

2 parts Blavod® Black Vodka
1 part Triple Sec
1 part Gold Rum

GLASS: SHOT

Shake with ice and strain

Duck Fuck

2 parts Gin
1 part Vodka
1 part Beer

GLASS: SHOT

Shake with ice and strain

Electric Kamikaze

1 part Triple Sec
1 part Vodka
1 part Blue Curaçao
1 part Lime Juice

{ GLASS: SHOT
Shake with ice and strain

Elvis Presley

1 part Vodka
1 part Frangelico®
1 part Crème de Banana
splash Irish Cream Liqueur

{ GLASS: SHOT
Shake with ice and strain

Emerald Rocket

1 part Vodka
1 part Coffee Liqueur
1 part Melon Liqueur
1 part Irish Cream Liqueur

{ GLASS: SHOT
Shake with ice and strain

The End of the World

1 part 151-Proof Rum
1 part Wild Turkey® 101
1 part Vodka

{ GLASS: SHOT
*Pour ingredients into glass
neatly (do not chill)*

Epidural

1 part Grain Alcohol
1 part Vodka
1 part Coconut-Flavored Rum
1 part Coconut Crème

{ GLASS: SHOT
Shake with ice and strain

Flamethrower

1 part Vodka
2 parts Cinnamon Schnapps

{ GLASS: SHOT
Shake with ice and strain

Flaming Cocaine

1 part Cinnamon Schnapps
1 part Vodka
splash Cranberry Juice Cocktail

GLASS: SHOT
Shake with ice and strain

Flaming Squeegee

1 part Rum
1 part Vodka
1 part Lemon Juice
1 part Orange Juice

GLASS: SHOT
Shake with ice and strain

Flügel

1 part Cranberry-Flavored Vodka
1 part Red Bull® Energy Drink

GLASS: SHOT
Pour ingredients into glass neatly (do not chill)

Fog

3 parts Vodka
1 part Fresh Lime Juice

GLASS: SHOT
Shake with ice and strain

Freaking Shot

1 part Raspberry Liqueur
1 part Vodka
1 part Cranberry Juice Cocktail

GLASS: SHOT
Shake with ice and strain

Freddy Krueger®

1 part Sambuca
1 part Jägermeister®
1 part Vodka

GLASS: SHOT
Shake with ice and strain

Frigid Alaskan Nipple

1 part Butterscotch Schnapps
1 part Rumple Minze®
2 parts Vodka

GLASS: SHOT
Shake with ice and strain

Fruity Pebbles®

1 part Vodka
1 part Blue Curaçao
1 part Milk
splash Grenadine

GLASS: SHOT

Shake with ice and strain

Fucking Hot

1 part Pepper-Flavored Vodka
1 part Cinnamon Schnapps

GLASS: SHOT

Pour ingredients into glass neatly (do not chill)

Fuzzy Monkey

1 part Vodka
1 part Peach Schnapps
1 part Crème de Banana
1 part Orange Juice

GLASS: SHOT

Shake with ice and strain

Fuzzy Russian

1 part Vodka
1 part Peach Schnapps

GLASS: SHOT

Shake with ice and strain

G. T. O.

1 part Vodka
1 part Rum
1 part Gin
1 part Southern Comfort®
1 part Amaretto
1 part Grenadine
4 parts Orange Juice

GLASS: SHOT

Shake with ice and strain
Note: Because this recipe includes many ingredients, it's easier to make in volume, about 6 shots.

Galactic Ale

2 parts Vodka
2 parts Blue Curaçao
1 part Lime Juice
splash Blackberry Liqueur

GLASS: SHOT

Shake with ice and strain

Gator Cum

1 part Vodka
1 part Crème de Cacao (Dark)
1 part Frangelico®

GLASS: SHOT
Shake with ice and strain

Getaway Car

3 parts Peach Schnapps
1 part Citrus-Flavored Vodka

GLASS: SHOT
Shake with ice and strain

Ghostbuster

1 part Vodka
1 part Melon Liqueur
1 part Pineapple Juice
1 part Orange Juice

GLASS: SHOT
Shake with ice and strain

Gingerbread Man

1 part Goldschläger®
1 part Irish Cream Liqueur
1 part Butterscotch Schnapps
1 part Vodka

GLASS: SHOT
Shake with ice and strain

Godhead

1 part Rum
1 part Vodka
1 part Raspberry Liqueur
splash Lime Juice
splash 151-Proof Rum

GLASS: SHOT
Shake with ice and strain

Golden Russian

1 part Vodka
1 part Galliano®

GLASS: SHOT
Shake with ice and strain

Grandpa Is Alive

2 parts Amaretto
1 part Vodka

GLASS: SHOT
Shake with ice and strain

Greek Lightning

1 part Ouzo
1 part Vodka
1 part Raspberry Liqueur

GLASS: SHOT
Shake with ice and strain

Green Apple Kamikazi

1 part Melon Liqueur
1 part Vodka
1 part Sour Mix
splash Lime Juice

GLASS: SHOT
Shake with ice and strain

Green Apple Toffee

1 part Vodka
1 part Butterscotch Schnapps
1 part Sour Apple Schnapps

GLASS: SHOT
Shake with ice and strain

Green Gummy Bear

1 part Orange-Flavored Vodka
1 part Melon Liqueur
splash Lemon-Lime Soda

GLASS: SHOT
Shake with ice and strain

Green Sneaker

2 parts Vodka
1 part Melon Liqueur
1 part Cointreau®
splash Cream

GLASS: SHOT
Shake with ice and strain

Grenade

1 part Vodka
1 part Triple Sec
1 part Grenadine

GLASS: SHOT

Shake with ice and strain

Gross One

1 part Vodka
1 part Gin
1 part Jack Daniel's®
1 part Amaretto
1 part Sambuca

GLASS: SHOT

Shake with ice and strain
*Note: Because this recipe includes many ingredients, it's easier to make in volume, about 6 shots.

Happy Juice

1 part Lemon Juice
1 part Vodka

GLASS: SHOT

Shake with ice and strain

Hawaiian Punch® from Hell

1 part Vodka
1 part Southern Comfort®
1 part Amaretto
splash Orange Juice
splash Lemon-Lime Soda
splash Grenadine

GLASS: SHOT

Shake with ice and strain
*Note: Because this recipe includes many ingredients, it's easier to make in volume, about 6 shots.

Hawoo-Woo

1 part Vodka
1 part Peach Schnapps
1 part Cranberry Juice Cocktail
1 part Pineapple Juice

GLASS: SHOT

Shake with ice and strain

Heilig

1 part Vodka
1 part Blueberry Schnapps
1 part Cranberry Juice Cocktail

GLASS: SHOT

Shake with ice and strain

Herman's Special

1 part Vodka
1 part Brandy
3 parts Peach Schnapps
splash Raspberry Liqueur

GLASS: SHOT

Shake with ice and strain

Hide the Banana

1 part Amaretto
1 part Melon Liqueur
1 part Citrus-Flavored Vodka

GLASS: SHOT

Shake with ice and strain

Honolulu Action

1 part Grenadine
1 part Melon Liqueur
1 part Blue Curaçao
1 part Irish Cream Liqueur
1 part Tequila
1 part Vodka
1 part 151-Proof Rum
top with Whipped Cream

GLASS: SHOT

Shake with ice and strain

Note: Because this recipe includes many ingredients, it's easier to make in volume, about 6 shots.

Honolulu Hammer Shooter

2 parts Vodka
1 part Amaretto
1 part Pineapple Juice

GLASS: SHOT

Shake with ice and strain

Hooter

1 part Citrus-Flavored Vodka
1 part Amaretto
1 part Orange Juice
1 part Grenadine

GLASS: SHOT

Shake with ice and strain

Horny Bastard

1 part Vodka
1 part Caramel Liqueur
splash Grenadine

GLASS: SHOT

Shake with ice and strain

Hot Damn

1 part Whiskey
1 part Orange Juice
1 part Rum
1 part Vodka

GLASS: SHOT

Shake with ice and strain

Hot Fusion

1 part Melon Liqueur
1 part Absolut® Peppar Vodka

GLASS: SHOT

Shake with ice and strain

Ice Blue Kamikaze

1 part Rumple Minze®
1 part Vodka
1 part Lemon-Lime Soda

GLASS: SHOT

Pour ingredients into glass neatly (do not chill)

Iceberg Shooter

1 part Crème de Menthe (White)
1 part Citrus-Flavored Vodka

GLASS: SHOT

Shake with ice and strain

Icy After Eight

2 parts Vodka
1 part Chocolate Syrup
1 part Crème de Menthe (Green)

GLASS: SHOT
Shake with ice and strain

Iguana

1 part Vodka
1 part Tequila
1 part Coffee Liqueur

GLASS: SHOT
Shake with ice and strain

Illusion

1 part Coconut-Flavored Rum
1 part Melon Liqueur
1 part Vodka
1 part Cointreau®
splash Pineapple Juice

GLASS: SHOT
Shake with ice and strain

International Incident

1 part Vodka
1 part Coffee Liqueur
1 part Amaretto
1 part Frangelico®
2 parts Irish Cream Liqueur

GLASS: SHOT
Shake with ice and strain

Irish Bulldog

1 part Irish Cream Liqueur
1 part Vodka

GLASS: SHOT
Shake with ice and strain

Irish Potato Famine

1 part Vodka
1 part Irish Whiskey
1 part Irish Cream Liqueur

GLASS: SHOT
Shake with ice and strain

Irish Quaalude

1 part Crème de Cacao (White)
1 part Frangelico®
1 part Citrus-Flavored Vodka

GLASS: SHOT
Shake with ice and strain

Italian Orgasm

1 part Vodka
1 part Amaretto
1 part Irish Cream Liqueur
1 part Frangelico®

GLASS: SHOT
Shake with ice and strain

Italian Russian

1 part Vodka
1 part Sambuca

GLASS: SHOT
Shake with ice and strain

Jamaican Bobsled

1 part Vodka
1 part Banana Liqueur

GLASS: SHOT
Shake with ice and strain

Jamboree

1 part Vodka
1 part Wild Berry Schnapps
1 part Cranberry Juice Cocktail

GLASS: SHOT
Shake with ice and strain

Jealous Queen

1 part Triple Sec
2 parts Vodka
dash Bitters
dash Salt

GLASS: SHOT
Shake with ice and strain

Jell-O® Shots

1 package instant Jell-O®
1 part Hot Water
1 part Vodka

(see flavor combinations)

GLASS: SHOT

Basic Recipe: Dissolve Jell-O® in hot water. Add Vodka. Pour into small paper cups and chill. Serve after the Jell-O® has set.
Flavor Combinations: *Cape Cods: Cranberry Jell-O® and Vodka; Lemonheads: Lemon Jell-O® and Vodka*

Jogger

1 part Citrus-Flavored Vodka
1 part Vodka
1 part Orange Juice
1 part Galliano®

GLASS: SHOT

Shake with ice and strain

Johnny on the Beach

3 parts Vodka
2 parts Melon Liqueur
2 parts Blackberry Liqueur
1 part Pineapple Juice
1 part Orange Juice
1 part Grapefruit Juice
1 part Cranberry Juice Cocktail

GLASS: SHOT

Shake with ice and strain
*Note: Because this recipe includes many ingredients, it's easier to make in volume, about 6 shots.

Johnny Appleseed

1 part Vodka
1 part Raspberry Liqueur
1 part Melon Liqueur
1 part Peach Schnapps
1 part Pineapple Juice

GLASS: SHOT

Shake with ice and strain
*Note: Because this recipe includes many ingredients, it's easier to make in volume, about 6 shots.

Johnny G Spot

1 part Vodka
1 part Blue Curaçao
1 part Orange Juice

GLASS: SHOT

Shake with ice and strain

Juicy Lips

1 part Vodka
1 part Crème de Banana
1 part Pineapple Juice

GLASS: SHOT

Shake with ice and strain

Juicy Volkheimer

1 part Vodka
1 part Coconut-Flavored Rum

GLASS: SHOT

Shake with ice and strain

Kamikaze

1 part Vodka
1 part Triple Sec
1 part Lime Juice

GLASS: SHOT

Shake with ice and strain

Key West Shooter

1 part Vodka
1 part Melon Liqueur
1 part Orange Juice
1 part Pineapple Juice

GLASS: SHOT

Shake with ice and strain

Killer Kool-Aid®

2 parts Vodka
1 part Amaretto
1 part Melon Liqueur
1 part Cranberry Juice Cocktail

GLASS: SHOT

Shake with ice and strain

Kimber Krush

1 part Vanilla-Flavored Vodka
1 part Rumple Minze®
1 part Irish Cream Liqueur
1 part Raspberry Liqueur

GLASS: SHOT

Shake with ice and strain

Kish Wacker

1 part Irish Cream Liqueur
1 part Crème de Cacao (Dark)
1 part Vodka
1 part Coffee Liqueur

GLASS: SHOT

Shake with ice and strain

Kiwiki

1 part Vodka
1 part Kiwi Schnapps
1 part Triple Sec

GLASS: SHOT

Shake with ice and strain

Kool-Aid®

1 part Vodka
1 part Amaretto
1 part Melon Liqueur
1 part Raspberry Liqueur

GLASS: SHOT

Shake with ice and strain

Kremlin Shooter

1 part Vodka
splash Grenadine

GLASS: SHOT

Shake with ice and strain

Kurant Shooter

1 part Melon Liqueur
1 part Currant-Flavored Vodka
2 parts Pineapple Juice

GLASS: SHOT

Shake with ice and strain

Kurant Stinger

1 part Bärenjäger®
1 part Currant-Flavored Vodka

GLASS: SHOT

Shake with ice and strain

The Lady in Red

1 part Peppermint Schnapps
1 part Peach Schnapps
1 part Vodka
1 part Grenadine

GLASS: SHOT

Shake with ice and strain

Lemon Drop Shooter

1 part Vodka
1 Lemon Wedge
dash Sugar

GLASS: SHOT

Shake the Vodka with ice and strain into a shot glass. Pour the Sugar onto the Lemon Wedge. Drink the shot and bite down on the Lemon Wedge.

Life Preserver

1 part Blue Curaçao
1 part Vodka
1 piece Cheerio's® cereal

GLASS: SHOT

Shake the Vodka and Blue Curaçao with ice and strain. Float the Cheerio in the center of the shot.

Light Green Panties

1 part Crème de Menthe (Green)
1 part Vodka
1 part Irish Cream Liqueur
splash Grenadine

GLASS: SHOT

Shake all but Grenadine with ice and strain into the glass. Place a few drops of Grenadine in the center of the drink.

Lime Lizard

1 part Vodka
1 part Rum
1 part Lime Juice
1 part Grenadine

GLASS: SHOT

Shake with ice and strain

Lipstick Lesbian

1 part Raspberry-Flavored Vodka
1 part Watermelon Schnapps
1 part Cranberry Juice Cocktail
1 part Sour Mix

GLASS: SHOT

Shake with ice and strain

Liquid Candy Cane

1 part Vodka
2 parts Cherry Liqueur
2 parts Peppermint Schnapps

GLASS: SHOT

Shake with ice and strain

Liquid Cocaine

1 part Grand Marnier®
1 part Southern Comfort®
1 part Vodka
1 part Amaretto
1 part Pineapple Juice

GLASS: SHOT

Shake with ice and strain

**Note: Because this recipe
includes many ingredients, it's
easier to make in volume,
about 6 shots.*

Liquid Heroin

1 part Vodka
1 part Rumple Minze®
1 part Jägermeister®

GLASS: SHOT

Shake with ice and strain

Liquid Screw

1 part Coconut-Flavored Rum
1 part Peach Schnapps
1 part Vodka
1 part Lemon-Lime Soda

GLASS: SHOT

Shake with ice and strain

A Little Nervous

1 part Vodka
1 part Peach Schnapps
1 part Blackberry Liqueur

GLASS: SHOT

Shake with ice and strain

Long Island Shooter

1 part Tequila Silver
1 part Vodka
1 part Light Rum
1 part Gin
1 part Triple Sec
1 part Cola
1 part Sour Mix

GLASS: SHOT

Shake with ice and strain

Mad Hatter

1 part Vodka
1 part Peach Schnapps
1 part Lemonade
1 part Cola

GLASS: SHOT

Shake with ice and strain

Mad Melon Shooter

1 part Watermelon Schnapps
1 part Vodka

GLASS: SHOT

Shake with ice and strain

Mage's Fire

2 parts Vodka
1 part Cinnamon Schnapps
1 part Blue Curaçao

GLASS: SHOT

Shake with ice and strain

Mattikaze

1 part Vodka
1 part Lime Juice
1 part Triple Sec
1 part Peach Schnapps

GLASS: SHOT

Shake with ice and strain

Meat and Potatoes

1 part Potato Vodka
1 Pepperoni Slice

GLASS: SHOT

Shake the Vodka with ice and strain into a shot glass. Garnish with a slice of Pepperoni.

Melon Ball Shooter

2 parts Melon Liqueur
1 part Vodka
1 part Orange Juice

GLASS: SHOT

Shake with ice and strain

Melon Kamikaze

1 part Vodka
1 part Melon Liqueur
1 part Sour Mix

GLASS: SHOT

Shake with ice and strain

Melonoma

2 parts Vodka
1 part Melon Liqueur

GLASS: SHOT

Shake with ice and strain

Memory Loss

1 part Vodka
1 part Raspberry Liqueur
1 part Banana Liqueur
1 part Cranberry Juice Cocktail
1 part Orange Juice

GLASS: SHOT

Shake with ice and strain

*Note: Because this recipe includes many ingredients, it's easier to make in volume, about 6 shots.

Mexican Kamikaze

2 parts Tequila
1 part Vodka
1 part Lemon Juice
1 part Lime Juice

GLASS: SHOT

Shake with ice and strain

Mexican Stand-Off

1 part Vodka
1 part Tequila
1 part Passoã®

GLASS: SHOT

Shake with ice and strain

Mexican Water

1 part Crown Royal® Whiskey
1 part Tequila Reposado
1 part Vodka

GLASS: SHOT

Shake with ice and strain

Mild Jizz

1 part Vodka
1 part Melon Liqueur
1 part Coconut-Flavored Rum
1 part Lemon-Lime Soda

GLASS: SHOT

Shake with ice and strain

Misty Blue Cumming

1 part Vodka
1 part Sloe Gin
1 part Blue Curaçao
1 part Peach Schnapps

GLASS: SHOT

Shake with ice and strain

Monkey Poop Shooter

1 part Vodka
1 part Crème de Banana
1 part Pineapple Juice
1 part Orange Juice
1 part Lime Cordial

GLASS: SHOT

Shake with ice and strain

**Note: Because this recipe
includes many ingredients, it's
easier to make in volume,
about 6 shots.*

Monsoon

1 part Currant-Flavored Vodka
1 part Amaretto
1 part Coffee Liqueur
1 part Frangelico®

GLASS: SHOT

Shake with ice and strain

Moose Fart

1 part Vodka
1 part Bourbon
1 part Coffee Liqueur
1 part Irish Cream Liqueur

GLASS: SHOT

Shake with ice and strain

Morning Wood

1 part Vodka
1 part Peach Schnapps
1 part Orange Juice
1 part Sour Mix
1 part Raspberry Liqueur

GLASS: SHOT

Shake with ice and strain
**Note: Because this recipe
includes many ingredients,
it's easier to make in volume,
about 6 shots.*

Mother Load

1 part Vodka
1 part Blackberry Liqueur
1 part Coconut-Flavored Rum

GLASS: SHOT

Shake with ice and strain

Mother Pucker Shooter

1 part Vodka
1 part Sour Apple Schnapps
splash Lemon-Lime Soda
splash Club Soda

GLASS: SHOT

Shake with ice and strain

Mouth Wash

1 part Crème de Menthe (White)
1 part Vodka
1 part Blue Curaçao

GLASS: SHOT

Shake with ice and strain

Mr. G

1 part Licor 43®
1 part Vodka
2 parts Grenadine

GLASS: SHOT

Shake with ice and strain

Mud Slide Shooter

1 part Vodka
1 part Coffee Liqueur
1 part Irish Cream Liqueur

{ GLASS: SHOT

Shake with ice and strain

Muddy Water

1 part Vodka
1 part Coffee Liqueur
1 part Irish Cream Liqueur

{ GLASS: SHOT

Shake with ice and strain

Muff Dive

1 part Vodka
1 part Peach Schnapps
1 part Cranberry Juice Cocktail

{ GLASS: SHOT

Shake with ice and strain

MVP's Strawberry Bomb

1 part Tequila Rose®
1 part Vodka
1 part Strawberry Liqueur

{ GLASS: SHOT

Shake with ice and strain

Neon Bull Frog

1 part Vodka
1 part Blue Curaçao
1 part Melon Liqueur
1 part Sour Mix

{ GLASS: SHOT

Shake with ice and strain

Nero's Delight

1 part Vodka
1 part Sambuca

{ GLASS: SHOT

Shake with ice and strain

Neuronium

1 part Crème de Menthe (White)
1 part Vodka
splash Grenadine

{ GLASS: SHOT

Shake all but Grenadine with ice and strain into the glass. Place a few drops of Grenadine in the center of the drink.

A Night at Naughty Nikki's

1 part Vodka
2 parts Lemon-Lime Soda
Skittles

{ GLASS: SHOT

Place the Skittles, or other fruity chewy candy, in the bottom of a shot glass, then pour Lemon-Lime Soda and Vodka.

Nuclear Kamikaze

3 parts Vodka
1 part Lime Juice
1 part Triple Sec
2 parts Melon Liqueur

{ GLASS: SHOT

Shake with ice and strain

Nuclear Waste

2 parts Vodka
1 part Melon Liqueur
1 part Triple Sec
splash Lime Juice

{ GLASS: SHOT

Shake with ice and strain

Opera House Special

1 part Tequila
1 part Gin
1 part Light Rum
1 part Vodka
1 part Pineapple Juice
1 part Orange Juice
1 part Sour Mix

{ GLASS: SHOT

Shake with ice and strain

*Note: Because this recipe includes many ingredients, it's easier to make in volume, about 6 shots.

Orange Crush Shooter

1 part Vodka
1 part Triple Sec
1 part Club Soda

GLASS: SHOT

Shake with ice and strain

Orgasm

1 part Vodka
1 part Amaretto
1 part Coffee Liqueur
1 part Irish Cream Liqueur

GLASS: SHOT

Shake with ice and strain

Pants on Fire

1 part Vodka
1 part Strawberry Liqueur
1 part Banana Liqueur
1 part Grapefruit Juice
1 part Orange Juice

GLASS: SHOT

Shake with ice and strain
*Note: Because this recipe
includes many ingredients,
it's easier to make in
volume, about 6 shots.

Panty Raid

2 parts Citrus-Flavored Vodka
1 part Chambord®
splash Lemon-Lime Soda
splash Pineapple Juice

GLASS: SHOT

Shake with ice and strain

Paralyzer Shooter

1 part Vodka
1 part Coffee Liqueur
1 part Cola
1 part Milk

GLASS: SHOT

Shake with ice and strain

PB&J

1 part Vodka
1 part Raspberry Liqueur
1 part Frangelico®

GLASS: SHOT

Shake with ice and strain

Peach Death

1 part Vodka
1 part Peach Schnapps
1 part Amaretto

GLASS: SHOT

Shake with ice and strain

Peach Nehi

1 part Vodka
1 part Peach Schnapps
1 part Cherry Liqueur
1 part Sour Mix
1 part Pineapple Juice
1 part Lemon-Lime Soda

GLASS: SHOT

Shake with ice and strain
*Note: Because this recipe includes many ingredients, it's easier to make in volume, about 6 shots.

Pearl Harbor

1 part Vodka
1 part Melon Liqueur
1 part Orange Juice

GLASS: SHOT

Shake with ice and strain

Pedra

1 part Tequila
1 part Vodka
1 part Dark Rum
1 part Irish Cream Liqueur
1 part Grenadine
1 part Absinthe

GLASS: SHOT

Shake with ice and strain
*Note: Because this recipe includes many ingredients, it's easier to make in volume, about 6 shots.

Pee Gee

1 part Cinnamon Schnapps
1 part Orange Juice
1 part Vodka

GLASS: SHOT

Shake with ice and strain

Peppermint

3 parts Pepper-Flavored Vodka
1 part Crème de Menthe (White)

GLASS: SHOT

Shake with ice and strain

Photon Torpedo

1 part After Shock® Cinnamon Schnapps
1 part Vodka

GLASS: SHOT

Shake with ice and strain

Pierced Fuzzy Navel

2 parts Peach Schnapps
1 part Vodka
1 part Orange Juice

GLASS: SHOT

Shake with ice and strain

Pigskin Shot

1 part Vodka
1 part Melon Liqueur
1 part Sour Mix

GLASS: SHOT

Shake with ice and strain

Piña Crana Kazi

2 parts Vodka
1 part Triple Sec
1 part Pineapple Juice

GLASS: SHOT

Shake with ice and strain

Pineberry

1 part Cranberry-Flavored Vodka
1 part Pineapple-Flavored Vodka

GLASS: SHOT

Shake with ice and strain

Pink Cadillac

2 parts Vodka
1 part Cherry Juice
1 part Lemonade
1 part Orange Juice

GLASS: SHOT

Shake with ice and strain

Pink Cotton Candy

1 part Vodka
1 part Amaretto
splash Grenadine

GLASS: SHOT

Shake with ice and strain

Pink Danger

1 part Butterscotch Schnapps
2 parts Vodka
3 parts Fruit Punch

GLASS: SHOT

Shake with ice and strain

Pink Floyd

1 part Vodka
1 part Peach Schnapps
1 part Cranberry Juice Cocktail
1 part Grapefruit Juice

GLASS: SHOT

Shake with ice and strain

Pink Lemonade Shooter

1 part Vodka
1 part Sour Mix
1 part Cranberry Juice Cocktail

GLASS: SHOT

Shake with ice and strain

Pink Nipple Shooter

3 parts Currant-Flavored Vodka
1 part Sambuca

GLASS: SHOT

Shake with ice and strain

Pink Ranger

2 parts Vodka
1 part Coconut-Flavored Rum
1 part Peach Schnapps
1 part Cranberry Juice Cocktail
1 part Pineapple Juice

GLASS: SHOT

Shake with ice and strain

Pinkeye

1 part Vodka
1 part Cranberry Juice Cocktail
1 part Sour Mix

GLASS: SHOT

Shake with ice and strain

Pleading Insanity

1 part Tequila Silver
1 part Vodka
1 part Dark Rum

GLASS: SHOT

Shake with ice and strain

Poco Loco Boom

1 part Vodka
1 part Tia Maria®
1 part Coconut Cream

GLASS: SHOT

Shake with ice and strain

Poison Apple

1 part Apple Brandy
1 part Vodka

GLASS: SHOT

Shake with ice and strain

Popper

1 part Vodka
3 parts Lemon-Lime Soda

GLASS: SHOT

Build in the glass with no ice

Porto Covo

1 part Vodka
1 part Absinthe
1 part Coconut-Flavored Liqueur
1 part Banana Liqueur

GLASS: SHOT

Shake with ice and strain

Power Drill

1 part Vodka
1 part Orange Juice
1 part Beer

GLASS: SHOT

Shake with ice and strain

Power Shot

2 parts Vodka
1 part Absolut® Peppar Vodka
dash Wasabi

GLASS: SHOT

Build in the glass with no ice

Prestone

1 part Melon Liqueur
2 parts Citrus-Flavored Vodka
2 parts Lemon-Lime Soda

GLASS: SHOT

Shake with ice and strain

Puke

1 part Jack Daniel's®
1 part Jim Beam®
1 part Yukon Jack®
1 part Vodka
1 part Tequila

GLASS: SHOT

Shake with ice and strain

Purple Elastic Thunder Fuck

1 part Vodka
1 part Crown Royal® Whiskey
1 part Southern Comfort®
1 part Amaretto
1 part Raspberry Liqueur
1 part Pineapple Juice
1 part Cranberry Juice Cocktail

GLASS: SHOT

Shake with ice and strain

*Note: Because this recipe includes many ingredients, it's easier to make in volume, about 6 shots.

Purple Haze

1 part Citrus-Flavored Vodka
1 part Raspberry Liqueur
1 part Lemon-Lime Soda

GLASS: SHOT

Shake with ice and strain

Purple Panther

3 parts Sour Apple–Flavored Vodka
1 part Blue Curaçao

GLASS: SHOT

Shake with ice and strain

Purple Penis

2 parts Vodka
1 part Blue Curaçao
1 part Raspberry Liqueur

GLASS: SHOT

Shake with ice and strain

Purple Rain Shooter

3 parts Cranberry-Flavored Vodka
1 part Blue Curaçao

GLASS: SHOT

Shake with ice and strain

Purple Viper

1 part Sloe Gin
1 part Vodka
2 parts Raspberry Liqueur

GLASS: SHOT

Shake with ice and strain

Pussy Juice

1 part Goldschläger®
1 part Vodka
1 part Vegetable Juice Blend

GLASS: SHOT

Shake with ice and strain

Quaalude

1 part Vodka
1 part Coffee Liqueur
1 part Irish Cream Liqueur
1 part Amaretto
1 part Frangelico®

GLASS: SHOT

Shake with ice and strain
*Note: Because this recipe
includes many ingredients, it's
easier to make in volume,
about 6 shots.*

Raging Indian

1 part Vodka
1 part Coffee Liqueur
1 part Orange Juice
1 part Mango Nectar

GLASS: SHOT

Shake with ice and strain

Raspberry Beret

1 part Vodka
1 part Raspberry Liqueur
1 part Cream

GLASS: SHOT

Shake with ice and strain

A Real Strong Dirty Rotten Scoundrel

1 part Cranberry-Flavored Vodka
½ part Melon Liqueur

GLASS: SHOT

Shake with ice and strain

Red Death

1 part Vodka
1 part Fire Water®
1 part Yukon Jack®
1 part 151-Proof Rum

GLASS: SHOT

Shake with ice and strain

Red Devil Shooter

1 part Vodka
1 part Southern Comfort®
1 part Amaretto
1 part Triple Sec
1 part Grenadine
1 part Orange Juice
1 part Sour Mix

GLASS: SHOT

Shake with ice and strain
*Note: Because this recipe includes many ingredients, it's easier to make in volume, about 6 shots.

Red-Eyed Hell

1 part Triple Sec
1 part Vodka
1 part 151-Proof Rum
2 parts Vegetable Juice Blend

GLASS: SHOT

Shake with ice and strain

Red Mosquito

1 part Vodka
1 part Hot Damn!® Cinnamon Schnapps

GLASS: SHOT

Shake with ice and strain

Roasted Toasted Almond Shooter

1 part Amaretto
1 part Coffee Liqueur
1 part Cream
1 part Vodka

GLASS: SHOT

Shake with ice and strain

Robot

2 parts Jack Daniel's®
1 part Vodka
1 part Grenadine

GLASS: SHOT

Shake with ice and strain

Rocket Fuel

2 parts 151-Proof Rum
1 part Vodka
1 part Blue Curaçao

GLASS: SHOT

Shake with ice and strain

Romulan Ale Shooter

1 part Vodka
1 part Tropical Punch Schnapps
1 part Cactus Juice Schnapps

GLASS: SHOT

Shake with ice and strain

Rosso di Sera

1 part Vodka
1 part Strawberry Liqueur
1 part Triple Sec

GLASS: SHOT

Shake with ice and strain

Rott Gut

1 part Cinnamon Schnapps
1 part Vodka

GLASS: SHOT

Shake with ice and strain

Royal

1 part Vodka
1 part Crème de Banana
1 part Blue Curaçao
1 part Lemon Juice

GLASS: SHOT

Shake with ice and strain

Royal Fuck

1 part Crown Royal® Whiskey
1 part Chambord®
1 part Peach Schnapps
1 part Pineapple-Flavored Vodka
1 part Cranberry Juice Cocktail

GLASS: SHOT

Shake with ice and strain

Ruby Red

2 parts Vodka
2 parts Cranberry Juice Cocktail
1 part Sour Mix

GLASS: SHOT

Shake with ice and strain

Rumka

1 part Vodka
1 part Spiced Rum

GLASS: SHOT

Shake with ice and strain

Russian Ballet

3 parts Vodka
1 part Crème de Cassis

GLASS: SHOT

Shake with ice and strain

Russian Kamikaze

2 parts Vodka
1 part Raspberry Liqueur

GLASS: SHOT

Shake with ice and strain

Russian Quaalude Shooter

1 part Vodka
1 part Frangelico®
1 part Irish Cream Liqueur
1 part Coffee Liqueur
1 part Cream

GLASS: SHOT

Shake with ice and strain

*Note: Because this recipe
includes many ingredients, it's
easier to make in volume,
about 6 shots.*

Russian Roulette

1 part Vodka
1 part Galliano®
1 part 151-Proof Rum

GLASS: SHOT

Shake with ice and strain

Russian Tongue

1 part Goldschläger®
1 part Rumple Minze®
1 part Vodka

GLASS: SHOT

Shake with ice and strain

Rusty Halo

1 part Vodka
1 part Amaretto
1 part Banana Liqueur
1 part Melon Liqueur

GLASS: SHOT

Shake with ice and strain

Sambuca Slide

2 parts Sambuca
1 part Vodka
1 part Light Cream

GLASS: SHOT

Shake with ice and strain

Scooby Shooter

2 parts Coconut-Flavored Rum
2 parts Peach Schnapps
2 parts Melon Liqueur
1 part Vodka
1 part Orange Juice
1 part Pineapple Juice

GLASS: SHOT

Shake with ice and strain
*Note: Because this recipe
includes many ingredients, it's
easier to make in volume,
about 6 shots.*

Scorpion Shooter

2 parts Vodka
1 part Blackberry Liqueur

GLASS: SHOT

Shake with ice and strain

Screamer

1 part Gin
1 part Rum
1 part Tequila
1 part Triple Sec
1 part Vodka

GLASS: SHOT

Shake with ice and strain
*Note: Because this recipe
includes many ingredients, it's
easier to make in volume,
about 6 shots.*

Screaming Orgasm

1 part Cream
1 part Vodka
1 part Amaretto
1 part Crème de Banana

GLASS: SHOT

Shake with ice and strain

Screaming Purple Jesus

1 part Vodka
1 part Grape Juice (Red)

GLASS: SHOT

Shake with ice and strain

Second Childhood

1 part Crème de Menthe (White)
1 part Vodka

GLASS: SHOT

Shake with ice and strain

Señor Freak

1 part Tequila Reposado
1 part Light Rum
1 part Vodka
1 part Lemon-Lime Soda

GLASS: SHOT

Shake with ice and strain

Seven Twenty-Seven

1 part Vodka
1 part Coconut-Flavored Liqueur

GLASS: SHOT

Shake with ice and strain

Sex in the Parking Lot

1 part Raspberry Liqueur
1 part Vodka
1 part Sour Apple Schnapps

GLASS: SHOT

Shake with ice and strain

Sex on a Pool Table

1 part Peach Schnapps
1 part Vodka
1 part Pineapple Juice
1 part Sour Mix
1 part Melon Liqueur

GLASS: SHOT

Shake with ice and strain

*Note: Because this recipe includes many ingredients, it's easier to make in volume, about 6 shots.

Sex On the Beach Shooter

1 part Vodka
1 part Peach Schnapps
1 part Orange Juice

GLASS: SHOT

Shake with ice and strain

Sex Under the Moonlight

2 parts Vodka
1 part Coffee
1 part Port
1 part Cream

GLASS: SHOT

Shake with ice and strain

Sex Up Against the Wall

2 parts Currant-Flavored Vodka
1 part Pineapple Juice
1 part Sour Mix

GLASS: SHOT

Shake with ice and strain

Shit Stain

1 part Crème de Cacao (Dark)
1 part Jägermeister®
1 part Vodka

GLASS: SHOT

Shake with ice and strain

Shogun Shooter

3 parts Citrus-Flavored Vodka
1 part Melon Liqueur

GLASS: SHOT

Shake with ice and strain

Short Vodka

1 part Triple Sec
1 part Orange-Flavored Vodka

GLASS: SHOT

Pour ingredients into glass neatly (do not chill)

Shot in the Back

3 parts Vodka
1 part Goldschläger®
dash Wasabi

GLASS: SHOT

Shake with ice and strain

Siberian Gold

2 part Vodka
2 part Goldschläger®
1 part Blue Curaçao

GLASS: SHOT

Shake with ice and strain

Siberian Toolkit

4 parts Vodka
1 part Whiskey

GLASS: SHOT

Shake with ice and strain

Siberian Walrus

2 parts Blue Curaçao
1 part Light Rum
1 part Vodka
1 part Jack Daniel's®
1 part Kirschwasser
1 part Orange Juice

GLASS: SHOT

Shake with ice and strain
*Note: Because this recipe includes many ingredients, it's easier to make in volume, about 6 shots.

Silk Panties

1 part Peach Schnapps
3 parts Vodka

GLASS: SHOT

Shake with ice and strain

Silver Bullet Shooter

2 parts Peppermint Schnapps
1 part Vodka

GLASS: SHOT

Shake with ice and strain

Silver Nipple

4 parts Sambuca
1 part Vodka

GLASS: SHOT

Shake with ice and strain

Silver Spider

1 part Vodka
1 part Rum
1 part Triple Sec
1 part Crème de Cacao (White)

GLASS: SHOT

Shake with ice and strain

Skandia Iceberg

1 part Crème de Menthe (White)
1 part Vodka

GLASS: SHOT

Shake with ice and strain

Skittles®

1 part Vodka
1 part Southern Comfort®
1 part Melon Liqueur
1 part Pineapple Juice
1 part Sour Mix

GLASS: SHOT

Shake with ice and strain

Sky Pilot

1 part Vodka
1 part Irish Cream Liqueur
1 part Peppermint Schnapps

GLASS: SHOT

Shake with ice and strain

Slammer

1 part Vodka
1 part Lemon-Lime Soda

GLASS: SHOT

Build in the glass with no ice

Slice of Apple Pie

3 parts Vodka
1 part Apple Juice

GLASS: SHOT

Shake with ice and strain

Slick and Sleezy

1 part Salsa
5 parts Vodka

GLASS: SHOT

Shake with ice and strain

Slippery Cricket

1 part Vodka
1 part Blue Hawaiian Schnapps
1 part Tropical Punch Schnapps

GLASS: SHOT

Shake with ice and strain

Slippery Saddle

1 part Vodka
1 part Licor 43®
1 part Orange Juice

GLASS: SHOT

Shake with ice and strain

Sloppy Bagina

1 part Vodka
1 part Irish Cream Liqueur
2 parts 151-Proof Rum
splash Lime Juice

GLASS: SHOT

Shake with ice and strain

Small Bomb

1 part Vodka
1 part Triple Sec
1 part Grenadine

GLASS: SHOT

Shake with ice and strain

Snoopy® Dog

2 parts Vodka
1 part Grenadine
1 part Amaretto
1 part Crème de Banana

GLASS: SHOT

Shake with ice and strain

Snot Rocket

1 part Apple Brandy
1 part Sour Apple Schnapps
1 part Vodka

GLASS: SHOT

Shake with ice and strain

Snow Drop Shooter

1 part Crème de Cacao (White)
1 part Vodka
1 part Triple Sec

GLASS: SHOT

Shake with ice and strain

Snow Shoe

1 part Vodka
1 part Peppermint Schnapps

GLASS: SHOT

Shake with ice and strain

Solar Flare

1 part Vodka
1 part Triple Sec

GLASS: SHOT

Shake with ice and strain

Son of a Peach

1 part Vodka
1 part Peach Schnapps
1 part Honey

GLASS: SHOT

Shake with ice and strain

Songbird

1 part Tequila Silver
1 part Vodka
1 part Crème de Banana

GLASS: SHOT

Shake with ice and strain

Soother

2 parts Amaretto
2 parts Melon Liqueur
1 part Vodka
1 part Sour Mix

GLASS: SHOT

Shake with ice and strain

Soul Taker

1 part Vodka
1 part Tequila
1 part Amaretto

GLASS: SHOT

Shake with ice and strain

Sour Grapes

1 part Vodka
1 part Raspberry Liqueur
1 part Sour Mix

GLASS: SHOT

Shake with ice and strain

Sourball

1 part Vodka
1 part Lemonade
1 part Orange Juice

GLASS: SHOT

Shake with ice and strain

Sperm

1 part Tequila
1 part Vodka
splash Cream

GLASS: SHOT

Shake all but Cream with ice and strain into the glass. Place a few drops of Cream in the center of the drink.

Spitfire

1 part Jack Daniel's®
1 part Rum
1 part Vodka

GLASS: SHOT

Shake with ice and strain

Sprawling Dubinsky

1 part Johnnie Walker® Red Label
1 part Johnnie Walker® Black Label
1 part Citrus-Flavored Vodka
splash Amaretto

GLASS: SHOT

Shake with ice and strain

Squishy

1 part Raspberry Liqueur
1 part Amaretto
1 part Vodka

GLASS: SHOT

Shake with ice and strain

Stained Blue Dress

1 part Vodka
1 part Blue Curaçao
splash Irish Cream Liqueur

GLASS: SHOT

Shake all but Irish Cream with ice and strain into the glass. Place a few drops of Irish Cream in the center of the drink.

Stardust

1 part Citrus-Flavored Vodka
1 part Peach Schnapps
1 part Blue Curaçao
1 part Sour Mix
1 part Pineapple Juice
1 part Grenadine

GLASS: SHOT

Shake with ice and strain

*Note: Because this recipe includes many ingredients, it's easier to make in volume, about 6 shots.

Start Me Up

2 parts Vodka
1 part Tequila
1 part Currant-Flavored Vodka
1 part Dark Rum

GLASS: SHOT

Shake with ice and strain

Stop Lights

3 parts Vodka
splash Midori®
splash Orange Juice
splash Cranberry Juice Cocktail

GLASS: SHOT

Shake Vodka with ice and strain equal parts into three shot glasses. Top the first glass with Midori®, the second with Orange Juice, and the third one with Cranberry Juice. Drink all three shots rapidly and in order.

Strong Bad

1 part Southern Comfort®
1 part Vanilla-Flavored Vodka
1 part Tonic Water

GLASS: SHOT

Shake with ice and strain

Suicide Stop Light

1 part Midori®
1 part Vodka
1 part After Shock®
Cinnamon Schnapps
splash Orange Juice

GLASS: SHOT

Fill the first of three shot glasses with Midori®, the second one with 1 part Vodka and 1 part Orange Juice, and the last one with After Shock®. Drink all three rapidly and in order.

Sunset at the Beach

2 parts Cranberry-Flavored Vodka
1 part Melon Liqueur
1 part Raspberry Liqueur
2 parts Pineapple Juice

GLASS: SHOT

Shake with ice and strain

Susu

2 parts Vodka
1 part Irish Cream Liqueur
1 part Crème de Cacao (Dark)
1 part Coffee Liqueur
1 part Grenadine
2 parts Milk

GLASS: SHOT

Shake with ice and strain

*Note: Because this recipe includes many ingredients, it's easier to make in volume, about 6 shots.

Swedish Color

1 part Banana Liqueur
1 part Blue Curaçao
1 part Vodka

GLASS: SHOT

Shake with ice and strain

Sweet Pickle

1 part Vodka
1 part Rumple Minze®
1 part Melon Liqueur

GLASS: SHOT

Shake with ice and strain

Sweet Pigeon

1 part Citrus-Flavored Vodka
2 parts Crème de Cacao (White)
1 part Blue Curaçao
2 parts Cream

GLASS: SHOT

Shake with ice and strain

Sweet Shit

1 part Vodka
1 part Amaretto
1 part Irish Cream Liqueur
1 part Coffee Liqueur
2 parts Chocolate Syrup

GLASS: SHOT

Shake with ice and strain

*Note: Because this recipe includes many ingredients, it's easier to make in volume, about 6 shots.

Swell Sex

1 part Vodka
1 part Coconut-Flavored Rum
1 part Melon Liqueur
1 part Cream
1 part Pineapple Juice

GLASS: SHOT

Shake with ice and strain

Swift Kick in the Balls

1 part Rum
1 part Vodka
1 part Lemon Juice

GLASS: SHOT

Shake with ice and strain

Tablazo

1 part Vodka
1 part Ginger Ale

GLASS: SHOT

Build in the glass with no ice

Take It and Vomit

1 part Vodka
1 part Peach Schnapps
1 part Blue Curaçao
1 part Grenadine
1 part Orange Juice

GLASS: SHOT

Shake with ice and strain

Tangaroa

3 parts Vodka
1 part Vanilla Liqueur

GLASS: SHOT

Shake with ice and strain

Tarzan® Scream

2 parts Vodka
2 parts 151-Proof Rum
1 part Caramel Syrup
splash Cream

GLASS: SHOT

Shake with ice and strain. Top with Cream.

Tear Drop

3 parts Pepper-Flavored Vodka
1 part Triple Sec

GLASS: SHOT

Shake with ice and strain

TGV

1 part Tequila
1 part Gin
1 part Vodka

GLASS: SHOT

Build in the glass with no ice

Thong

2 parts Vodka
1 part Triple Sec
1 part Cream
1 part Orange Juice
1 part Crème de Noyaux
1 part Grenadine

GLASS: SHOT

Shake with ice and strain
Note: Because this recipe includes many ingredients, it's easier to make in volume, about 6 shots.

Thumb Press

2 parts Vodka
2 parts Midori®
1 part 151-Proof Rum
splash Grenadine

{ GLASS: SHOT

Shake with ice and strain

Tie Me to the Bedpost

1 part Midori®
1 part Citrus-Flavored Vodka
1 part Coconut-Flavored Rum
1 part Sour Mix

{ GLASS: SHOT

Shake with ice and strain

Toffee Apple

1 part Vodka
1 part Butterscotch Schnapps
1 part Apple Brandy

{ GLASS: SHOT

Shake with ice and strain

Tokyo Rose

1 part Vodka
1 part Sake
1 part Melon Liqueur

{ GLASS: SHOT

Shake with ice and strain

Top Banana Shooter

1 part Crème de Cacao (White)
1 part Vodka
1 part Coffee
1 part Crème de Banana

{ GLASS: SHOT

Shake with ice and strain

Toro

1 part Spiced Rum
1 part Vodka
1 part Sour Mix

{ GLASS: SHOT

Shake with ice and strain

Toxic Refuse

1 part Vodka
1 part Triple Sec
1 part Midori®
splash Lime Juice

GLASS: SHOT

Shake with ice and strain

Traffic Light

1 part Orange Juice
1 part Peach Schnapps
1 part Grenadine
1 part Blue Curaçao
1 part Vodka

GLASS: SHOT

Shake with ice and strain
*Note: Because this recipe
includes many ingredients, it's
easier to make in volume,
about 6 shots.*

Transmission Overhaul

1 part Vodka
1 part Amaretto
1 part Southern Comfort®
1 part Mountain Dew®
1 part Orange Juice
1 part Grenadine

GLASS: SHOT

Stir gently with ice and strain
*Note: Because this recipe
includes many ingredients, it's
easier to make in volume,
about 6 shots.*

Tree Frog

1 part Citrus-Flavored Vodka
1 part Blue Hawaiian Schnapps
2 parts Grapefruit Juice

GLASS: SHOT

Shake with ice and strain

Triplesex

1 part Vodka
1 part Triple Sec
1 part Sour Mix
1 part Pineapple Juice

GLASS: SHOT

Shake with ice and strain

Tropical Hooter

1 part Citrus-Flavored Vodka
1 part Raspberry Liqueur
1 part Watermelon Schnapps
1 part Lemon-Lime Soda

GLASS: SHOT
Shake with ice and strain

True Canadian

1 part Vodka
1 part Maple Syrup

GLASS: SHOT
Shake with ice and strain

Turn Up the Volume

1 part Citrus-Flavored Vodka
1 part Blue Curaçao
1 part Peach Schnapps

GLASS: SHOT
Shake with ice and strain

Twister Shooter

1 part Vodka
1 part Cherry Brandy
1 part Ouzo

GLASS: SHOT
Shake with ice and strain

Unabomber

1 part Gin
1 part Vodka
1 part Triple Sec
1 part Lime Juice

GLASS: SHOT
Shake with ice and strain

Unholy Water

1 part Gin
1 part Spiced Rum
1 part Tequila Silver
1 part Vodka

GLASS: SHOT
Shake with ice and strain

Upside Down Apple Pie Shot

1 part Apple Juice
1 part Cinnamon Schnapps
1 part Vodka
Whipped Cream

GLASS: SHOT

Shake all but the Whipped Cream with ice and strain into a shot glass. Sit facing away from the bar and lean your head back onto the bar. Pour the shot into your mouth, followed by a squirt of Whipped Cream, and then sit up quickly. A towel might be handy.

Upside Down Kamikaze

2 parts Triple Sec
2 parts Vodka
1 part Lime Juice
Whipped Cream

GLASS: SHOT

Shake with ice and strain into a shot glass. Sit facing away from the bar and lean your head back onto the bar. Pour the shot into your mouth, followed by a squirt of Whipped Cream, and then sit up quickly. A towel might be handy.

Urine Sample Shooter

1 part Galliano®
1 part Midori®
1 part Vodka

GLASS: SHOT

Shake with ice and strain

Viagra® Shooter

1 part Vodka
1 part Blue Curaçao
1 part Irish Cream Liqueur

GLASS: SHOT

Shake with ice and strain

Victoria's Shot

2 parts Vodka
2 parts Passion Fruit Liqueur
1 part Pineapple Juice
splash Lime Juice
pinch Powdered Sugar

GLASS: SHOT

Shake with ice and strain

Village

1 part Vodka
1 part Passion Fruit Liqueur
1 part Pineapple Juice
1 part Aperol™

GLASS: SHOT

Shake with ice and strain

Vine Climber

2 parts Vodka
2 parts Melon Liqueur
1 part Sour Mix

GLASS: SHOT

Shake with ice and strain

Viper

1 part Vodka
1 part Amaretto
1 part Malibu® Rum
1 part Midori®
1 part Pineapple Juice

GLASS: SHOT

Shake with ice and strain

Virgin Breaker

1 part Vodka
1 part Whiskey
1 part Sambuca
1 part Orange Juice
1 part Grenadine

GLASS: SHOT

Shake with ice and strain
**Note: Because this recipe
includes many ingredients, it's
easier to make in volume,
about 6 shots.*

Vodka Passion

1 part Orange-Flavored Vodka
1 part Passion Fruit Juice

GLASS: SHOT

Shake with ice and strain

Volvo®

1 part Cointreau®
1 part Grand Marnier®
1 part Vodka
1 part Cognac
1 part Apricot Brandy

GLASS: SHOT

Shake with ice and strain
Note: Because this recipe includes many ingredients, it's easier to make in volume, about 6 shots.

Voodoo Doll

1 part Vodka
1 part Raspberry Liqueur

GLASS: SHOT

Shake with ice and strain

Waffle

1 part Vodka
1 part Butterscotch Schnapps
1 part Orange Juice

GLASS: SHOT

Shake with ice and strain

Wandering Minstrel Shooter

1 part Crème de Menthe (White)
1 part Brandy
1 part Vodka
1 part Coffee

GLASS: SHOT

Shake with ice and strain

Washington Red Apple

1 part Canadian Whiskey
1 part Sour Apple Schnapps
1 part Vodka
1 part Cranberry Juice Cocktail

GLASS: SHOT

Shake with ice and strain

Watermelon Shot

1 part Vodka
1 part Amaretto
1 part Southern Comfort®
1 part Orange Juice

GLASS: SHOT

Shake with ice and strain

White Cap

1 part Vodka
1 part Cream
1 part Coffee
1 part Port

GLASS: SHOT

Shake with ice and strain

White Death

1 part Crème de Cacao (White)
1 part Vodka
1 part Raspberry Liqueur

GLASS: SHOT

Shake with ice and strain

White Knuckle Ride

2 parts Coffee
1 part Vodka

GLASS: SHOT

Shake with ice and strain

Wicked Stepmother

2 parts Pepper-Flavored Vodka
1 part Amaretto

GLASS: SHOT

Shake with ice and strain

Widow Maker

1 part Vodka
1 part Jägermeister®
1 part Coffee Liqueur
splash Grenadine

GLASS: SHOT

Shake with ice and strain

Wild Berry Pop-Tart®

1 part Wild Berry Schnapps
1 part Vodka
1 part Strawberry Liqueur

GLASS: SHOT

Shake with ice and strain

Wild Child

1 part Sour Apple Schnapps
1 part Vodka
1 part Lemon-Lime Soda

GLASS: SHOT

Build in the glass with no ice

Wild Thing Shooter

2 parts Vodka
1 part Apricot Brandy
1 part Lemon-Lime Soda

GLASS: SHOT

Build in the glass with no ice

Windex® Shooter

1 part Blue Curaçao
1 part Vodka

GLASS: SHOT

Shake with ice and strain

Windy

1 part Vodka
1 part Blue Curaçao
1 part Pineapple Juice
1 part Sour Mix

GLASS: SHOT

Shake with ice and strain

Woo-Shoo

2 parts Cranberry-Flavored Vodka
1 part Peach Schnapps

GLASS: SHOT

Shake with ice and strain

Woo Woo Shooter

1 part Vodka
1 part Peach Schnapps
1 part Cranberry Juice Cocktail

GLASS: SHOT

Shake with ice and strain

Xaibalba

1 part Vodka
1 part Butterscotch Schnapps
1 part Vanilla Liqueur
1 part Chocolate Syrup

GLASS: SHOT

Shake with ice and strain

Y2K Shot

1 part Vodka
1 part Melon Liqueur
1 part Raspberry Liqueur

GLASS: SHOT

Shake with ice and strain

Yellow Bow Tie

2 parts Vodka
2 parts Amaretto
1 part Triple Sec
1 part Fresh Lime Juice

GLASS: SHOT

Shake with ice and strain

Yellow Cake

1 part Vanilla-Flavored Vodka
1 part Triple Sec
1 part Pineapple Juice

GLASS: SHOT

Shake with ice and strain

Yellow Snow

3 parts Pineapple-Flavored Vodka
1 part Pineapple Juice

GLASS: SHOT

Shake with ice and strain

Yoda®

1 part Vodka
1 part Blue Curaçao
1 part Sour Mix
1 part Midori®
2 parts Sour Apple Schnapps

GLASS: SHOT

Shake with ice and strain

Zool

1 part Peach Schnapps
1 part Vodka
1 part Amaretto

GLASS: SHOT

Shake with ice and strain

LAYERED SHOTS

CHAPTER

SHAKE
WITH
ICE &
STRAIN

8

CREATING A LAYERED EFFECT IN A SHOT
TAKES A STEADY HAND AND LOTS OF
PRACTICE. WITH THE BACK OF A BAR
SPOON, A KNOWLEDGE OF WHICH LIQUEURS
ARE HEAVIER THAN OTHERS, AND NERVES
OF STEEL, YOU CAN CREATE ART IN A VERY
SMALL GLASS.

DRINK UP!

69er in a Pool

1 part Vodka
1 part 151-Proof Rum
splash Lemon Juice
splash Tabasco® Sauce

GLASS: SHOT

Layer in a shot glass

Alligator Bite

1 part Jägermeister®
1 part Raspberry Liqueur
1 part Vodka
splash Orange Juice
1 part Melon Liqueur

GLASS: SHOT

Layer in a shot glass

Apple Pie

1 part Vodka
1 part Apple Juice

GLASS: SHOT

Layer in a shot glass

Backfire

1 part Coffee Liqueur
1 part Irish Cream Liqueur
1 part Vodka

GLASS: SHOT

Layer in a shot glass

Bertie Bichberg

1 part Vodka
1 part Crème de Banana
1 Maraschino Cherry

GLASS: SHOT

Layer in a shot glass

Bloodeye

½ part Raspberry Liqueur
1 part Citrus-Flavored Vodka
½ part Cranberry Liqueur

GLASS: SHOT

Layer in a shot glass

Blue Ice Breathe

1 part Citrus-Flavored Vodka
1 part Blue Curaçao
1 part Bitter Lemon

{ GLASS: SHOT

Layer in a shot glass

Blue Kisok

2 parts Blue Curaçao
1 part Vodka
splash Lime Juice
fill with Lemon-Lime Soda

{ GLASS: SHOT

Layer in a shot glass

Bulgaria United

1 part Grenadine
1 part Crème de Menthe (Green)
1 part Vodka

{ GLASS: SHOT

Layer in a shot glass

Cerebellum

4 parts Vodka
1 part Grenadine
1 part Irish Cream Liqueur

{ GLASS: SHOT

Layer in a shot glass

Concrete

1 part Vodka
1 part Irish Cream Liqueur

{ GLASS: SHOT

Layer in a shot glass

E.T.

1 part Melon Liqueur
1 part Irish Cream Liqueur
1 part Vodka

{ GLASS: SHOT

Layer in a shot glass

Fahrenheit 5,000

1 part Firewater®
1 part Absolut® Peppar Vodka
3 splashes Tabasco® Sauce

{ GLASS: SHOT

Layer in a shot glass

Flamboyance

½ part Apricot Brandy
1 part Vodka
splash Grand Marnier®

{ GLASS: SHOT

Layer in a shot glass

Gold Rush

1 part Swiss Chocolate Almond Liqueur
1 part Vodka
1 part Yukon Jack®

{ GLASS: SHOT

Layer in a shot glass

Hard Rocka

1 part Vodka
1 part Melon Liqueur
1 part Irish Cream Liqueur

{ GLASS: SHOT

Layer in a shot glass

Lsd

1 part Cherry Brandy
1 part Vodka
1 part Passoã®

{ GLASS: SHOT

Layer in a shot glass

Lube Job

1 part Vodka
1 part Irish Cream Liqueur

{ GLASS: SHOT

Layer in a shot glass

Oreo® Cookie

1 part Coffee Liqueur
1 part Crème de Cacao (White)
1 part Irish Cream Liqueur
splash Vodka

GLASS: SHOT

Layer in a shot glass

Pipeline

1 part Tequila
1 part Vodka

GLASS: SHOT

Layer in a shot glass

Race War

1 part Crème de Cacao (White)
1 part Irish Cream Liqueur
1 part Vodka

GLASS: SHOT

Layer in a shot glass

Rock 'n' Roll

1 part Chocolate Mint Liqueur
1 part Vodka

GLASS: SHOT

Layer in a shot glass

Russian Candy

1 part Vodka
1 part Peach Schnapps
1 part Grenadine

GLASS: SHOT

Layer in a shot glass

Saipa

1 part Banana Liqueur
1 part Vodka

GLASS: SHOT

Layer in a shot glass

Solar Plexus

2 parts Vodka
1 part Cherry Brandy
1 part Campari®

GLASS: SHOT

Layer in a shot glass

Spot Shooter

1 part Vodka
1 part Coffee
splash Irish Cream Liqueur

GLASS: SHOT

Layer in a shot glass. Place a few drops of Irish Cream in the center of the drink.

Texas Chainsaw Massacre

1 part Strawberry Liqueur
1 part Vodka

GLASS: SHOT

Layer in a shot glass

Thin Blue Line

1 part Vodka
1 part Triple Sec
splash Blue Curaçao

GLASS: SHOT

Layer the Triple Sec on top of the Vodka, then gently drip the Blue Curaçao. It will settle between the Vodka and the Triple Sec, forming a thin blue line.

Whistling Gypsy

1 part Tia Maria®
1 part Irish Cream Liqueur
1 part Vodka

GLASS: SHOT

Layer in a shot glass

CHAPTER

SHAKE
WITH
ICE &
STRAIN

9

CLASSIC DRINKS ARE CONSIDERED TO BE THOSE
THAT HAVE WITHSTOOD THE TEST OF TIME. MANY
OF THESE RECIPES HAVE CHANGED OVER THE YEARS
AS COMPONENTS BECAME SCARCE (PEYCHAUD'S®
BITTERS), DISCONTINUED (CRÈME YVETTE®), OR
OUTLAWED (ABSINTHE). ALTHOUGH EACH OF THE
RECIPES IN THIS SECTION CAN BE FOUND IN A
MODERN-DAY BARTENDER'S GUIDE, WHAT MAKES
THEM UNIQUE IS THAT THEY CAN ALSO BE FOUND IN
BARTENDER GUIDES DATING TO BEFORE 1940.

CLASSIC DRINKS

DRINK UP!

Black Eye

1½ parts Vodka
½ part Blackberry Brandy

GLASS: COCKTAIL

Shake with ice and strain

Blue Devil

1 part Vodka
1 part Blue Curaçao
fill with Sweet & Sour Mix
splash Cherry Juice

GLASS: HIGHBALL

Build over ice and stir

Blue Moon Cocktail

1½ parts Citrus-Flavored Vodka
1 part Vanilla-Flavored Vodka
1 part Blue Curaçao

GLASS: COCKTAIL

Shake with ice and strain

Bohemian Martini

1 part Anisette
1 part Vodka

GLASS: COCKTAIL

Shake with ice and strain

Catastrophe

1 part Goldschläger®
splash Strawberry Liqueur
splash Cranberry-Flavored Vodka

GLASS: HIGHBALL

Build over ice and stir

Creole Cocktail

1 part Coconut-Flavored Rum
¾ part Vodka
1 part Orange Juice
splash Grenadine

GLASS: COCKTAIL

Shake with ice and strain

Earthquake

1 part Vodka
1 part Amaretto
1 part Southern Comfort®
½ part Sweetened Lime Juice

GLASS: COCKTAIL
Shake with ice and strain

Eclipse

1 part Vodka
splash Crème de Cacao (White)
splash Strawberry Liqueur
1 part Cream

GLASS: HIGHBALL
Shake with ice and strain over ice

Emerald Isle

1 part Vodka
2 parts Melon Liqueur
fill with Mountain Dew®

GLASS: HIGHBALL
Build over ice and stir

Gin Stinger

2 parts Vodka
1 part Crème de Cacao (White)
1 part Crème de Menthe (Green)

GLASS: COCKTAIL
Shake with ice and strain

Havana

1 part Vodka
1 part Banana Juice
1 part Wild Berry–Flavored Schnapps
2 parts Lemonade
1 part Orange Juice

GLASS: HIGHBALL
Build over ice and stir

Hurricane Cocktail

1¼ parts Brandy
¾ part Pernod®
¾ part Vodka

GLASS: COCKTAIL
Shake with ice and strain

Monte Cristo Cocktail

1 part Cointreau®
1 part Lemon-Flavored Vodka

{ GLASS: OLD-FASHIONED

Shake with ice and strain over ice

Pall Mall Martini

2 parts Vodka
½ part Crème de Menthe (White)
½ part Dry Vermouth
½ part Sweet Vermouth

{ GLASS: COCKTAIL

Shake with ice and strain

Pierre Special

1 part Vodka
1 part Coconut-Flavored Rum
½ part Passion Fruit Liqueur
½ part Lime Cordial

{ GLASS: OLD-FASHIONED

Shake with ice and strain

Pink Elephant

1 part Vodka
1 part Galliano®
1 part Crème de Noyaux
1 part Orange Juice
1 part Cream
splash Grenadine

{ GLASS: CHAMPAGNE FLUTE

Shake with ice and strain

Russian

1 part Crème de Cacao (White)
1 part Gin
1 part Vodka

{ GLASS: COCKTAIL

Shake with ice and strain

Sunshine

1½ parts Vodka
½ part Triple Sec
fill with Grapefruit Juice

{ GLASS: OLD-FASHIONED

Build over ice and stir

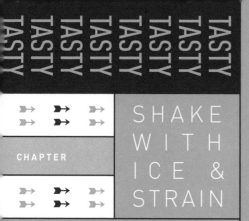

CHAPTER

SHAKE
WITH
ICE &
STRAIN

10

X-RATED DRINKS

WHAT MAKES A DRINK X-RATED?
ACCORDING TO THE SUPREME COURT,
YOU'LL KNOW IT WHEN YOU SEE IT!

DRINK UP!

Absolut® Royal Fuck

1 part Crown Royal® Whiskey
½ part Absolut® Currant-Flavored Vodka
½ part Peach Schnapps
splash Cranberry Juice Cocktail
splash Pineapple Juice

GLASS: WHISKEY SOUR

Shake with ice and strain over ice

Absolut® Sex

1 part Absolut® Currant-Flavored Vodka
½ part Cranberry Juice Cocktail
½ part Melon Liqueur
2 parts Lemon-Lime Soda

GLASS: HIGHBALL

Build over ice and stir

Adios Motherfucker

1 part Gin
1 part Light Rum
1 part Triple Sec
1 part Vodka
fill with Sour Mix

GLASS: COLLINS

Build over ice and stir

American Clusterfuck

1 part Light Rum
1 part Dark Rum
1 part Tequila
1 part Vodka
1 part Cranberry Juice Cocktail
splash Tropical Punch Schnapps

GLASS: COLLINS

Build over ice and stir

Apple Screw

1 part Apple Liqueur
1 part Vodka
fill with Orange Juice

GLASS: HIGHBALL

Build over ice and stir

Ass

2 parts Vodka
1 part Lemon-Lime Soda
1 part Orange Juice
splash Grenadine

GLASS: HIGHBALL

Build over ice and stir

Bald Pussy

1 part Citrus-Flavored Vodka
1 part Vodka
1 part Triple Sec
1½ parts Blueberry Schnapps
1½ parts Melon Liqueur
splash Lime Juice
splash Lemon-Lime Soda

GLASS: HIGHBALL

Build over ice and stir

Ballbreaker

2 parts Vodka
1 part Dry Vermouth
1 part Tequila Silver
1 part Raspberry Syrup
2 parts Vegetable Juice Blend

GLASS: OLD-FASHIONED

Shake with ice and pour

Banana Assmaster

1 part Vodka
2 parts Milk
1 Banana
4 scoops Ice Cream

GLASS: COLLINS

Build over ice and stir

Bishop's Nipple

1 part Orange-Flavored Vodka
1 part Raspberry Liqueur
1 part Lime Cordial
fill with Lemon-Lime Soda

GLASS: COLLINS

Build over ice and stir

Bitch Ass

1½ parts Coconut-Flavored Rum
1½ parts Vanilla-Flavored Vodka
splash Cranberry Juice Cocktail
1 part Orange Juice
1 part Pineapple Juice

GLASS: HURRICANE
Build over ice and stir

Blue Motherfucker

1 part Blue Curaçao
1 part Gin
1 part Light Rum
1 part Tequila Silver
1 part Vodka
splash Lemon-Lime Soda
splash Sour Mix

GLASS: COLLINS
Build over ice and stir

Blue Screw

1½ parts Orange-Flavored Vodka
1 part Blue Curaçao
fill with Orange Juice

GLASS: HIGHBALL
Build over ice and stir

Buttcrack

1 part RedRum®
1 part Citrus-Flavored Vodka

GLASS: COLLINS
Build over ice and stir

Clusterfuck

1 part Southern Comfort®
1 part Vodka
splash Grenadine
1 part Orange Juice
1 part Pineapple Juice

GLASS: HIGHBALL
Build over ice and stir

Comfortable Screw

1 part Vodka
1 part Southern Comfort®
fill with Orange Juice

GLASS: HIGHBALL

Shake with ice and pour

Comfortable Screw Up Against a Fuzzy Wall

½ part Vodka
¾ part Southern Comfort®
½ part Peach Schnapps
¼ part Galliano®
fill with Orange Juice

GLASS: HIGHBALL

Shake with ice and pour

Comfortable Screw Up Against a Wall

¾ part Vodka
¾ part Southern Comfort®
¼ part Galliano®
fill with Orange Juice

GLASS: HIGHBALL

Shake with ice and pour

Cool Summer Sex

1 part Currant-Flavored Vodka
1 part Melon Liqueur
1 part Fresh Lime Juice
fill with Lemon-Lime Soda

GLASS: COLLINS

Build over ice and stir

Cum Fuck Me Punch

1 part Amaretto
½ part Southern Comfort®
½ part Vodka
1 part Pineapple Juice
1 part Orange Juice
1 part Sour Mix
1 part Grenadine

GLASS: COLLINS

Build over ice and stir

Dick Hard

1 part Vodka
1 part Gin
1 part Light Rum
fill with Lemon-Lime Soda
1 Lime Wedge

GLASS: HIGHBALL

Build over ice and stir

Dickey Wallbanger

1 part Tequila Silver
1 part Vodka
fill with Orange Juice

GLASS: OLD-FASHIONED

Build over ice and stir

Dirty Screwdriver

1½ parts Vodka
fill with Orange Juice
2 splashes Cinnamon Schnapps

GLASS: HIGHBALL

Build over ice and stir

French Nipple

1 part Coffee Liqueur
1 part Amaretto
1 part Vodka
fill with Milk

GLASS: COLLINS

Build over ice and stir

French Screw

1 part Vodka
1 part Raspberry Liqueur
fill with Orange Juice

GLASS: HIGHBALL

Build over ice and stir

Frog Cum

1 part Vodka
1 part Melon Liqueur
1 part Lemonade
1 part Club Soda

GLASS: OLD-FASHIONED

Build over ice and stir

Fruity Fuck

½ part Vodka
1 part Melon Liqueur
2 parts Orange Juice
2 parts Pineapple Juice
1 part Passion Fruit Liqueur
½ part Lime Juice

GLASS: COLLINS

Build over ice and stir

Fuck in the Graveyard

1 part Vodka
1 part Rum
1 part Blueberry Schnapps
1 part Sour Apple Schnapps
1 part Blue Curaçao
1 part Raspberry Liqueur
fill with Cranberry Juice Cocktail
splash Orange Juice

GLASS: HIGHBALL

Shake with ice and pour

Fuck Me Hard

1 part Vodka
1 part Triple Sec
1 part Amaretto
2 parts Raspberry Liqueur
1 part Southern Comfort®
splash Cranberry Juice Cocktail
splash Orange Juice

GLASS: OLD-FASHIONED

Shake with ice and pour

Fuzzy Ass

2 parts Citrus-Flavored Vodka
1½ parts Peach Schnapps
1 part Sour Mix
splash Grenadine
1 part Triple Sec
fill with Lemon-Lime Soda

GLASS: COLLINS

Build over ice and stir

Fuzzy Fucker

1 part Peach Schnapps
1 part Vodka
1 part Southern Comfort®
2 parts Orange Juice

GLASS: HIGHBALL
Build over ice and stir

Fuzzy Nipple

1½ parts Vodka
1½ parts Peach Schnapps
splash Triple Sec
fill with Orange Juice

GLASS: HIGHBALL
Build over ice and stir

Fuzzy Screw

1 part Vodka
1 part Peach Schnapps
fill with Orange Juice

GLASS: HIGHBALL
Build over ice and stir

Fuzzy Screw Up Against a Wall

1 part Vodka
1 part Peach Schnapps
splash Galliano®
fill with Orange Juice

GLASS: HIGHBALL
Build over ice and stir

Golden Mountain Screw

1 part Banana Liqueur
2 parts Vodka
fill with Mountain Dew®

GLASS: HIGHBALL
Build over ice and stir

Golden Screw

1½ parts Vodka
dash Angostura® Bitters
fill with Orange Juice

GLASS: HIGHBALL
Build over ice and stir

Good as Sex

1 part Blue Curaçao
1 part Pisang Ambon® Liqueur
1 part Passoã
¾ part Orange-Flavored Vodka
fill with Lemonade

GLASS: COLLINS

Build over ice and stir

Hard Fuck

1 part Melon Liqueur
1 part Vodka
1 part Blue Curaçao
1 part Blueberries
fill with Orange Juice

GLASS: HIGHBALL

Build over ice and stir

Hawaiian Screw

1 part Vodka
1 part Rum
1 part Orange Juice
1 part Pineapple Juice

GLASS: HIGHBALL

Build over ice and stir

Italian Screw

1½ parts Vodka
1 part Galliano®
fill with Orange Juice

GLASS: HIGHBALL

Build over ice and stir

Let's Get Drunk and Screw

2 parts Vodka
1 part Raspberry Liqueur
fill with Cranberry Juice Cocktail

GLASS: COLLINS

Build over ice and stir

Mongolian Motherfucker

1 part Citrus-Flavored Vodka
1 part Coconut-Flavored Rum
½ part Blue Curaçao
½ part Peach Schnapps
splash Melon Liqueur
splash Grand Marnier®
splash Banana Liqueur
splash Orange Juice
splash Pineapple Juice
splash Lemonade
splash Piña Colada Mix

GLASS: HIGHBALL

Shake with ice and strain over ice

Mountain Screw

2 parts Vodka
fill with Mountain Dew®

GLASS: COLLINS

Build over ice and stir

Mud Fuck

2 parts Vodka
½ part Chocolate Syrup
2 parts Dr Pepper®
1 part Milk

GLASS: COUPETTE

Combine all ingredients in a blender with ice. Blend until smooth.

Naked Pretzel

¾ part Vodka
1 part Melon Liqueur
½ part Crème de Cassis
fill with Pineapple Juice

GLASS: OLD-FASHIONED

Shake with ice and strain over ice

Naked Twister

1 part Melon Liqueur
½ part Vodka
½ part Tuaca®
fill with Pineapple Juice
splash Lemon-Lime Soda

GLASS: BEER MUG

Build over ice and stir

Oral Sex on the Beach

1 part Melon Liqueur
1 part Raspberry Liqueur
½ part Vodka
fill with Orange Juice

GLASS: HIGHBALL

Shake with ice and strain over ice

Passionate Screw

2 parts Vodka
1 part Orange Juice
2 dashes Bitters

GLASS: COLLINS

Build over ice and stir

Perfect Screw

1¼ part Peach Schnapps
¼ part Vodka
fill with Orange Juice

GLASS: HIGHBALL

Shake with ice and pour

Pussy on Your Face

1 part Melon Liqueur
¾ part Strawberry-Flavored Vodka
¾ part Banana Liqueur
1 part Sour Mix
1 part Orange Juice
1 part Pineapple Juice

GLASS: HURRICANE

Build over ice and stir

Raspberry Screw

1 part Vodka
1 part Raspberry Liqueur
1 part Orange Juice
1 part Lemon-Lime Soda

GLASS: COLLINS

Build over ice and stir

Red Hot Lover

2 parts Vodka
2 parts Peach Schnapps
splash Grenadine
1 part Strawberry Juice
1 part Orange Juice

{ GLASS: COLLINS

Shake with ice and pour

Russian Pussy

1 part Vodka
1 part Crème de Cacao (White)

{ GLASS: OLD-FASHIONED

Shake with ice and strain over ice

Sand in Your Crack

½ part Vodka
½ part Blue Curaçao
½ part Melon Liqueur
4 parts Pineapple Juice

{ GLASS: COUPETTE

Combine all ingredients in a blender with ice. Blend until smooth.

Screaming Multiple Climax

2 parts Vodka
1 part Crème de Cacao (White)
1 part Amaretto
1 part Frangelico®
1 part Crème de Banana
fill with Cream

{ GLASS: HURRICANE

Shake with ice and pour

Screaming Nipple Twister

2 parts Vodka
fill with Dr Pepper®
1 scoop Ice Cream

{ GLASS: COLLINS

Build over ice and stir

Screw You

1 part Vodka
1 part Coffee Liqueur
1 part Strawberry Liqueur

{ GLASS: HIGHBALL

Combine all ingredients in a blender with ice. Blend until smooth.

Screwed Driver

1½ parts Orange-Flavored Vodka
fill with Lemonade
splash Cranberry Juice Cocktail

GLASS: OLD-FASHIONED

Build over ice and stir

Screwed Strawberry Stripper

1 part Vodka
2 parts Strawberry Liqueur
fill with Orange Juice

GLASS: COLLINS

Build over ice and stir

Sex by the Lake

1 part Vodka
1 part Peach Schnapps
1 part Pineapple Juice
1 part Orange Juice

GLASS: COLLINS

Build over ice and stir

Sex in a Jacuzzi

2 parts Vodka
1 part Cranberry Juice Cocktail
1 part Orange Juice
1 part Pineapple Juice
fill with Lemon-Lime Soda
splash Raspberry Liqueur
splash Orange Soda

GLASS: HIGHBALL

Build over ice and stir

Sex in the City

2 parts Blue Curaçao
1½ parts Peach Schnapps
1½ parts Vodka
1 part Pineapple Juice
1 part Raspberry Juice

GLASS: COLLINS

Shake with ice and pour

Sex in the Forest

1 part Coconut-Flavored Rum
1 part Peach Schnapps
splash Vodka
splash Crème de Menthe (White)
fill Lemon-Lime Soda
splash Cream

GLASS: HIGHBALL

Build over ice and stir

Sex in the Jungle

1½ parts Vodka
1 part Blue Curaçao
1 part Melon Liqueur
1 part Coconut-Flavored Rum
1 part Fresh Lime Juice
1 part Pineapple Juice
1 part Orange Juice

GLASS: HURRICANE

Shake with ice and pour

Sex on an Arizona Beach

1 part Vodka
1 part Peach Schnapps
splash Grapefruit Juice
splash Lime Juice
splash Grenadine

GLASS: OLD-FASHIONED

Shake with ice and strain over ice

Sex on Daytona Beach

1 part Vodka
1 part Peach Schnapps
½ part Grenadine
¼ part Heavy Cream
fill with Pineapple Juice

GLASS: HIGHBALL

Shake with ice and pour

Sex on Malibu Beach

½ part Vodka
½ part Coconut-Flavored Rum
½ part Peach Schnapps
1 part Cranberry Juice Cocktail
1 part Orange Juice
splash Grenadine

GLASS: HIGHBALL

Shake with ice and pour

Sex on the Beach

1 part Vodka
1 part Peach Schnapps
1 part Cranberry Juice Cocktail
1 part Orange Juice

GLASS: HIGHBALL

Shake with ice and pour

Sex on the Beach in Winter

1 part Vodka
1 part Peach Schnapps
½ part Coconut Crème
1 part Cranberry Juice Cocktail
1 part Pineapple Juice

GLASS: COUPETTE

Combine all ingredients in a blender with ice. Blend until smooth.

Sex on the Beach with a California Blonde

1 part Vodka
½ part Midori®
½ part Raspberry Liqueur
1 part Pineapple Juice
1 part Cranberry Juice Cocktail

GLASS: COLLINS

Shake with ice and pour

Sex on the Beach with a Friend

1 part Crème de Cassis
1 part Midori®
1 part Pineapple Juice
1 part Vodka

GLASS: HIGHBALL

Shake with ice and pour

Sex on the Brain

1 part Peach Schnapps
1 part Vodka
1 part Midori®
1 part Pineapple Juice
1 part Orange Juice
splash Sloe Gin

{ GLASS: HURRICANE

Shake with ice and pour

Sex on the Farm

¼ part Vodka
¼ part Amaretto
¼ part Peach Schnapps
¼ part Coconut-Flavored Rum
¼ part Midori®
splash Grenadine
1 part Orange Juice
1 part Pineapple Juice

{ GLASS: COLLINS

Shake with ice and pour

Sex on the Grass

1 part Vodka
1 part Peach Schnapps
½ part Southern Comfort®
½ part Blue Curaçao
1 part Melon Liqueur

{ GLASS: HIGHBALL

Shake with ice and pour

Sex on the Sofa

1 part Vodka
1 part Peach Schnapps
fill with Orange Juice

{ GLASS: OLD-FASHIONED

Shake with ice and strain over ice

Sexual Deviant

1 part Citrus-Flavored Vodka
¾ part Melon Liqueur
½ part Raspberry Liqueur
2 parts Orange Juice
2 parts Pineapple Juice
1 part Margarita Mix

GLASS: HIGHBALL

Shake with ice and strain over ice

Sexual Peak

½ part Amaretto
½ part Vodka
¼ part Peach Schnapps
1 part Orange Juice
1 part Pineapple Juice
splash Sour Mix

GLASS: COLLINS

Shake with ice and pour

Sexual Trance

1 part Citrus-Flavored Vodka
½ part Midori®
½ part Raspberry Liqueur
1 part Orange Juice
1 part Pineapple Juice
splash Sour Mix

GLASS: COLLINS

Shake with ice and pour

Sexy Blue-Eyed Boy

1 part Blue Curaçao
1 part Vodka
1 part Crème de Cacao (Dark)
1 part Rum Cream Liqueur
1 scoop Ice Cream

GLASS: COUPETTE

Combine all ingredients in a blender with ice. Blend until smooth.

Sexy Green Frogs

1 part Vodka
1 part Triple Sec
1 part Melon Liqueur
fill with Lemon-Lime Soda

GLASS: HIGHBALL

Build over ice and stir

Shag in the Sand

1½ parts Southern Comfort®
1½ parts Sloe Gin
1 part Vodka
1 part Maraschino Liqueur
½ part Red Curaçao
fill with Orange Juice

GLASS: HURRICANE

Shake with ice and pour

Slow Comfortable Screw 151 Times in the Dark

1 part Vodka
1 part Sloe Gin
1 part Southern Comfort®
1 part Galliano®
1 part Tequila
1 part Dark Rum
splash 151-Proof Rum
fill with Orange Juice

GLASS: COLLINS

Build over ice and stir

Slow Comfortable Screw Between the Sheets

1 part Sloe Gin
1 part Southern Comfort®
1 part Vodka
1 part Triple Sec
fill with Orange Juice

GLASS: COLLINS

Build over ice and stir

Slow Comfortable Screw Up Against a Fuzzy Wall

1 part Vodka
1 part Southern Comfort®
1 part Sloe Gin
1 part Peach Schnapps
½ part Galliano®
fill with Orange Juice

GLASS: HIGHBALL

Build over ice and stir

Slow Comfortable Screw Up Against the Wall

1 part Sloe Gin
1 part Southern Comfort®
1 part Vodka
splash Galliano®
fill with Orange Juice

GLASS: HIGHBALL

Build over ice and stir

Slow Fuzzy Screw

1 part Vodka
1 part Sloe Gin
1 part Peach Schnapps
fill with Orange Juice

GLASS: HIGHBALL

Build over ice and stir

Slow Fuzzy Screw Up Against the Wall

1 part Vodka
1 part Sloe Gin
1 part Peach Schnapps
fill with Orange Juice
splash Galliano®

GLASS: HIGHBALL

Build over ice and stir

Slow Screw Mildly Comfortable, Slightly Wild

GLASS: HURRICANE

Shake with ice and pour

1 part Vodka
1 part Sloe Gin
¾ part Bourbon
¾ part Southern Comfort®
1 part Lemonade
1 part Orange Juice

Slow Screw Up Against the Wall

GLASS: HIGHBALL

Build over ice and stir

1 part Vodka
1 part Sloe Gin
fill with Orange Juice
splash Galliano®

Stop and Go Naked

GLASS: OLD-FASHIONED

Shake with ice and pour

2 parts Triple Sec
1 part Silver Tequila
1 part Vodka
1 part Light Rum
1 part Gin

Sweet Sex

GLASS: HURRICANE

Shake with ice and pour

1 part Raspberry-Flavored Vodka
1 part 99-Proof Banana Liqueur
1 part Coconut-Flavored Rum
1 part Tequila Rose®
1 part Watermelon Schnapps
splash Grenadine
fill with Orange Juice

Thunderfuck

1 part Vodka
1 part Amaretto
1 part Melon Liqueur
1 part Rum
1 part Sour Mix
1 part Orange Juice

GLASS: HIGHBALL

Shake with ice and strain

Tropical Screw

1 part Vodka
½ part Triple Sec

GLASS: HIGHBALL

Build over ice and stir

Twenty-Dollar Blowjob

¾ part Vodka
¾ part Southern Comfort®
¾ part Peach Schnapps
2 parts Cranberry Juice Cocktail
2 parts Sour Mix
½ part Orange Juice

GLASS: COLLINS

Build over ice and stir

Twisted Asshole

1 part Vodka
1 part Melon Liqueur
½ part Peach Schnapps
splash Blue Curaçao
1 part Pineapple Juice
1 part Orange Juice

GLASS: COLLINS

Shake with ice and pour

Twisted Screw

2 parts Vodka
fill with Orange Juice
splash Banana Juice

GLASS: HIGHBALL

Build over ice and stir

Wild Screw

1 part Vodka
1 part Bourbon
fill with Orange Juice

{ GLASS: COLLINS

Build over ice and stir

Wild Squirrel Sex

½ part Lemon-Flavored Vodka
½ part Strawberry-Flavored Vodka
½ part Orange-Flavored Vodka
½ part Raspberry-Flavored Vodka
1 part Amaretto
1 part Sour Mix
1 part Cranberry Juice Cocktail
splash Grenadine

{ GLASS: BEER MUG

Build over ice and stir

TIKI DRINKS

SHAKE
WITH
ICE &
STRAIN

CHAPTER

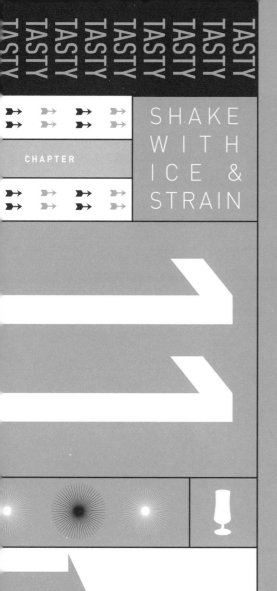

11

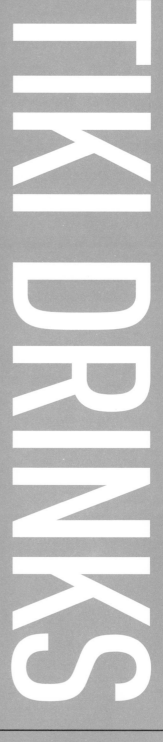

HERE ARE SOME COLORFUL, FRUITY TROPICAL DRINKS THAT WILL HELP YOU PRETEND YOU'RE ON THE BEACH—EVEN IN MID-JANUARY.

DRINK UP!

2-Tonga

1 part Cranberry-Flavored Vodka
1½ parts Red Curaçao
1½ parts Mango Schnapps
4 parts Orange Juice
1 part Fresh Lime Juice

GLASS: HURRICANE

Shake with ice and strain over ice

Ambros Lighthouse

2 parts Vodka
1 part Parfait Amour
1 part Coconut-Flavored Liqueur
fill with Banana Juice

GLASS: HURRICANE

Build over ice and stir

Anchors Away

1 part Vodka
1 part Amaretto
1 part Blackberry Liqueur
fill with Orange Juice

GLASS: HURRICANE

Combine all ingredients in a blender with ice. Blend until smooth.

Banana Chi Chi

1 part Vodka
1 part Cherry Juice
1 part Banana Juice
fill with Piña Colada Mix
splash Orange Juice

GLASS: HIGHBALL

Combine all ingredients in a blender with ice. Blend until smooth.

Banana Punch

2 parts Vodka
1½ splashes Banana Liqueur
½ part Lime Juice
fill with Carbonated Water

GLASS: COLLINS

Build over ice and stir

Baywatch

1 part Vodka
1 part Galliano®
fill with Orange Juice
splash Cream

GLASS: HURRICANE

Build over ice and stir

Beach Bum

1½ parts Vodka
1 part Apple Juice
1 part Banana Liqueur
2 parts Pineapple Juice
fill with Fruit Punch

GLASS: COLLINS

Shake with ice and pour

Beach Sunday

2 parts Peach-Flavored Vodka
1 part Chambord®
3 parts Cranberry Juice Cocktail

GLASS: HIGHBALL

Build over ice and stir

Beach Sweet

2 parts Vodka
1 part Apricot Brandy
½ part Fresh Lime Juice
3 parts Banana Juice

GLASS: OLD-FASHIONED

Combine all ingredients in a blender with ice. Blend until smooth.

Beachcomber

1 part Vodka
1½ parts Light Rum
6 Strawberries
1 Banana
½ part Coconut Cream
splash Lime Juice
½ part Grenadine

GLASS: HIGHBALL

Combine all ingredients in a blender with ice. Blend until smooth.

Beachside

1 part Vodka
1 part Melon Liqueur
1 part Strawberry Daiquiri Mix
1 part Orange Juice
1 part Pineapple Juice

{ GLASS: HIGHBALL

Shake with ice and strain over ice

Berry Buster

1½ parts Currant-Flavored Vodka
½ part Raspberry Liqueur
2 parts Cranberry Juice Cocktail

{ GLASS: COUPETTE

Shake with ice and strain over ice

Berry Me in the Sand

1 part Vodka
½ part Blackberry Liqueur
½ part Triple Sec
fill with Orange Juice

{ GLASS: HIGHBALL

Build over ice and stir

Black Magic

1½ parts Vodka
¾ part Coffee Liqueur
splash Lemon Juice

{ GLASS: OLD-FASHIONED

Build over ice and stir

Bolduc on the Beach

1 part Vodka
1 part Orange Juice
1 part Grapefruit Juice

{ GLASS: HIGHBALL

Shake with ice and pour

Cocoa Beach

1 part Vodka
1 part Blue Curaçao
2 parts Piña Colada Mix
1 part Lemonade
1 part Pineapple Juice

GLASS: HURRICANE

Shake with ice and strain over ice

Daytona Beach

1 part Vodka
1 part Cherry Juice
1 part Wild Berry Schnapps
2 parts Lemonade
1 part Orange Juice

GLASS: HIGHBALL

Shake with ice and pour

El Niño

1 part Vodka
1 part Peach Schnapps
½ part Blue Curaçao
2 parts Pineapple Juice
2 parts Orange Juice
splash Club Soda

GLASS: HURRICANE

Shake all but Club Soda with ice and strain into the glass over ice. Top with Club Soda.

Fun on the Beach

1 part Vodka
1 part Melon Liqueur
splash Raspberry Liqueur
1 part Pineapple Juice
1 part Cranberry Juice Cocktail

GLASS: HIGHBALL

Build over ice and stir

Gilligan's Island®

1 part Vodka
1 part Peach Schnapps
3 parts Orange Juice
3 parts Cranberry Juice Cocktail

{ GLASS: COLLINS

Shake with ice and strain over ice

Hawaiian Punch®

½ part Vodka
½ part Southern Comfort®
½ part Amaretto
½ part Sloe Gin
1 part Orange Juice
1 part Pineapple Juice

{ GLASS: HURRICANE

Build over ice and stir

Hawaiian® Surf City

1 part Vodka
1 part Wild Berry Schnapps
1 part Peach Nectar
2 parts Lemonade
1 part Pineapple Juice

{ GLASS: HIGHBALL

Build over ice and stir

Hoi Punch

2 parts Vodka
½ part Crème de Cassis
½ part Light Rum
fill with Lemon Juice
1½ parts Simple Syrup

{ GLASS: COLLINS

Shake with ice and strain over ice

Hurricane Leah

¼ part Light Rum
¼ part Gin
¼ part Vodka
¼ part Tequila
¼ part Blue Curaçao
splash Cherry Brandy
1 part Sour Mix
1 part Orange Juice

GLASS: HURRICANE

Shake with ice and strain over ice

Iceberg Vacation

1½ parts Blue Curaçao
1½ parts Vodka
1 part Cream
1 part Crème de Menthe (White)
1 part Fresh Lime Juice
fill with Lemon-Lime Soda

GLASS: HURRICANE

Build over ice and stir

Kangeroo Jumper

1 part Vodka
1 part Rum
1 part Coconut Crème
½ part Blue Curaçao
fill with Passion Fruit Juice

GLASS: COUPETTE

Shake with ice and strain over ice

Malibu Beach

1 part Vodka
1 part Coconut-Flavored Rum
1 part Orange Juice
1 part Pineapple Juice

GLASS: HIGHBALL

Build over ice and stir

Myrtle Beach

1 part Vodka
1 part Blue Curaçao
1 part Piña Colada Mix
1 part Lemonade
1 part Orange Juice

GLASS: HIGHBALL

Shake with ice and strain over ice

Oslo Breeze

1 part Vodka
1 part Aquavit
dash Orange Bitters
fill with Cider

GLASS: COUPETTE

Build over ice and stir

Peach on the Beach

1½ parts Vodka
½ part Peach Schnapps
fill with Pineapple Juice

GLASS: HIGHBALL

Shake with ice and pour

Puerto Rican Punch

¾ part Vodka
¾ part Gin
¾ part Sloe Gin
¾ part Peach Schnapps
1 part Orange Juice
1 part Pineapple Juice
splash Grenadine

GLASS: HURRICANE

Build over ice and stir

Rio Bamba

1 part Vodka
1 part Gin
½ part Passion Fruit Liqueur
½ part Peach Schnapps
½ part Cream
1 part Pineapple Juice
1 part Orange Juice

GLASS: HURRICANE

Shake with ice and pour

Sandbar Sleeper

1 part Vodka
1 part Irish Crème Liqueur
1 part Coffee Liqueur
1 part Frangelico®
½ part Milk

GLASS: HIGHBALL

Shake with ice and strain over ice

Sandcastle

2 parts Citrus-Flavored Vodka
1 part Grenadine
fill with Pineapple Juice

GLASS: COLLINS

Shake with ice and pour

South Padre Island

1 part Vodka
¾ part Peach Schnapps
1 part Sour Mix
fill with Cranberry Juice Cocktail
splash Orange Juice
splash Pineapple Juice

GLASS: HURRICANE

Build over ice

Sunset at the Beach

1½ parts Cranberry-Flavored
 Vodka
½ part Melon Liqueur
½ part Raspberry Liqueur
3 parts Pineapple Juice
fill with Lemon-Lime Soda

GLASS: COLLINS

*Shake all but Lemon-Lime Soda
with ice and strain into the glass.
Top with Lemon-Lime Soda.*

Sunset on the Beach

½ part Vodka
1 part Peach Schnapps
1 part Melon Liqueur
1 part Coconut Cream
1 part Sour Mix
fill with Orange Juice

GLASS: HURRICANE

Shake with ice and strain over ice

Survivor Island

1 part Sloe Gin
1 part Melon Liqueur
1 part Currant-Flavored Vodka
fill with Orange Juice

GLASS: HIGHBALL

Shake with ice and strain over ice

Thunder Cloud

½ part Crème de Noyaux
½ part Blue Curaçao
½ part Amaretto
¾ part Vodka
2 parts Sour Mix
fill with Lemon-Lime Soda

GLASS: HURRICANE

Build over ice and stir

Tropical Kick

1 part Coconut-Flavored Rum
1 part Pineapple-Flavored Vodka
1 part Light Rum
½ part Tropical Punch Schnapps
½ part Raspberry Liqueur
fill with Pineapple Juice

GLASS: HURRICANE

Shake with ice and pour

Tropical Nat

2 parts Spiced Rum
1 part Vodka
1 part Orange Juice
1 part Cranberry Juice Cocktail
splash Pineapple Juice

GLASS: HURRICANE

Build over ice

Wiki Waki

1 part Light Rum
1 part Amaretto
½ part Tequila Silver
½ part Vodka
½ part Triple Sec
1 part Pineapple Juice
1 part Orange Juice

GLASS: HURRICANE

Shake with ice and pour

Winter Tropic

2 parts Vodka
1 part Cranberry Juice Cocktail
1 part Strawberry Daiquiri Mix

GLASS: HURRICANE

Build over ice and stir

Yo Ho

1 part Vodka
1½ parts Amaretto
1½ parts Grapefruit Juice
splash Amaretto
1 Banana

{ GLASS: COLLINS

Combine all ingredients in a blender with ice. Blend until smooth.

Zombies in the Night

1 part Vodka
1 part Apricot Brandy
1 part Wild Berry Schnapps
1 part Orange Juice
1 part Pineapple Juice

{ GLASS: HIGHBALL

Shake with ice and pour

SHAKE
WITH
ICE &
STRAIN

CHAPTER

12

COOLERS

START WITH VODKA, ADD A LIQUOR, OR
LIQUEUR, AND SOME JUICE FOR FLAVOR AND
THEN FILL THE GLASS WITH SODA—VIOLÁ!

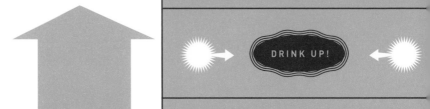

DRINK UP!

3001

1 part Vodka
1 part Blue Curaçao
splash Lime Juice
fill with Lemon-Lime Soda

{ GLASS: COLLINS

Mix with ice

Absolut® Limousine

2 parts Absolut® Citrus-Flavored Vodka
1 part Lime Juice
fill with Tonic Water

{ GLASS: COLLINS

Build over ice and stir

Absolutely Screwed Up

1 part Triple Sec
fill with Ginger Ale

{ GLASS: COLLINS

Build over ice and stir

Alien Secretion

1 part Melon Liqueur
1 part Vodka
2 parts Pineapple Juice
fill with Club Soda

{ GLASS: COLLINS

Build over ice and stir

Amaretto Cooler

1½ parts Amaretto
1½ parts Vanilla-Flavored Vodka
fill with Cola

{ GLASS: HIGHBALL

Build over ice and stir

Annie

1 part Vodka
1 part Cranberry Liqueur
½ part Cream
splash Lime Juice
fill with Club Soda

GLASS: COLLINS

Build over ice and stir

Apricot Breeze

1 part Vodka
3 parts Apricot Nectar
fill with Tonic Water

GLASS: HURRICANE

Build over ice and stir

Aquafresh

1½ parts Vodka
½ part Crème de Menthe (Green)
fill with Club Soda

GLASS: OLD-FASHIONED

Build over ice and stir

Auto da Fe

1½ parts Vodka
splash Lime Juice
fill with Club Soda

GLASS: COLLINS

Build over ice and stir

Backstage Pass

1 part Orange-Flavored Vodka
½ part Triple Sec
½ part Cherry Brandy
1 part Citrus-Flavored Rum
2 parts Orange Juice
fill with Club Soda

GLASS: HIGHBALL

Shake all but Club Soda with ice and strain into the glass. Top with Club Soda.

Banana Balm

1½ parts Vodka
½ part Banana Liqueur
splash Lime Juice
fill with Club Soda

{ GLASS: COLLINS

Shake all but Club Soda with ice and strain into the glass. Top with Club Soda.

Banker's Doom

1 part Whiskey
1 part Vodka
1 part Melon Liqueur
fill with Club Soda

{ GLASS: COLLINS

Shake all but Club Soda with ice and strain into the glass. Top with Club Soda.

Barramundy

1 part Vodka
½ part Blackberry Liqueur
½ part Raspberry Liqueur
1 part Cranberry Juice Cocktail
fill with Club Soda

{ GLASS: HIGHBALL

Build over ice and stir

Beach Ball Cooler

1½ parts Vodka
1 part Lime
½ part Crème de Cacao (White)
fill with Ginger Ale

{ GLASS: COLLINS

Shake all but Ginger Ale with ice and strain into the glass. Top with Ginger Ale.

Beach Beauty

1½ parts Vodka
1½ parts Orange Juice
1 part Crème de Banana
splash Grenadine
fill with Tonic Water

{ GLASS: COLLINS

Build over ice and stir

Beasley

1 part Brandy
1 part Tequila
1 part Triple Sec
1 part Vodka
2 parts Vanilla Liqueur
½ part Lemon Juice
fill with Tonic Water

GLASS: COLLINS

Shake all but Club Soda with ice and strain into the glass. Top with Club Soda.

Bee

1 part Vodka
1 part Banana Liqueur
fill with Ginger Ale

GLASS: HIGHBALL

Build over ice and stir

Big Ol' Girl

1 part Triple Sec
1 part Vodka
splash Lime Juice
fill with Club Soda

GLASS: COLLINS

Build over ice and stir

Billie Holiday

1 part Vodka
fill with Ginger Ale
splash Grenadine

GLASS: COLLINS

Build over ice and stir

Bingo

1 part Vodka
1 part Mandarine Napoléon® Liqueur
1 part Apricot Brandy
fill with Club Soda

GLASS: COLLINS

Build over ice and stir

Blue Ice Mountain

2 parts Blue Curaçao
1 part Vodka
fill with Club Soda

GLASS: HIGHBALL

Build over ice and stir

Blue in the Face

1 part Vodka
1 part Gin
1 part Light Rum
1 part Blue Curaçao
splash Sugar
fill with Tonic Water

GLASS: WHISKEY SOUR

*Layer over ice. Drink through
a straw.*

Blue Rose

1 part Blue Curaçao
1 part Blavod® Black Vodka
1 part Currant-Flavored Vodka
fill with Tonic Water

GLASS: COLLINS

Build over ice and stir

Blue Water

1½ parts Vodka
¼ part Blue Curaçao
fill with Club Soda

GLASS: HIGHBALL

Build over ice and stir

Blueberry Kick

1 part Vodka
2 parts Blueberry Schnapps
splash Cream
fill with Club Soda

GLASS: COLLINS

Build over ice and stir

The Bottom Line

1½ parts Vodka
½ part Lime Juice
fill with Tonic Water

GLASS: HIGHBALL

Build over ice and stir

Cantaloupe Dizzy

1 part Vodka
1 part Melon Liqueur
1 part Peach Schnapps
fill with Club Soda

GLASS: PARFAIT

Build over ice and stir

Cherry Cooler

2 parts Cherry Vodka
1 Lemon Slice
fill with Cola

GLASS: COLLINS

Build over ice and stir

Chilton

1 part Vodka
splash Margarita Mix
fill with Club Soda

GLASS: HIGHBALL

Build over ice and stir

Cielo

1¼ parts Vodka
¾ part Crème de Cassis
2 dashes Bitters
fill with Ginger Ale

GLASS: COLLINS

Build over ice and stir

Citron Cooler

1½ parts Citrus-Flavored Vodka
½ part Lime Cordial
fill with Tonic Water

GLASS: COLLINS

Build over ice and stir

Clouseau

1 part Vodka
1 part Coffee Liqueur
fill with Ginger Ale

GLASS: HIGHBALL

Build over ice and stir

Cotton Panties

1 part Vodka
2 parts Peach Schnapps
1 part Half and Half
fill with Tonic Water

GLASS: COLLINS

Build over ice and stir

Dusty Dog

2 parts Vodka
½ part Crème de Cassis
splash Lemon Juice
fill with Ginger Ale

GLASS: HIGHBALL

Build over ice and stir

Flaming Soda

1 part Vodka
½ part Melon Liqueur
½ part Triple Sec
fill with Club Soda

GLASS: HIGHBALL

Build over ice and stir

Flying High

1 part Vodka
1 part Fresh Lime Juice
½ part Crème de Banana
fill with Orange Soda

GLASS: COLLINS

Build over ice and stir

Frontal Lobotomy

½ part Jack Daniel's®
½ part Tequila
½ part Vodka
1 part Jägermeister®
fill with Club Soda

GLASS: COLLINS

Shake all but Club Soda with ice and strain into the glass. Top with Club Soda.

Fuzzy Feeling

1 part Orange-Flavored Vodka
⅔ part Blackberry Liqueur
½ part Lemon Juice
fill with Club Soda

GLASS: HIGHBALL

Build over ice and stir

Gables Collins

1½ parts Vodka
1 part Crème de Noyaux
1 part Pineapple Juice
1 part Lemon Juice
fill with Club Soda
1 Lemon Slice

GLASS: COLLINS

Shake all but Club Soda with ice and strain into the glass. Top with Club Soda.

Geting

1 part Vodka
½ part Banana Liqueur
fill with Ginger Ale

GLASS: HIGHBALL

Build over ice and stir

Gingervitas

1 part Citrus-Flavored Vodka
1 part Dry Vermouth
fill with Ginger Ale

GLASS: COLLINS

Build over ice and stir

Gospodin

1 part Vodka
2/3 part Apricot Brandy
fill with Club Soda

GLASS: COLLINS

Build over ice and stir

Green Dinosaur

1 part Rum
1 part Vodka
1 part Tequila
1 part Gin
1 part Melon Liqueur
splash Lemon Juice
fill with Club Soda

GLASS: HIGHBALL

Build over ice and stir

Gumball

1 part Blue Curaçao
½ part Vodka
½ part Crème de Banana
fill with Ginger Ale

GLASS: COLLINS

Build over ice and stir

Headless Horseman

2 parts Vodka
3 dashes Bitters
fill with Ginger Ale
1 Orange Slice

GLASS: COLLINS

Build over ice and stir

High Valley Sneeker

1 part Vodka
½ part Banana Liqueur
½ part Jägermeister®
fill with Ginger Ale

GLASS: HIGHBALL

Build over ice and stir

Hillbilly Buttkicker

1 part Southern Comfort®
1 part Gin
1 part Vodka
1 part Orange Juice
fill with Ginger Ale
1 part Grenadine

GLASS: COLLINS

Build over ice and stir

Incognito

1½ parts Vodka
1 part Apricot Brandy
fill with Ginger Ale

GLASS: COLLINS

Build over ice and stir

Island Soda

2 parts Vodka
½ part Banana Liqueur
2 parts Pineapple Juice
fill with Ginger Ale

GLASS: COLLINS

Build over ice and stir

Jealous Husband

½ part Vodka
⅔ part Peach Schnapps
⅔ part Triple Sec
3 parts Cranberry Juice Cocktail
fill with Ginger Ale

GLASS: HIGHBALL

Build over ice and stir

Joy Ride

1½ parts Citrus-Flavored Vodka
1 part Campari®
3 parts Sour Mix
1 part Sugar
fill with Club Soda

GLASS: HURRICANE

Shake all but Club Soda with ice and strain over ice into the glass. Top with Club Soda.

Kurant Collins

2 parts Currant-Flavored Vodka
1 part Lemon Juice
dash Powdered Sugar
fill with Club Soda

GLASS: COLLINS

Shake all but Club Soda with ice and strain over ice into the glass. Top with Club Soda.

L.A. Iced Tea

1 part Vodka
1 part Triple Sec
1 part Melon Liqueur
1 part Gin
1 part Rum
fill with Club Soda

GLASS: COLLINS

Shake all but Club Soda with ice and strain over ice into the glass. Top with Club Soda.

Lappland

1 part Vodka
1 part Apricot Brandy
1 part Sour Mix
fill with Ginger Ale

GLASS: COLLINS

Build over ice and stir

Lili

1 Lime Twist
dash Sugar
Juice from half a Lime
1 part Vodka
1 part Triple Sec
fill with Club Soda

GLASS: COLLINS

Muddle the Lime, Sugar, and Lime Juice in the bottom of a collins glass. Fill the glass with ice and add the Vodka and Triple Sec. Fill with Club Soda.

Long Vodka

2 parts Vodka
½ part Lime Juice
4 dashes Angostura® Bitters
fill with Tonic Water

GLASS: COLLINS

Build over ice and stir

Machete

1 part Vodka
2 parts Pineapple Juice
fill with Tonic Water

GLASS: COLLINS

Build over ice and stir

Mandarin Delight

1½ parts Orange-Flavored Vodka
fill Tonic Water
1 Lime Wedge

GLASS: COLLINS

Build over ice and stir

Mark Pilkinton

1½ parts Vodka
¾ part Triple Sec
1 part Sour Mix
fill with Raspberry Ginger Ale

GLASS: HIGHBALL

Build over ice and stir

Melba Tonic

2 parts Vodka
½ part Peach Schnapps
½ part Grenadine
½ part Simple Syrup
fill with Tonic Water

GLASS: COLLINS

Build over ice and stir

Melon Patch

1 part Melon Liqueur
½ part Triple Sec
½ part Vodka
fill with Club Soda

GLASS: HIGHBALL

Shake all but Club Soda with ice and strain into the glass. Top with Club Soda.

Montgomery

1 part Vodka
¼ part Grenadine
2 parts Sour Mix
fill with Ginger Ale

GLASS: COLLINS

Build over ice and stir

Morning Fizz

1½ parts Vodka
1 part Simple Syrup
3 parts Grapefruit Juice
fill with Club Soda

GLASS: WHITE WINE

*Shake all but Club Soda with ice
and strain into the glass. Top
with Club Soda.*

Naked Truth

⅔ part Vodka
1 part Melon Liqueur
1 part Lemon Juice
dash Powdered Sugar
fill with Club Soda

GLASS: COLLINS

*Shake all but Club Soda with ice
and strain into the glass. Top
with Club Soda.*

Napoli

1 part Vodka
1 part Campari®
½ part Dry Vermouth
splash Sweet Vermouth
fill with Club Soda

GLASS: HIGHBALL

*Shake all but Club Soda with ice
and strain into the glass. Top
with Club Soda.*

Night Fever

1 part Blue Curaçao
1 part Vodka
½ part Cachaca
fill with Club Soda

GLASS: COLLINS

*Shake all but Club Soda with ice
and strain into the glass. Top
with Club Soda.*

Nirvana

1½ parts Orange-Flavored Vodka
½ part Melon Liqueur
½ part Passion Fruit Liqueur
splash Lime Cordial
fill with Club Soda

GLASS: CHAMPAGNE FLUTE

*Shake all but Club Soda with ice
and strain into the glass. Top
with Club Soda.*

Nuclear Fizz

¾ part Vodka
½ part Melon Liqueur
½ part Triple Sec
splash Lime Juice
fill with Club Soda

GLASS: COLLINS

*Shake all but Club Soda with ice
and strain into the glass. Top
with Club Soda.*

Pacific Exchange

1½ parts Vodka
½ part Raspberry Liqueur
⅔ part Plum Brandy
⅔ part Lemon Juice
fill with Club Soda

GLASS: HIGHBALL

*Shake all but Club Soda with ice
and strain into the glass. Top
with Club Soda.*

Paddlesteamer

1 part Vodka
1 part Southern Comfort®
2 parts Orange Juice
fill with Ginger Ale

GLASS: COLLINS

*Shake all but Ginger Ale with
ice and strain into the glass. Top
with Ginger Ale.*

Passione al Limone

1½ parts Vodka
½ part Passion Fruit Liqueur
½ part Simple Syrup
fill with Club Soda

GLASS: COLLINS

*Shake all but Club Soda with ice
and strain into the glass. Top
with Club Soda.*

Phat Louie

2 parts Vanilla-Flavored Vodka
½ part Grenadine
fill with Ginger Ale

GLASS: COLLINS

Build over ice and stir

Plugged on Fruit

1 part Orange-Flavored Vodka
1 part Blue Curaçao
1 part Peach Schnapps
1 part Lime Juice
1 part Lemon Juice
fill with Club Soda

GLASS: HIGHBALL

Shake all but Club Soda with ice and strain into the glass. Top with Club Soda.

Pond Scum

1 part Vodka
fill with Club Soda
½ part Irish Cream Liqueur

GLASS: HIGHBALL

Build over ice. Top with Irish Cream Liqueur.

Province Town

1 part Vodka
½ part Citrus-Flavored Vodka
2 parts Grapefruit Juice
2 parts Cranberry Juice Cocktail
fill with Club Soda

GLASS: COLLINS

Shake all but Club Soda with ice and strain into the glass. Top with Club Soda.

Rangoon Ruby

2 parts Vodka
2 parts Cranberry Juice Cocktail
½ part Lime Juice
fill with Club Soda

GLASS: HIGHBALL

Build over ice and stir

Raspberry Watkins

1½ parts Vodka
½ part Raspberry Liqueur
¼ part Lime Cordial
splash Grenadine
fill with Club Soda

GLASS: COLLINS

Shake all but Club Soda with ice and strain into the glass. Top with Club Soda.

Red Devil's Poison

1½ parts Citrus-Flavored Vodka
½ part Parfait Amour
1 part Lemon Juice
fill with Tonic Water

GLASS: COLLINS

Build over ice and stir

Red Rock West

1 part Crème de Cassis
1 part Raspberry Liqueur
1 part Vodka
fill with Club Soda

GLASS: HIGHBALL

Build over ice and stir

Red Tonic

2 parts Vodka
1 part Grenadine
1 part Lemon Juice
fill with Tonic Water

GLASS: HIGHBALL

Build over ice and stir

Royal Eagle

1½ parts Currant-Flavored Vodka
½ part Blackberry Liqueur
½ part Kirschwasser
⅔ part Lemon Juice
fill with Ginger Ale

GLASS: HIGHBALL

Shake all but Ginger Ale with ice and strain into the glass. Top with Ginger Ale.

Seadoo

1 part Vodka
splash Cranberry Juice Cocktail
fill with Club Soda

GLASS: COLLINS

Build over ice and stir

South-of-the-Border Iced Tea

1 part Vodka
1 part Coffee Liqueur
fill with Club Soda

GLASS: COLLINS

Build over ice and stir

Soviet Sunset

1 part Lemon-Flavored Vodka
1 part Triple Sec
1 part Sweetened Lime Juice
fill with Club Soda

GLASS: HIGHBALL

Build over ice and stir

Spritzer

1½ parts Vodka
fill with Club Soda

GLASS: HIGHBALL

Build over ice and stir

Sweet Tart Cooler

1 part Vodka
1 part Cherry Juice
1 part Wild Berry Schnapps
1 part Lemonade
1 part Orange Juice
1 part Lemon-Lime Soda

GLASS: HIGHBALL

Build over ice and stir

Thermometer

2 parts Vodka
1 part Cranberry Juice Cocktail
fill with Club Soda

GLASS: HIGHBALL

Build over ice and stir

Valencia Lady

2 parts Vodka
splash Blue Curaçao
splash Cranberry Juice Cocktail
fill with Club Soda

GLASS: HIGHBALL

Build over ice and stir

Very Berry Tonic

1 part Currant-Flavored Vodka
½ part Raspberry Liqueur
fill with Tonic Water

GLASS: COLLINS

Build over ice and stir

Viktor

2 parts Currant-Flavored Vodka
1 part Lime Juice
fill with Ginger Ale

GLASS: HIGHBALL

Build over ice and stir

Vodka Cooler

2 parts Vodka
dash Powdered Sugar
fill with Carbonated Water

GLASS: COLLINS

Build over ice and stir

Vodka Highball

2 parts Vodka
½ part Dry Vermouth
fill with Ginger Ale

GLASS: OLD-FASHIONED

Build over ice and stir

Vodka Rickey

2 parts Vodka
½ part Sweetened Lime Juice
fill with Club Soda

GLASS: HIGHBALL

Build over ice and stir

Wasp

1 part Vodka
1 part Banana Liqueur
fill with Ginger Ale

GLASS: COLLINS

Build over ice and stir

Wild at Heart

1 part Brandy
1 part Vodka
1 part Triple Sec
1 part Gin
fill with Ginger Ale

GLASS: COLLINS

Build over ice and stir

Zanzibar Cooler

2 parts Vodka
1 part Peach Liqueur
dash Brown Sugar
fill with Ginger Ale

GLASS: COLLINS

Build over ice and stir

TASTY
TASTY
TASTY
TASTY
TASTY
TASTY
TASTY
TASTY
TASTY
TASTY

SHAKE
WITH
ICE &
STRAIN

CHAPTER

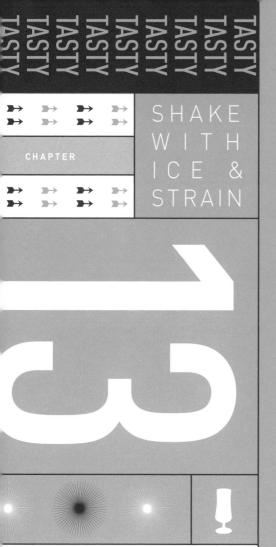

13

TALL DRINKS

DRINKS THAT ARE SERVED IN A TALL GLASS
THAT DON'T FIT INTO ANY OTHER CATEGORY
FALL INTO THIS "CATCHALL" CATEGORY OF
TALL DRINKS.

DRINK UP!

007

1 part Orange-Flavored Vodka
1 part Lemon-Lime Soda
1 part Orange Juice

GLASS: COLLINS

Mix with ice

187 Urge

1 part Jack Daniel's®
1 part Vodka
fill with Dr Pepper®

GLASS: COLLINS

Mix with ice

319 Special

1 part Vodka
1 part Orange Juice
1 part Lemon-Lime Soda
splash Lime Juice

GLASS: COLLINS

Mix with ice

.357 Magnum

1 part Vodka
1 part Spiced Rum
fill with Lemon-Lime Soda
1½ parts Amaretto

GLASS: COLLINS

Mix with ice and float Amaretto on top

The 5th Element

½ part 151-Proof Rum
½ part Southern Comfort®
½ part Vodka
1 part Pineapple Juice
1 part Lemon-Lime Soda

GLASS: BEER MUG

Build over ice and stir

50/50

2½ parts Vanilla-Flavored Vodka
splash Grand Marnier®
fill with Orange Juice

GLASS: COLLINS

Build over ice and stir

500 Proof

½ part Vodka
½ part Southern Comfort®
½ part Bourbon
½ part 151-Proof Rum
1 part Orange Juice
½ part Simple Syrup

{ GLASS: COLLINS

Shake with ice and strain over ice

'57 T-Bird with Florida Plates

1 part Vodka
1 part Amaretto
1 part Grand Marnier®
fill with Orange Juice

{ GLASS: COLLINS

Build over ice and stir

612 Delight

1 part Vodka
1 part Diet Lemonade
fill with Cola

{ GLASS: COLLINS

Build over ice and stir

The Abba

2 parts Citrus-Flavored Vodka
fill with Lemon-Lime Soda

{ GLASS: COLLINS

Build over ice and stir

Abbie Dabbie

2 parts Vodka
2 parts Melon Liqueur
3 parts Apple Juice

{ GLASS: COLLINS

Build over ice and stir

Abe Froman

3 parts Vodka
½ part Grenadine
fill with Lemonade

{ GLASS: COLLINS

Build over ice and stir

A-Bomb

2 parts Tequila
1 part Vodka
3 parts Root Beer Schnapps
fill with Root Beer
1 scoop Ice Cream

GLASS: BEER MUG

Combine all but Ice Cream in a large beer mug over ice and stir. Top with a scoop of Ice Cream and drizzle Root Beer Schnapps over the top.

Abso Bloody Lutly

1½ parts Absolut® Vodka
4 parts Tomato Juice
splash Worcestershire Sauce
dash Horseradish

GLASS: COLLINS

Shake with ice and strain over ice

Absolut® Apple

1 part Absolut® Vodka
1 part Sour Apple Schnapps
3 parts Lemon-Lime Soda
3 parts Apple Juice

GLASS: COLLINS

Build over ice and stir

Absolut® Can Dew

2 parts Absolut® Vodka
1 part Blue Curaçao
½ part Mountain Dew®

GLASS: COLLINS

Build over ice and stir

Absolut® Hollywood

1½ parts Absolut® Vodka
1 part Raspberry Liqueur
fill with Pineapple Juice

GLASS: COLLINS

Build over ice and stir

Absolut® Lemonade

1 part Absolut® Citrus-Flavored Vodka
1 part Amaretto
splash Sour Mix
splash Lemon-Lime Soda

GLASS: COLLINS

Build over ice and stir

Absolut® Nothing

1 part Absolut® Vodka
fill with Lemon-Lime Soda

GLASS: COLLINS

Build over ice and stir

Absolut® Orgasm

2 parts Absolut® Vodka
1 part Triple Sec
fill with Lemon-Lime Soda
1 part Sour Mix

GLASS: COLLINS

Build over ice and stir

Absolut® Power Juice

2 parts Absolut® Vodka
2 parts Peach Schnapps
1 part Raspberry Liqueur
1 part Lemonade

GLASS: COLLINS

Build over ice and stir

Absolut® Russian

1 part Absolut® Vodka
3 parts Tonic Water
splash Currant Syrup

GLASS: COLLINS

Build over ice and stir

Absolut® Slut

1 part Absolut® Vodka
2 parts Orange Juice
2 parts Pineapple Juice

GLASS: COLLINS

Build over ice and stir

Absolut® Stress

½ part Absolut® Vodka
½ part Coconut-Flavored Rum
½ part Peach Schnapps
1 part Orange Juice
1 part Pineapple Juice
1 part Cranberry Juice Cocktail

GLASS: COLLINS

Build over ice and stir

Absolut® Summer

1½ parts Absolut® Citrus-Flavored Vodka
⅔ part Blue Curaçao
3 parts Grapefruit Juice
3 parts Orange Juice

GLASS: COLLINS

Build over ice and stir

Absolut® Summertime

1½ parts Absolut® Citrus-Flavored Vodka
¾ part Sour Mix
½ part Lemon-Lime Soda
3 parts Club Soda
1 Lemon Wedge

GLASS: COLLINS

Shake with ice and strain over ice

Absolut® Viking

1 part Absolut® Currant-Flavored Vodka
1 part Crème de Cassis
fill with Ginger Ale

GLASS: COLLINS

Build over ice and stir

Absolutely Horny

1 part 99-Proof Banana Liqueur
1 part Crown Royal® Whiskey
1 part Peach Schnapps
1 part Vodka
1½ parts Cranberry Juice Cocktail
1½ parts Pineapple Juice

GLASS: COLLINS

Build over ice and stir

Ace

1 part Vodka
1 part Rum
2 parts Pineapple Juice
2 parts Orange Juice
1 part Fresh Lime Juice
½ part Grenadine
½ part Sugar

GLASS: HURRICANE

Shake with ice and strain over ice

Adios

1 part Dry Gin
1 part Vodka
1 part Rum
1 part Blue Curaçao
1 part Sour Mix
fill with Lemonade

GLASS: COLLINS

Build over ice and stir

Adios Mother

1 part Vodka
1 part Gin
1 part Light Rum
1 part Blue Curaçao
2 parts Sour Mix
fill with Lemon-Lime Soda

GLASS: HURRICANE

Build over ice and stir

After Party

1 part Vodka
2 parts Pineapple Juice
2 parts Cranberry Juice Cocktail
2 parts Ginger Ale
dash Sugar

GLASS: COLLINS

Build over ice and stir

Agent G

1 part Vodka
1 part Rum
1 part Gin
1 part Southern Comfort®
1 part Yukon Jack®
2 parts Grenadine
fill with Grapefruit Juice

GLASS: COLLINS

Build over ice and stir

Agent Orange

1 part Vodka
1 part Rum
1 part Gin
1 part Southern Comfort®
1 part Yukon Jack®
1 part Sour Apple Schnapps
1 part Melon Liqueur
fill with Orange Juice
splash Grenadine

{ GLASS: COLLINS

Build over ice and stir

Alabama Riot

2 parts Southern Comfort®
1 part Peppermint Schnapps
1 part Vodka
fill with Fruit Punch
1 part Lime Juice

{ GLASS: COLLINS

Shake with ice and strain over ice

Alaska White

2 parts Tequila
2 parts Vodka
1 part Gin
1 part Sambuca
fill with Lemon-Lime Soda

{ GLASS: COLLINS

Build over ice and stir

Alex's Super Stinger

1 part Honey
3 parts Rum
3 parts Vodka
fill with Apple Juice

{ GLASS: COLLINS

Build over ice and stir

All Night Long

½ part Vodka
½ part Coconut-Flavored Rum
½ part Coffee Liqueur
½ part Crème de Cacao (White)
4 parts Pineapple Juice
2 parts Sour Mix

GLASS: HURRICANE

Shake with ice and strain over ice

Almost Heaven

1 part Currant-Flavored Vodka
3 parts Amaretto
3 parts Raspberry Liqueur
splash Pineapple Juice
splash Cranberry Juice Cocktail

GLASS: COLLINS

Shake with ice and strain over ice

Amando IV

1½ parts Citrus-Flavored Vodka
⅔ part Blue Curaçao
2 parts Orange Juice
1 part Lemon Juice
splash Simple Syrup

GLASS: COLLINS

Shake with ice and strain over ice

Amaretto Stiletto

2 parts Amaretto
1 part Vodka
1 part Lemon-Lime Soda
1 part Lime Juice
1 part Sour Mix

GLASS: COLLINS

Build over ice and stir

Amaretto Vodka Collins

1 part Vodka
1 part Amaretto
½ part Sour Mix
fill with Lemon-Lime Soda

GLASS: COLLINS

Build over ice and stir

Amaya

1 part Vodka
1 part Apricot Brandy
½ part Grenadine
½ part Passion Fruit Nectar
2 parts Orange Juice

GLASS: HURRICANE

Shake with ice and strain over ice

Amazing Pepper

2 parts Amaretto
1 part Vodka
fill with Cola

GLASS: COLLINS

Build over ice and stir

Ambulance

2 parts Vodka
1 part Coffee Liqueur
1½ parts Coffee
fill with Cola

GLASS: COLLINS

Build over ice and stir

Amorosae

1 part Parfait Amour
1 part Vodka
splash Crème de Cassis
splash Lime Juice
fill with Lemon-Lime Soda

GLASS: COLLINS

Shake with ice and strain over ice

Anastavia

1 part Vodka
splash Triple Sec
splash Grenadine
1 part Orange Juice
splash Lemon Juice

GLASS: COLLINS

Shake with ice and pour

Andersson

1 part Vodka
1 part Melon Liqueur
fill with Milk

GLASS: COLLINS

Build over ice and stir

Andy Pandy

1 part Vodka
1 part Peach Schnapps
1 part Blue Curaçao
1 part Lemonade
1 part Orange Juice

GLASS: COLLINS

Build over ice and stir

Anti-Arctic

1½ parts Citrus-Flavored Vodka
½ part Triple Sec
fill with Iced Tea

GLASS: COLLINS

Shake with ice and pour

Apple Cider Surprise

2 parts Vodka
1 part Apple Juice
1 part Ginger Ale

GLASS: COLLINS

Build over ice and stir

Apple-Dew

1 part Apple Liqueur
1 part Vodka
fill with Mountain Dew®

GLASS: COLLINS

Build over ice and stir

Apple Knocker

1½ parts Vodka
splash Lemon Juice
splash Strawberry Liqueur
fill with Apple Cider

GLASS: COLLINS

Shake with ice and strain over ice

Apple-Snake Nuts

1 part Vodka
1 part Amaretto
1 part Sour Apple Schnapps
1 part Triple Sec
splash Sweetened Lime Juice

{ GLASS: COLLINS

Shake with ice and pour

Apricanza

1 part Vodka
½ part Apricot Brandy
fill with Lemon-Lime Soda
splash Grenadine

{ GLASS: COLLINS

Build over ice and stir

Aquamarine

1 part Vodka
½ part Peach Schnapps
splash Blue Curaçao
splash Triple Sec
fill with Apple Juice

{ GLASS: COLLINS

Build over ice and stir

Arbogast

1 part Vodka
½ part Rumple Minze®
½ part Coffee Liqueur
½ part Irish Cream Liqueur
fill with Milk

{ GLASS: COLLINS

Shake with ice and pour

Arcadian Lovemaker

1 part Citrus-Flavored Vodka
1 part Sloe Gin
1 part Southern Comfort®
1 part Orange Juice

{ GLASS: COLLINS

Shake with ice and pour

Arctic Circle

2 parts Vodka
1 part Lime Juice
3 parts Ginger Ale

GLASS: COLLINS

Build over ice and stir

Ashtray

1 part Vodka
1 part Blavod® Black Vodka
1½ parts Blackberry Liqueur
2 parts Milk
2 parts Blackberry Juice

GLASS: COLLINS

Shake with ice and pour

Assassin

1 part Lemon-Flavored Rum
1 part Citrus-Flavored Vodka
1 part Lemon-Lime Soda
1 part Orange Juice

GLASS: COLLINS

Build over ice and stir

ASU Girls

1½ parts Vodka
½ part Peach Schnapps
fill with Pineapple Juice

GLASS: COLLINS

Build over ice and stir

Atomic Kool-Aid®

½ part Melon Liqueur
½ part Vodka
½ part Amaretto
splash Grenadine
1 part Orange Juice
1 part Pineapple Juice

GLASS: COLLINS

Shake with ice and pour

Atomic Lokade

1 part Vodka
½ part Blue Curaçao
½ part Triple Sec
fill with Lemonade

GLASS: COLLINS

Build over ice and stir

Atomic Shit

1 part Vodka
1 part Grapefruit Juice
fill with Lemonade
splash Jack Daniel's®

GLASS: COLLINS

Build over ice and stir

Attitude

1 part Amaretto
1 part Southern Comfort®
1 part Lemon-Flavored Vodka
1 part Melon Liqueur
½ part Sloe Gin
fill with Orange Juice
splash Cranberry Juice Cocktail

GLASS: HURRICANE

Shake with ice and strain over ice

Attitude Adjustment

1 part Vodka
1 part Gin
1 part Triple Sec
1 part Amaretto
1 part Peach Schnapps
1 part Sour Mix
splash Cranberry Juice Cocktail

GLASS: COLLINS

Shake with ice and strain over ice

Avalon

3 parts Vodka
1 part Pisang Ambon® Liqueur
1½ parts Lemon Juice
fill with Apple Juice

GLASS: COLLINS

Build over ice and stir

Aviator Fuel

1 part Vodka
1 part Lemonade
1 part Lemon-Lime Soda

GLASS: COLLINS

Build over ice and stir

Azteken Punch

1½ parts Pineapple Juice
1 part Vodka
1 part Crème de Cacao (Dark)
fill with Orange Juice

GLASS: COLLINS

Build over ice and stir

Bacio & Kiss

1 part Vodka
splash Lychee Liqueur
splash Peach Schnapps
2 parts Grapefruit Juice
2 parts Cranberry Juice Cocktail

GLASS: COLLINS

Shake with ice and strain over ice

Bad Attitude

½ part Rum
½ part Vodka
½ part Gin
½ part Tequila
½ part Triple Sec
1 part Amaretto
1 part Pineapple Juice
1 part Orange Juice
1 part Cranberry Juice Cocktail
splash Grenadine

GLASS: COLLINS

Build over ice and stir

Bahama Mama

½ part Coffee-Flavored Vodka
1 part Dark Rum
1 part Coconut-Flavored Rum
1 part Lemon Juice
fill with Pineapple Juice
splash 151-Proof Rum

GLASS: COLLINS

Build over ice and stir

Bahia de Plata

1 part Dark Rum
1 part Vodka
1 part Triple Sec
fill with Pineapple Juice
splash Grenadine

GLASS: COLLINS

Build over ice and stir

Baja Mar

1½ parts Dark Rum
¼ part Vodka
¼ part Crème de Banana
fill with Orange Juice
splash Grenadine

GLASS: COLLINS

Build over ice and stir

Ballet Russe

1½ parts Vodka
½ part Crème de Cassis
3 parts Sour Mix

GLASS: COLLINS

Build over ice and stir

Baltic

1 part Vodka
½ part Passion Fruit Juice
splash Blue Curaçao
fill with Orange Juice

GLASS: COLLINS

Build over ice and stir

Baltic Murder Mystery

1 part Vodka
1 part Crème de Cassis
fill with Lemon-Lime Soda

GLASS: COLLINS

Build over ice and stir

Baltimore Zoo

1 part Vodka
1 part Rum
1 part Tequila
1 part Triple Sec
1 part Sweetened Lime Juice
1 part Grenadine
1 part Sour Mix
1 part Root Beer
1 part 151-Proof Rum

GLASS: COLLINS

Build over ice and stir

Bamby

1 part Dark Rum
1 part Vodka
1 part Crème de Menthe (Green)
1 part Crème de Banana
fill with Pineapple Juice

GLASS: COLLINS

Build over ice and stir

Banana Rama

1 part Vodka
1 part Banana Liqueur
½ part Coconut-Flavored Rum
fill with Milk

GLASS: COLLINS

Build over ice and stir

Barbie®

1 part Gin
1 part Vodka
fill with Lime Soda
splash Grenadine

GLASS: COLLINS

Build over ice and stir

Barney's® Revenge

1 part Vodka
1 part Blue Curaçao
splash Apricot Brandy
fill with Raspberry-Flavored Seltzer

GLASS: COLLINS

Build over ice and stir

Barracuda

2 parts Vodka
2 parts Grapefruit Juice
1 part Tonic Water

GLASS: COLLINS

Build over ice and stir

Bartender in a Cup

2 parts Vodka
1 part Triple Sec
1 part Pineapple Juice
1 part Orange Juice
1 part Sour Mix
1 part Grenadine

GLASS: COLLINS

Shake with ice and pour

Baseball Pleasure

2 parts Vodka
1½ parts Whiskey
1½ parts Amaretto
fill with Orange Juice

GLASS: COLLINS

Build over ice and stir

Bay of Passion

1 part Vodka
2 parts Pineapple Juice
1 part Passion Fruit Liqueur

GLASS: COLLINS

Build over ice and stir

Beatle Juice

½ part Gin
½ part Tequila Reposado
½ part Light Rum
½ part Vodka
1 part Melon Liqueur
splash Grenadine
fill with Sour Mix
top with Lemon-Lime Soda

GLASS: HURRICANE

Shake all but Soda with ice and strain into a Hurricane glass. Top with Soda.

Beekers Fruit

1 part Jack Daniel's®
1 part Vodka
1 part Sloe Gin
1 part Pineapple Juice
1 part Passion Fruit Nectar

GLASS: COLLINS

Build over ice and stir

Beep

1 part Vodka
3 parts Orange Juice
fill with Lemon-Lime Soda

GLASS: COLLINS

Build over ice and stir

Beetlejuice

1 part Vodka
1 part Melon Liqueur
1 part Blue Curaçao
1 part Raspberry Liqueur
1 part Cranberry Juice Cocktail
fill with Sour Mix

GLASS: COLLINS

Build over ice and stir

Before the Kiss

½ part Vodka
½ part Triple Sec
1 part Melon Liqueur
1 part Pear Syrup
fill with Apple Juice

GLASS: COLLINS

Shake all but Apple Juice with ice and strain into the glass. Top with Apple Juice.

Bejia Flor

1½ parts Vodka
¼ part Parfait Amour
¼ part Southern Comfort®
splash Crème de Banana
splash Apricot Brandy
fill with Lemon-Lime Soda

GLASS: COLLINS

Build over ice

Bent Bum

1½ parts Gin
1½ parts Vodka
1 part Orange Juice
1 part Grapefruit Juice
splash Cola

GLASS: COLLINS

Build over ice and stir

Berry Lemonade

1 part Vodka
splash Strawberry Liqueur
fill with Lemonade

GLASS: COLLINS

Build over ice and stir

Best Year

1 part Vodka
½ part Blue Curaçao
½ part Licor 43
½ part Lime Juice
fill with Pineapple Juice

GLASS: COLLINS

Shake with ice and pour

Bette Davis Eyes

1 part Vodka
½ part Blue Curaçao
½ part Coconut-Flavored Liqueur
fill with Lemon-Lime Soda

GLASS: COLLINS
Build over ice and stir

The Betty Ford

1½ parts Citrus-Flavored Vodka
fill with Lemon-Lime Soda
½ part Grenadine

GLASS: COLLINS
Build over ice

Big Apple

2 parts Vodka
fill with Apple Juice
splash Crème de Menthe (White)

GLASS: COLLINS
Build over ice and stir

Billy Belly Bomber

1 part Vodka
3 parts Pineapple Juice
splash Lemon Juice

GLASS: COLLINS
Build over ice and stir

Bitter Sweet Symphon-Tea

1½ parts Citrus-Flavored Vodka
splash Orange Liqueur
fill with Iced Tea
splash Lemon Juice

GLASS: COLLINS
Shake with ice and strain over ice

Black Jacket

1 part Coffee Liqueur
splash Vodka
splash Crème de Noyaux
⅔ part Cream

GLASS: COLLINS
Shake with ice and pour

Black-Eyed Susan

1 part Vodka
1 part Light Rum
1 part Triple Sec
splash Lime Juice
1 part Pineapple Juice
1 part Orange Juice

GLASS: COLLINS

Shake with ice and strain over ice

Blast-Off

1 part Vodka
½ part Cointreau®
½ part Galliano®
4 parts Orange Juice
2 parts Pineapple Juice

GLASS: COLLINS

Build over ice and stir

Bleeker

1 part Vodka
½ part Lillet®
½ part Triple Sec
1 Egg White

GLASS: COLLINS

Shake with ice and pour

Bloody Caesar

1½ parts Vodka
fill with Clamato® Juice
1 dash Tabasco® Sauce
2 dashes Worcestershire Sauce
1 Lime Wedge
1 Celery Stick
dash Salt
dash Pepper

GLASS: COLLINS

Build over ice and stir

Blue Aegean

1 part Blue Curaçao
1 part Vodka
1 part Triple Sec
fill with Pineapple Juice

GLASS: COLLINS

Build over ice and stir

Blue Bunny

1 part Rum
1 part Vodka
splash Sour Mix
splash Blue Curaçao

GLASS: COLLINS

Shake with ice and strain over ice

Blue Ice with Wings

1 part Vodka
¾ part Blue Curaçao
½ part Coconut-Flavored Liqueur
½ part Sour Mix
fill with Red Bull® Energy Drink

GLASS: HURRICANE

Build over ice and stir

Blue Jeans

1 part Vodka
1 part Blue Curaçao
1 part Grapefruit Juice
1 part Pineapple Juice

GLASS: COLLINS

Build over ice and stir

Blue Malibu®

½ part Gin
½ part Rum
½ part Vodka
½ part Blue Curaçao
2 parts Sour Mix
splash Lemon-Lime Soda

GLASS: COLLINS

Build over ice and stir

Blue Nuke

1 part Vodka
1 part 151-Proof Rum
1 part Gin
1 part Blue Curaçao
1 part Blueberry Schnapps
fill with Sour Mix

GLASS: COLLINS

Build over ice and stir

Blue Owl

½ part Vodka
1 part Blue Curaçao
1 part Crème de Banana
splash Cherry Brandy
fill with Lemonade

GLASS: COLLINS

Shake with ice and pour

Blue Paradiso

1½ parts Blue Curaçao
1½ parts Orange-Flavored Vodka
½ part Coconut-Flavored Rum
fill with Pineapple Juice

GLASS: HURRICANE

Shake with ice and pour

Blue Spider

2 parts Cranberry-Flavored Vodka
fill with Red Bull® Energy Drink

GLASS: COLLINS

Build over ice and stir

Blue Suede Juice

1 part Citrus-Flavored Vodka
¼ part Blue Curaçao
¾ part Triple Sec
fill with Sour Mix
splash Lemon-Lime Soda

GLASS: COLLINS

Build over ice and stir

Blue Sweden

1 part Blue Curaçao
1 part Vodka
1 part Crème de Banana
fill with Orange Juice

GLASS: COLLINS

Build over ice and stir

Blueberry Hill

½ part Vodka
½ part Raspberry Liqueur
¼ part Blackberry Liqueur
1 part Sour Mix
splash Peach Schnapps
fill with Lemonade

GLASS: COLLINS

Build over ice and stir

The Blues

1 part Vodka
1 part Coconut-Flavored Rum
¾ part Blue Curaçao
½ part Triple Sec
fill with Pineapple Juice

GLASS: COLLINS

Shake with ice and strain over ice

Boca Chica

½ part Vodka
splash Pisang Ambon® Liqueur
splash Coconut-Flavored Liqueur
1 part Guava Juice
splash Passion Fruit Nectar

GLASS: COLLINS

Shake with ice and strain over ice

Bodega Blues

1 part Melon Liqueur
1 part Vodka
1 part Peach Schnapps
1 part Orange Juice
1 part Passion Fruit Juice

GLASS: COLLINS

Build over ice and stir

Boogie Beck

1 part Vodka
1 part Amaretto
1 part Southern Comfort®
½ part Fresh Lime Juice
1 part Pineapple Juice
1 part Orange Juice

{ GLASS: COLLINS

Build over ice and stir

Boot Blaster

1 part Light Rum
1 part Gin
1 part Vodka
1 part Triple Sec
fill with Lemonade
splash Cola

{ GLASS: COLLINS

Build over ice and stir

Bootlegger Tea

¾ part Vodka
¾ part Rum
¾ part Triple Sec
1 part Sour Mix
1 part Lemon-Lime Soda
splash Grenadine

{ GLASS: COLLINS

Build over ice and stir

Borisov

1 part Jack Daniel's®
1 part Vodka
½ part Brandy
½ part Campari®
½ part Cognac
fill with Red Bull® Energy Drink

{ GLASS: COLLINS

Build over ice and stir

Bottleneck

1 part Vodka
1 part Parfait Amour
1 part Crème de Banana
1 part Melon Liqueur
splash Fresh Lime Juice
fill with Lemon-Lime Soda

GLASS: COLLINS

Build over ice and stir

Brain Candy

1 part Vodka
1 part Crème de Menthe (White)
fill with Mountain Dew®

GLASS: COLLINS

Build over ice and stir

Brainwash

1 part Gin
1 part Vodka
1 part Jägermeister®
1 part Blue Curaçao
fill with Pineapple Juice

GLASS: COLLINS

Shake with ice and pour

Bridge to the Moon

1 part Currant-Flavored Vodka
1 part Apple Liqueur
1 part Passion Fruit Liqueur
fill with Lemon-Lime Soda

GLASS: COLLINS

Build over ice and stir

Bridget in the Buff

2 parts Vodka
1½ parts Raspberry Liqueur
fill with Lemon-Lime Soda
splash Sour Mix

GLASS: COLLINS

Build over ice and stir

Broken-Down Golf Cart

1 part Vodka
1 part Melon Liqueur
1 part Amaretto
fill with Cranberry Juice Cocktail

{ GLASS: COLLINS

Shake with ice and pour

Brown Derby

1¼ parts Vodka
fill with Cola

{ GLASS: COLLINS

Build over ice and stir

Bubblicious®

⅔ part Crème de Cacao (White)
½ part Vanilla-Flavored Vodka
⅔ part Southern Comfort®
½ part Sour Mix
1 part Pineapple Juice
1 part Orange Juice

{ GLASS: COLLINS

Shake with ice and pour

Bugix

1½ parts Vodka
½ part Crème de Banana
1 part Pineapple Juice
1 part Strawberry Juice

{ GLASS: HURRICANE

Shake with ice and pour

Burning Bitch!

1 part Vodka
1 part Irish Cream Liqueur
½ part Lemon Juice
splash Maraschino Cherry Juice

{ GLASS: COLLINS

Shake with ice and pour

Bye-Bye Honey

1 part Citrus-Flavored Rum
1 part Orange-Flavored Vodka
2 parts Blue Curaçao
1 part Orange Juice
fill with Lemon-Lime Soda

GLASS: COLLINS

Build over ice and stir

Bye-Bye New York

1 part Vodka
1 part Dark Rum
1 part Hazelnut Syrup
fill with Orange Juice

GLASS: COLLINS

Build over ice and stir

Cactus Breeze

1 part Vodka
1 part Cranberry Juice Cocktail
1 part Pineapple Juice
1 part Sour Mix

GLASS: COLLINS

Build over ice and stir

Caesar

1 part Vodka
4 parts Clamato® Juice
splash Tabasco® Sauce
splash Worcestershire Sauce

GLASS: COLLINS

Build over ice and stir

California Dreaming

½ part Vodka
½ part Coffee Liqueur
½ part Vanilla Liqueur
2 parts Sour Mix
1½ parts Cola

GLASS: COLLINS

Build over ice and stir

California Gold Rush

2 parts Vodka
1½ parts Goldschläger®
fill with Lemon-Lime Soda

{ GLASS: COLLINS
Build over ice and stir

California Screwdriver

1½ parts Grand Marnier®
2 parts Vodka
1 part Club Soda
1 part Orange Juice

{ GLASS: COLLINS
Build over ice and stir

Camurai

1 part Vodka
½ part Blue Curaçao
½ part Coconut Cream
fill with Sparkling Water

{ GLASS: COLLINS
Build over ice and stir

Cape Driver
(or Screw Codder)

1 part Vodka
1 part Cranberry Juice Cocktail
1 part Orange Juice

{ GLASS: COLLINS
Build over ice and stir

Captain Kirsch

1 part Vodka
1 part Kirschwasser
1 part Black Currant Syrup
fill with Lemonade

{ GLASS: COLLINS
Build over ice and stir

Caputo Special

1 part Gin
1 part Vodka
1 part Tequila
1 part Blue Curaçao
1 part Peach Schnapps
fill with Lemon-Lime Soda
splash Lime Juice

GLASS: COLLINS
Build over ice and stir

Caribbean Breeze

2 parts Coconut-Flavored Rum
1 part Vodka
fill with Orange Juice
splash Grenadine

GLASS: COLLINS
Build over ice and stir

Carlin

1 part Citrus-Flavored Vodka
1 part Triple Sec
3 parts Fresh Lime Juice

GLASS: COLLINS
Shake with ice and pour

Carman's Dance

1 part Vodka
1 part Gin
1 part Cranberry Juice Cocktail
1½ parts Strawberry Daiquiri Mix
fill with Orange Juice

GLASS: MASON JAR
Build over ice and stir

Casco Bay Lemonade

1½ parts Citrus-Flavored Vodka
fill with Sour Mix
splash Cranberry Juice Cocktail
splash Lemon-Lime Soda

GLASS: COLLINS
Build over ice and stir

Cave Blue

1½ parts Blue Curaçao
1 part Vodka
fill with Pineapple Juice

GLASS: COLLINS

Build over ice and stir

Cervino

1 part Vodka
½ part Coffee Liqueur
½ part Coconut-Flavored Liqueur
fill with Pineapple Juice

GLASS: COLLINS

Build over ice and stir

Cherry Cough Syrup

1 part Vodka
1 part Peach Schnapps
1 part Triple Sec
1 part Grenadine

GLASS: COLLINS

Build over ice and stir

Cherry-Bucko

1 part Cherry Brandy
½ part Vodka
½ part Lemon Juice
½ part Lime Juice
fill with Lemonade

GLASS: COLLINS

Build over ice and stir

Citrus Breeze

1½ parts Citrus-Flavored Vodka
1 part Cranberry Juice Cocktail
1 part Grapefruit Juice

GLASS: COLLINS

Build over ice and stir

Club Coke

1½ parts Vodka
½ part Peach Schnapps
2 parts Orange Juice
fill with Cola

GLASS: COLLINS

Build over ice and stir

Collins

1½ parts Vodka
3 parts Sour Mix
1 part Club Soda

GLASS: COLLINS

Build over ice and stir

Costa Dorada

1 part Vodka
1 part Spiced Rum
½ part Strawberry Liqueur
fill with Lemon-Lime Soda

GLASS: COLLINS

Build over ice and stir

Costanza

1½ parts Vodka
½ part Peach Schnapps
½ part Grenadine
fill with Carrot Juice

GLASS: COLLINS

Build over ice and stir

Cran Daddy

1 part Vanilla-Flavored Vodka
1 part Lemon-Lime Soda
1 part Cranberry Juice Cocktail

GLASS: HURRICANE

Build over ice and stir

Creamsicle®

1½ parts Vanilla-Flavored Vodka
1½ parts Milk
fill with Orange Juice

GLASS: COLLINS

Shake with ice and strain over ice

Croc Punch

1 part Melon Liqueur
1 part Crème de Banana
1 part Vodka
1 part Parfait Amour
fill with Lemon-Lime Soda
splash Lime Juice

GLASS: HURRICANE

Build over ice and stir

Crystal Cranberry

1 part Vodka
¼ part Bourbon
¼ part Gin
¼ part Amaretto
1 part Orange Juice
1 part Cranberry Juice Cocktail

GLASS: COLLINS

Build over ice and stir

Curbfeeler

1 part Peach Schnapps
1 part Light Rum
1 part Vodka
fill with Iced Tea

GLASS: COLLINS

Build over ice and stir

D J Special

1 part Vodka
1 part Triple Sec
1 part Amaretto
1 part Southern Comfort®
1 part Sloe Gin
fill with Pineapple Juice

GLASS: COLLINS

Build over ice and stir

D.P.R.

1 part Vodka
1 part Triple Sec
fill with Cranberry Juice Cocktail
splash Club Soda

GLASS: COLLINS

Build over ice and stir

Damn Gumby®

1 part Melon Liqueur
1 part Vodka
fill with Hard Apple Cider

GLASS: BEER MUG

Build in the glass with no ice

Darth Maul®

1 part Gin
1 part Light Rum
1 part Tequila Silver
1 part Vodka
1 part Triple Sec
1 part Jägermeister®
2 splashes Grenadine
fill with Sour Mix

GLASS: COLLINS

Shake with ice and pour

Darth Vader®

½ part Vodka
½ part Gin
½ part Light Rum
½ part Tequila Silver
½ part Triple Sec
1 part Jägermeister®
fill with Sour Mix

GLASS: COLLINS

Shake with ice and pour

Deep Blue Sea

2 parts Vodka
2 parts Blue Curaçao
1 part Passion Fruit Juice
1 part Grapefruit Juice

GLASS: COLLINS

Shake with ice and strain over ice

Delkozak

2 parts Vodka
1 part Grapefruit Juice
1 part Lemon Juice
1 part Lime Juice
1 part Orange Juice

GLASS: COLLINS

Build over ice and stir

Derby Daze

1 part Vodka
1 part Kiwi Schnapps
1 part Blackberry Liqueur

{ GLASS: HURRICANE

Shake with ice and strain over ice

Desert Sunrise

¾ part Vodka
1 part Orange Juice
1 part Pineapple Juice
splash Grenadine

{ GLASS: COLLINS

Build over ice

Diamond-Studded Screwdriver

1½ parts Vodka
fill with Orange Soda

{ GLASS: COLLINS

Build over ice and stir

Diaz

1½ parts Vanilla-Flavored Vodka
2 parts Apple Juice
2 parts Ginger Ale

{ GLASS: COLLINS

Build over ice and stir

Dirty Mop

½ part Blavod® Black Vodka
½ part Blue Curaçao
½ part Passoã®
1½ parts Orange Juice
1½ parts Cranberry Juice Cocktail

{ GLASS: COLLINS

Build over ice and stir

Diva

1½ parts Vodka
½ part Lime Juice
splash Maraschino Cherry Juice
fill with Lemon-Lime Soda

{ GLASS: COLLINS

Build over ice and stir

Double Vision

1 part Currant-Flavored Vodka
1 part Citrus-Flavored Vodka
fill with Apple Juice

{ GLASS: COLLINS
Build over ice and stir

Drink of the Year

1 part Vodka
½ part Triple Sec
½ part Raspberry Syrup
splash Blue Curaçao

{ GLASS: COLLINS
Shake with ice and pour

Dumpster™ Juice

1 part Vodka
1 part Light Rum
1 part Raspberry Liqueur
1 part Melon Liqueur
1 part Cranberry Juice Cocktail
1 part Orange Juice
1 part Pineapple Juice

{ GLASS: COLLINS
Shake with ice and pour

Electric Lemonade

1¼ parts Vodka
½ part Blue Curaçao
2 parts Sour Mix
splash Lemon-Lime Soda

{ GLASS: COLLINS
Build over ice and stir

Electric Lizard

1 part Melon Liqueur
1 part Vodka
fill with Sour Mix

{ GLASS: COLLINS
Build over ice and stir

Electric Tea

1 part Vodka
1 part Gin
1 part Light Rum
1 part Tequila
1 part Blue Curaçao
2 parts Sour Mix
1½ parts Lemon-Lime Soda

{ GLASS: COLLINS

Shake with ice and pour

Emerald Lily

1 part Vodka
1 part Rum
½ part Crème de Menthe (Green)
½ part Fresh Lime Juice
fill with Pineapple Juice

{ GLASS: HURRICANE

Build over ice and stir

Excitabull

1 part Vodka
1 part Peach Schnapps
fill with Red Bull® Energy Drink
splash Cranberry Juice Cocktail

{ GLASS: COLLINS

Build over ice and stir

Eye

1 part Vodka
⅔ part Passion Fruit Liqueur
⅔ part Triple Sec
2 parts Passion Fruit Juice
1 part Orange Juice

{ GLASS: COLLINS

Shake with ice and pour

Fino Mint

½ part Vodka
⅔ part Coffee Liqueur
½ part Peppermint Liqueur
fill with Milk

{ GLASS: COLLINS

Shake with ice and strain over ice

First Sight

1 part Blue Curaçao
1 part Vodka
1 part Tequila Reposado
fill with Lemon-Lime Soda

GLASS: COLLINS

Build over ice and stir

Flaming Jesse (Tropical Sunshine)

1 part Coconut-Flavored Rum
½ part Vodka
½ part Irish Cream Liqueur
fill with Orange Juice

GLASS: COLLINS

Build over ice and stir

Flubber

1 part Sambuca
2 parts Vodka
fill with Orange Juice

GLASS: COLLINS

Build over ice and stir

Flying Kangaroo

1½ parts Pineapple Juice
1 part Vodka
1 part Light Rum
1 part Orange Juice
½ part Cream
½ part Coconut-Flavored Liqueur

GLASS: COLLINS

Shake with ice and strain over ice

Forest Funk

1½ parts Citrus-Flavored Vodka
¾ part Peach Schnapps
fill with Grapefruit Juice

GLASS: COLLINS

Build over ice and stir

Forever Yours

1½ parts Vodka
1 part Passion Fruit Liqueur
1 part Fresh Lime Juice
fill with Orange Juice

GLASS: COLLINS

Shake with ice and pour

Fresh

1 part Citrus-Flavored Vodka
1 part Amaretto
1½ parts Orange Juice
fill with Apple Cider

GLASS: COLLINS

Build over ice and stir

Froggy Potion

1 part Rum
1 part Vodka
1 part Gin
1 part Tequila
fill with Orange Juice
splash Cola

GLASS: COLLINS

Build over ice and stir

Frosty Death

2 parts Peppermint Schnapps
1 part Vodka

GLASS: COLLINS

Shake with ice and strain

Frosty Rain

1 part Vodka
1 part Parfait Amour
1 part Triple Sec
fill with Lemonade
splash Crème de Banana

GLASS: COLLINS

Build over ice and stir

Fruit Tickler

1 part Peach Schnapps
⅔ part Melon Liqueur
⅔ part Vodka
1 part Orange Juice
1 part Cranberry Juice Cocktail
fill with Lemon-Lime Soda

GLASS: COLLINS

Build over ice and stir

Fruity Bitch

1½ parts Vodka
1½ parts Triple Sec
1 part Peach Schnapps
fill with Fruit Punch
splash Cola

GLASS: COLLINS

Build over ice and stir

Fubar

1 part Gin
2 parts Rum
2 parts Tequila
2 parts Vodka
fill with Apple Cider

GLASS: COLLINS

Build over ice and stir

Funkmaster 2000

1 part Peach Schnapps
2 parts Vodka
fill with Cranberry Juice Cocktail

GLASS: COLLINS

Build over ice and stir

Funky Filly

¾ part Vodka
¾ part Melon Liqueur
¾ part Cherry Liqueur
¾ part Triple Sec
2 parts Cranberry Juice Cocktail
2 parts Lemon-Lime Soda
1½ parts Lime Juice

GLASS: HURRICANE

Build over ice and stir

Furry Reggae

1 part Coconut-Flavored Liqueur
½ part Vodka
½ part Peach Schnapps
fill with Orange Juice

{ GLASS: COLLINS

Build over ice and stir

Fuzzy Hippo

1 part Peach Schnapps
1 part Vodka
2 parts Hypnotiq®
splash Lemon-Lime Soda
fill with Pineapple Juice

{ GLASS: HURRICANE

Build over ice and stir

A Fuzzy Thing

2 parts Citrus-Flavored Vodka
1 part Triple Sec
1½ parts Peach Schnapps
splash Orange Juice
splash Pineapple Juice
splash Sour Mix

{ GLASS: COLLINS

Build over ice and stir

G String

2 parts Vodka
1 part Blue Curaçao
1 part Blackberry Liqueur
2 parts Lemonade
2 parts Lime Juice
2 parts Sour Mix

{ GLASS: COLLINS

Shake with ice and pour

Gekko

1 part Vodka
1 part Crème de Cassis
2 parts Grapefruit Juice
fill with Ginger Ale

{ GLASS: COLLINS

Build over ice and stir

Gentle Ben

1 part Gin
1 part Vodka
1 part Tequila
fill with Orange Juice
1 Orange Slice
1 Maraschino Cherry

GLASS: COLLINS

Build over ice and stir

Genuine Risk

½ part Vodka
½ part Coffee Liqueur
½ part Amaretto
½ part Coconut-Flavored Liqueur
½ part Frangelico®
3 parts Cream

GLASS: COLLINS

Build over ice and stir

Get'cha Laid

1 part Vodka
2 parts Peach Schnapps
1 part Cranberry Juice Cocktail
1 part Orange Juice

GLASS: COLLINS

Build over ice and stir

Gettin' Loose

1½ parts Amaretto
2 parts Vodka
fill with Lemon-Lime Soda

GLASS: COLLINS

Build over ice and stir

Gibbs

1 part Vodka
1 part Watermelon Schnapps
fill with Lemon-Lime Soda

GLASS: COLLINS

Build over ice and stir

Gideon's Green Dinosaur

1 part Dark Rum
1 part Vodka
1 part Triple Sec
1 part Tequila
1 part Melon Liqueur
fill with Mountain Dew®

GLASS: COLLINS

Build over ice and stir

Giraffe

1 part Melon Liqueur
1 part Vodka
fill with Pineapple Juice
splash Cranberry Juice Cocktail

GLASS: HURRICANE

Build over ice and stir

Glass Tower

1 part Vodka
1 part Peach Schnapps
1 part Rum
1 part Triple Sec
½ part Sambuca
fill with Lemon-Lime Soda

GLASS: COLLINS

Build over ice and stir

Golden Girl

1 part Apricot Brandy
1 part Vodka
fill with Orange Juice

GLASS: COLLINS

Shake with ice and pour

Golden Moment

1 part Orange-Flavored Vodka
splash Goldschläger®
splash Apricot Brandy
splash Vanilla Liqueur
fill with Orange Juice

GLASS: COLLINS

Shake with ice and strain over ice

Gombay Smash

1 part Light Rum
1 part Dark Rum
1 part Vodka
½ part Triple Sec
1 part Pineapple Juice
1 part Apricot Brandy
dash Powdered Sugar

GLASS: COLLINS

Shake with ice and strain over ice

Goober

1½ parts Vodka
1½ parts Blackberry Liqueur
1½ parts Melon Liqueur
1 part Triple Sec
1 part Grenadine
1 part Pineapple Juice
1 part Orange Juice

GLASS: COLLINS

Shake with ice and strain over ice

Good Fortune

1¼ parts Citrus-Flavored Vodka
¾ part Alizé® Gold Passion
fill with Lemonade

GLASS: HURRICANE

Shake with ice and strain over ice

Goodnight Joyce

2 parts Vodka
1 part Raspberry Liqueur
fill with Orange Juice
splash Cranberry Juice Cocktail

GLASS: HURRICANE

Build over ice and stir

Google Juice

1 part Vodka
1 part Amaretto
1 part Cranberry-Flavored Vodka
fill with Cranberry Juice Cocktail

GLASS: HURRICANE

Build over ice and stir

Gorilla Punch

1 part Vodka
½ part Blue Curaçao
2 parts Orange Juice
2 parts Pineapple Juice
1 Maraschino Cherry

GLASS: COLLINS

Shake with ice and strain over ice

Grape Gazpacho

1 part Vodka
1 part Apricot Brandy
1 part Ginger Ale
1 part Grape Juice (White)

GLASS: COLLINS

Build over ice and stir

Green Doo-Doo

1 part Coffee Liqueur
1 part Melon Liqueur
½ part Peppermint Schnapps
½ part Vodka
fill with Cream

GLASS: COLLINS

Build over ice and stir

Green Eyes

1 part Vodka
1 part Blue Curaçao
2 parts Orange Juice

GLASS: COLLINS

Build over ice and stir

Green Hell

1 part Blue Curaçao
1 part Gin
1 part Vodka
1 part Rum
1 part Triple Sec
1 part Tequila Silver
fill with Orange Juice

GLASS: HURRICANE

Build over ice and stir

Green Peace

1 part Vodka
1 part Dry Vermouth
1 part Pisang Ambon® Liqueur
1 part Apricot Brandy
fill with Pineapple Juice

GLASS: COLLINS
Build over ice and stir

Green Scorpion

1 part Jack Daniel's®
1 part Vodka
2 splashes Blue Curaçao
fill with Lemon-Lime Soda

GLASS: COLLINS
Build over ice and stir

Green Tuberia

2 parts Vodka
1 part Melon Liqueur
1 part Lemon Juice
fill with Lemon-Lime Soda

GLASS: COLLINS
Build over ice and stir

Green Whale

1½ parts Blue Curaçao
splash Vodka
dash Sugar
1 part Pineapple Juice
1 part Orange Juice

GLASS: COLLINS
Shake with ice and pour

Grendel

½ part Vodka
½ part Rum
½ part Cointreau®
½ part Blue Curaçao
½ part Crème de Menthe (White)
½ part Advocaat
1 part Cream
fill with Lemonade

GLASS: COLLINS
Shake with ice and pour

Grinch

1½ part Melon Liqueur
1 part Malibu® Rum
1 part Gin
1 part Vodka
1 part Lemon-Lime Soda
1 part Sour Mix
1 part Blue Curaçao

GLASS: HURRICANE

Build over ice and stir

The Gummy Bear

2 parts Vodka
1 part Lemon-Lime Soda
2 parts Fruit Punch

GLASS: BEER MUG

Build over ice and stir

Hail Mary

2 parts Vodka
splash Grenadine
fill with Orange Juice
splash Tabasco® Sauce
1 Egg

GLASS: COLLINS

Shake with ice and pour

Hairy Sunrise

¾ part Tequila
¾ part Vodka
½ part Triple Sec
fill with Orange Juice
splash Grenadine

GLASS: COLLINS

Build over ice and stir

Halaballoosa

2 parts Citrus-Flavored Vodka
1 part Jamaican Rum
2 parts Blue Curaçao
1 part Orange Juice
1 part Clamato®

GLASS: COLLINS

Shake with ice and pour

Hale & Hearty

½ part Vodka
½ part Blue Curaçao
1½ parts Maple Syrup
splash Honey
fill with Grapefruit Juice

GLASS: COLLINS

Shake with ice and strain over ice

Halfway Special

1 part Citrus-Flavored Vodka
1 part Coconut-Flavored Rum
1 part Blackberry Liqueur
fill with Orange Juice
splash Grenadine

GLASS: HURRICANE

Build over ice and stir

Hamlet

1 part Vodka
½ part Campari®
fill with Orange Juice

GLASS: COLLINS

Build over ice and stir

Harvey Wallbanger

1 part Vodka
½ part Galliano®
fill with Orange Juice

GLASS: COLLINS

Shake with ice and pour

Hawaiian Hurricane Volcano

1 part Amaretto
1 part Southern Comfort®
1 part Vodka
splash Grenadine

GLASS: COLLINS

Shake with ice and pour

Healing Garden

1½ parts Vodka
⅔ part Galliano®
⅔ part Benedictine®
fill with Pineapple Juice

{ GLASS: COLLINS
Shake with ice and pour

Hector Special

1½ parts Vodka
1 part Tequila Silver
1 part Grenadine
fill with Orange Juice

{ GLASS: COLLINS
Build over ice and stir

Hi Rise

1 part Vodka
splash Cointreau®
1 part Sour Mix
fill with Orange Juice
splash Grenadine

{ GLASS: COLLINS
Build over ice and stir

Hitchhiker

1 part Vodka
1 part Mandarine Napoléon® Liqueur
½ part Crème de Banana
½ part Campari®
½ part Coconut-Flavored Liqueur
fill with Lemonade

{ GLASS: COLLINS
Build over ice and stir

Hollywood & Vine

1½ parts Citrus-Flavored Vodka
⅔ part Orange Liqueur
⅔ part Lime Juice
fill with Grapefruit Juice
dash Powdered Sugar

{ GLASS: COLLINS
Shake with ice and strain over ice

Hollywood Tea

1 part Gin
1 part Light Rum
1 part Tequila
1 part Vodka
fill with Lemon-Lime Soda

GLASS: COLLINS

Build over ice and stir

Homicidal Maniac

2 parts Peach Schnapps
2 parts Vodka
1 part Cranberry Juice Cocktail
1 part Apple Juice

GLASS: BEER MUG

Shake with ice and pour

Honey Dew This

1½ parts Vodka
½ part Melon Liqueur
splash Crème de Banana
fill with Pineapple Juice

GLASS: COLLINS

Shake with ice and strain over ice

Honey Driver

1½ parts Vodka
1 part Melon Liqueur
fill with Orange Juice
splash Honey

GLASS: COLLINS

Shake with ice and strain over ice

Hong Kong Fuey

1 part Tequila Silver
1 part Vodka
1 part Light Rum
1 part Melon Liqueur
1 part Gin
½ part Lime Cordial
fill with Lemonade

GLASS: COLLINS

Shake with ice and pour

Hot Land

1½ parts Absolut® Peppar Vodka
2 splashes Amaretto
¾ part Peach Schnapps
fill with Orange Juice

GLASS: COLLINS

Build over ice and stir

Hotel Riviera

1 part Vodka
1 part Blackberry Liqueur
½ part Sour Mix
fill with Lemon-Lime Soda

GLASS: COLLINS

Build over ice and stir

Hulk Smash!

1 part Vodka
1 part Gin
1 part Melon Liqueur
fill with Mountain Dew®

GLASS: COLLINS

Build over ice and stir

Humboldt Sunset

1½ parts Orange-Flavored Vodka
½ part Lemon Juice
1 part Pineapple Juice
1 part Cranberry Juice Cocktail

GLASS: COLLINS

Build over ice and stir

Iced Lemon

1 part Vodka
1 part Sour Mix
½ part Vanilla Liqueur
fill with Lemon-Lime Soda

GLASS: COLLINS

Build over ice and stir

Illusions

1 part Melon Liqueur
1 part Coconut-Flavored Rum
1 part Cointreau®
½ part Vodka
fill with Pineapple Juice

GLASS: COLLINS

Shake with ice and pour

Intercourse

2 parts Vodka
1 part Orange Juice
1 part Hawaiian Punch®
1 part Mountain Dew®

GLASS: COLLINS

Build over ice and stir

Irish Whip

1 part Vodka
1 part Pernod®
1 part 151-Proof Rum
1 part Crème de Menthe (White)
1 part Lemon-Lime Soda
1 part Orange Juice

GLASS: BEER MUG

Shake with ice and pour

Italian Canary

½ part Vodka
½ part Amaretto
½ part Rum
½ part Vanilla Liqueur
2 parts Sour Mix
fill with Lemon-Lime Soda

GLASS: COLLINS

Build over ice and stir

The Italian Job

2 parts Vodka
1 part Cointreau®
1 part Pineapple Juice
1 part Orange Juice
splash Cream

GLASS: MASON JAR

Build over ice and stir

Jade Isle

2 parts Melon Liqueur
1 part Blue Curaçao
1 part Currant-Flavored Vodka
1 part Sour Mix
1 part Lemon-Lime Soda
1 Maraschino Cherry

GLASS: HURRICANE

Build over ice and stir

Jamaican Sunrise

2 parts Vodka
2 parts Peach Schnapps
fill with Orange Juice
1 part Cranberry Juice Cocktail

GLASS: COLLINS

Build over ice

Java's Punch

1 part Vodka
1 part Pisang Ambon® Liqueur
1 part Coconut-Flavored Liqueur
fill with Orange Juice

GLASS: COLLINS

Build over ice and stir

Jinx

2 parts Vodka
1 part Blueberry Schnapps
½ part Irish Cream Liqueur
2 parts Lemon-Lime Soda
1 part Grape Juice (Red)

GLASS: COLLINS

Build over ice and stir

Joe Falchetto

1 part Vodka
½ part Triple Sec
½ part Vanilla Liqueur
½ part Strawberry Syrup
fill with Pineapple Juice

GLASS: COLLINS

Shake with ice and strain over ice

John Cooper Deluxe

2 parts Vodka
1 part Orange Juice
1 part Root Beer

GLASS: COLLINS

Build over ice and stir

John Daly

1¼ part Citrus-Flavored Vodka
¼ part Triple Sec
1 part Lemonade
1 part Iced Tea

GLASS: COLLINS

Build over ice and stir

Johnnie Red

1 part Vodka
½ part Parfait Amour
½ part Crème de Banana
fill with Orange Juice
splash Grenadine

GLASS: COLLINS

Build over ice and stir

Jolly Jumper

1 part Whiskey
1 part Vodka
1 part Gin
1 part Passion Fruit Liqueur
fill with Orange Juice

GLASS: COLLINS

Build over ice and stir

Juicy Lucy

1 part Vodka
1 part Gin
1 part Blue Curaçao
1 part Orange Juice
1 part Lemon-Lime Soda

GLASS: BEER MUG

Build over ice and stir

Jungle Juice

1 part Vodka
1 part Rum
½ part Triple Sec
splash Sour Mix
1 part Cranberry Juice Cocktail
1 part Orange Juice
1 part Pineapple Juice

GLASS: COLLINS
Build over ice and stir

Kermit®

½ part Vodka
½ part Whiskey
½ part Gin
fill with Orange Juice
1 part Blue Curaçao

GLASS: COLLINS
Build over ice and stir

Kermit® Green

1 part Vodka
1 part Melon Liqueur
fill with Lemon-Lime Soda

GLASS: COLLINS
Build over ice and stir

Kermit's® Revenge

1 part Rum
1 part Tequila
1 part Vodka
1 part Gin
1 part Triple Sec
1 part Crème de Menthe (White)
fill with Lemonade

GLASS: HURRICANE
Build over ice and stir

Kinky Monday

1 part Vodka
½ part Blackberry Liqueur
½ part Crème de Cassis
½ part Raspberry Liqueur
1 part Fresh Lime Juice
fill with Lemon-Lime Soda

GLASS: COLLINS

Build over ice and stir

Kiss of Blue

1 part Citrus-Flavored Vodka
1 part Blue Curaçao
1 part Lime Cordial
fill with Orange Juice

GLASS: COLLINS

Shake with ice and pour

Kitchen Sink

1 part Blue Curaçao
1 part Gin
1 part Light Rum
1 part Sour Apple Schnapps
1 part Vodka
1 part Triple Sec
splash Lemon-Lime Soda
splash Sour Mix
splash Lemon Juice
splash Melon Liqueur

GLASS: COLLINS

Build over ice and stir

KMart® Screwdriver

2 parts Vodka
fill with Orange Soda

GLASS: COLLINS

Build over ice and stir. Use the cheapest Vodka available and a store brand Soda.

Knoxville Lemonade

1 part Vodka
1 part Peach Schnapps
fill with Lemonade
splash Ginger Ale

GLASS: COLLINS

Build over ice and stir

Kodachrome

1 part Vodka
1 part Blue Curaçao
splash Lemonade
splash Orange Juice
splash Cranberry Juice Cocktail

GLASS: COLLINS

Shake with ice and pour

Kosmo

1½ parts Orange-Flavored Vodka
½ part Triple Sec
fill with Cranberry Juice Cocktail
splash Lime Juice
splash Lemon Juice

GLASS: COLLINS

Shake with ice and pour

Krazy Kool-Aid®

1 part Currant-Flavored Vodka
1 part Amaretto
1 part Melon Liqueur
fill with Pineapple Juice

GLASS: COLLINS

Shake with ice and pour

Kurant Mellow

1 part Southern Comfort®
1 part Currant-Flavored Vodka
fill with Lemon-Lime Soda

GLASS: COLLINS

Build over ice and stir

L.A. Sunrise

1 part Vodka
½ part Crème de Banana
1 part Pineapple Juice
1 part Orange Juice
splash Dark Rum

GLASS: COLLINS

Build over ice

A Laid-Back Drink

1 part Vodka
1 part Lemon-Lime Soda
1 part Orange Juice

GLASS: COLLINS

Build over ice and stir

Lake Water

½ part Gin
½ part Jack Daniel's®
½ part Tequila
½ part Vodka
1 part Blueberry Schnapps
1 part Cola
1 part Lemon-Lime Soda

GLASS: COLLINS

Build over ice and stir

Leaving Las Vegas

1 part Triple Sec
1 part Vodka
1 part Light Rum
1 part Gin
fill with Lemonade
splash Lemon-Lime Soda

GLASS: HURRICANE

Build over ice and stir

Lemon Fizz

1½ parts Vodka
1½ parts Triple Sec
2 parts Carbonated Water
fill with Lemonade
1 Lemon Wedge

GLASS: HURRICANE

Build over ice and stir

Limelon

1 part Melon Liqueur
1 part Vodka
fill with Limeade

GLASS: COLLINS

Build over ice and stir

Linux®

1½ parts Vodka
½ part Lime Juice
fill with Cola

GLASS: COLLINS

Build over ice and stir

Lipstick

1 part Vodka
½ part Apricot Brandy
½ part Grenadine
1 part Lemon Juice
fill with Orange Juice

GLASS: COLLINS

Shake with ice and pour

Liquid Bomb

½ part Vodka
½ part Citrus-Flavored Rum
1 part Alizé®
1 part Peach Schnapps
1 part Cranberry Juice Cocktail
1 part Orange Juice

GLASS: COLLINS

Build over ice and stir

Loose Caboose

2 parts Vodka
1 part Cranberry Juice Cocktail
1 part Lemonade
splash Grenadine
1 Maraschino Cherry

GLASS: COLLINS

Build over ice and stir

Losing Your Cherry

1½ parts Vodka
½ part Cherry Brandy
1 part Sour Mix
1 part Lemonade

GLASS: COLLINS

Build over ice and stir

Love Juice

½ part Vodka
½ part Passion Fruit Liqueur
¼ part Pisang Ambon® Liqueur
1 part Pineapple Juice
1 part Orange Juice
½ part Grenadine

GLASS: COLLINS

Build over ice and stir

Love on the Lawn

1 part Blue Curaçao
1 part Cranberry-Flavored Vodka
fill with Orange Juice
splash Grenadine

GLASS: COLLINS

Shake with ice and pour

Lunapop

¾ part Vodka
½ part Crème de Menthe (Green)
¼ part Vanilla Liqueur
splash Amaretto
fill with Milk

GLASS: COLLINS

Build over ice and stir

M.V.P.

1 part Vodka
½ part Melon Liqueur
½ part Coconut-Flavored Rum
fill with Pineapple Juice

GLASS: HURRICANE

Build over ice and stir

Made in Heaven

1 part Cream
1 part Vodka
1 part Coconut-Flavored Liqueur
1 part Strawberry Liqueur
fill with Lemon-Lime Soda

GLASS: HURRICANE

Build over ice and stir

Mandarin Sunrise

1½ parts Orange-Flavored Vodka
1 part Peach Schnapps
2 parts Pineapple Juice
1 part Orange Juice

GLASS: COLLINS

Build over ice and stir

Maracas

1½ parts Vodka
¼ part Blackberry Liqueur
splash Parfait Amour
fill with Pineapple Juice

GLASS: COLLINS

Build over ice and stir

Marion Barry

½ part Blackberry Liqueur
1½ parts Currant-Flavored Vodka
fill with Cranberry Juice Cocktail
1 part Cola

GLASS: COLLINS

Shake with ice and pour

Masroska

2 parts Vodka
1 part Orange Juice
2 parts Apple Juice

GLASS: COLLINS

Build over ice and stir

Mattapoo

1 part Vodka
½ part Melon Liqueur
1 part Grapefruit Juice
1 part Pineapple Juice

GLASS: COLLINS

Build over ice and stir

Maverick

1½ parts Vodka
½ part Amaretto
½ part Triple Sec
2 splashes Galliano®
fill with Pineapple Juice

GLASS: COLLINS

*Shake with ice and strain
over ice*

Meema

1 part Amaretto
1 part Peach Schnapps
1 part Vodka
fill with Cranberry Juice Cocktail

GLASS: COLLINS

Build over ice and stir

Melon Highball

1½ parts Melon Liqueur
1 part Vodka
fill with Orange Juice

GLASS: COLLINS

*Shake with ice and strain
over ice*

Melon Illusion

2 parts Melon Liqueur
½ part Vodka
½ part Triple Sec
1 part Lemon Juice
fill with Pineapple Juice

GLASS: COLLINS

*Shake with ice and strain
over ice*

Mentholyzer

1 part Vodka
1 part Tia Maria®
¼ part Crème de Menthe (White)
2 parts Cream
fill with Cola

GLASS: COLLINS

Build over ice and stir

Miami Ice

½ part Vodka
½ part Peach Schnapps
½ part Gin
½ part Rum
2 parts Sour Mix
fill with Orange Juice

GLASS: COLLINS

Shake with ice and pour

Mizzy

splash Melon Liqueur
splash Citrus-Flavored Vodka
¼ part Pineapple Juice
splash Simple Syrup
fill with Orange Juice

GLASS: COLLINS

Shake with ice and pour

Monkey Poop

¾ part Vodka
¾ part Crème de Banana
½ part Lime Cordial
1 part Pineapple Juice
1 part Orange Juice

GLASS: COLLINS

Shake with ice and strain over ice

Moon Tea

1 part Gin
1 part Rum
1 part Triple Sec
1 part Vodka
fill with Orange Juice

GLASS: COLLINS

Shake with ice and pour

Mount Red

1 part Vodka
1 part Light Rum
1 part Gin
1 part Peach Schnapps
fill with Cranberry Juice Cocktail
splash Lime Juice

GLASS: COLLINS
Build over ice and stir

Mouse Trap

2 parts Vodka
1½ parts Triple Sec
2 parts Orange Juice
1½ parts Grenadine
fill with Lemon-Lime Soda

GLASS: COLLINS
Build over ice and stir

Mr. Freeze

1 part Black Haus® Blackberry Schnapps
1 part Vodka
1 part Blue Curaçao
3 parts Sour Mix
1 part Lemon-Lime Soda

GLASS: COLLINS
Build over ice and stir

Naval Lint

2 parts Amaretto
1 part Vodka
splash Lime Juice
fill with Cola

GLASS: COLLINS
Build over ice and stir

Needle in Your Eye

1 part Gin
1 part Vodka
splash Lemon Juice
splash Lime Juice
splash Orange Juice
fill Lemon-Lime Soda

GLASS: COLLINS
Build over ice and stir

Neon Tea

½ part Gin
½ part Sour Apple Schnapps
½ part Vanilla-Flavored Vodka
½ part Light Rum
¼ part Triple Sec
1 part Sour Mix
¼ part Melon Liqueur

GLASS: COLLINS

Shake with ice and pour

Nickel

1 part Currant-Flavored Vodka
1 part Melon Liqueur
1 part Orange Juice
1 part Lemon-Lime Soda

GLASS: COLLINS

Build over ice and stir

Nikko

1½ parts Vodka
½ part Blue Curaçao
½ part Pineapple Juice
fill with Orange Juice

GLASS: COLLINS

Build over ice and stir

No Reason to Live

1 part Tequila
1 part Vodka
1 part Gin
1 part Sambuca
2 splashes Tabasco® Sauce
fill with Orange Juice

GLASS: COLLINS

Build over ice and stir

Norwegian Iceberg

2 parts Vodka
fill with Lemon-Lime Soda
1 part Blue Hawaiian Schnapps

GLASS: BEER MUG

Build over ice and stir

Nuclear Meltdown

1 part Gin
1 part Tequila Silver
1 part Vodka
1 part Light Rum
1 part Sour Mix
1 part Melon Liqueur
fill with Lemon-Lime Soda

GLASS: COLLINS

Build over ice and stir

Nuclear Sensation

1 part Dry Gin
1 part Vodka
1 part Rum
1 part Blue Curaçao
fill with Sour Mix

GLASS: COLLINS

Build over ice and stir

O&O

2 parts Orange-Flavored Vodka
fill with Orange Soda

GLASS: COLLINS

Shake with ice and pour

OOO

1 part Orange-Flavored Vodka
1 part Orange Juice
1 part Orange Soda

GLASS: HURRICANE

Build over ice and stir

Orange Passion

1 part Vodka
2 parts Passion Fruit Liqueur
fill with Orange Juice

GLASS: COLLINS

Build over ice and stir

Orlando

1 part Vodka
½ part Crème de Banana
1 part Pineapple Juice
1 part Cream
fill with Orange Juice

GLASS: HURRICANE

Shake with ice and pour

Oslo Nights

1 part Citrus-Flavored Vodka
1 part Blue Curaçao
1 part Aquavit
1 part Cider
1 part Lime Juice
fill with Lemonade

GLASS: COLLINS

Build over ice and stir

Pan Galactic Gargle Blaster

1 part Vodka
1 part Tia Maria®
½ part Cherry Brandy
splash Lime Juice
1 part Lemon-Lime Soda
1 part Apple Cider

GLASS: HURRICANE

Build over ice and stir

Panty Dropper

1 part Vodka
1 part Coconut-Flavored Rum
1 part Peach Schnapps
1 part Pineapple Juice
1 part Orange Juice

GLASS: COLLINS

Build over ice and stir

Passionate Cherry

1½ parts Cherry Brandy
½ part Vodka
fill with Sour Mix

GLASS: COLLINS

Shake with ice and strain over ice

Passover

1 part Vodka
2 parts Passion Fruit Juice
fill with Grapefruit Juice

GLASS: COLLINS

Build over ice and stir

Peach Beseech

1 part Vodka
1½ parts Peach Schnapps
½ part Crème de Cacao (White)
fill with Milk

GLASS: COLLINS

Shake with ice and pour

Peach Bomber

1½ parts Peach Schnapps
1 part Vodka
½ part Blue Curaçao
1 part Pineapple Juice
1 part Orange Juice

GLASS: COLLINS

Shake with ice and pour

Peachface

1 part Vodka
1 part Peach Schnapps
fill with Cranberry Juice Cocktail

GLASS: COLLINS

Build over ice and stir

Peachy

1 part Vodka
1 part Peach Schnapps
1 part Melon Liqueur
1 part Orange Juice
1 part Pear Juice

GLASS: COLLINS

Shake with ice and pour

Pegasus

1 part Vodka
1 part Peach Schnapps
½ part Lime Juice
½ part Lemon Juice
½ part Cherry Juice
fill with Red Bull® Energy Drink

GLASS: COLLINS
Build over ice and stir

Phantasm

1½ parts Vodka
½ part Galliano®
½ part Cream
fill with Cola

GLASS: COLLINS
Build over ice and stir

Phillips Screwdriver

2 parts Vodka
fill with SunnyD® Orange Drink

GLASS: COLLINS
Shake with ice and pour

Pimp Punch

1 part Raspberry Liqueur
1 part Currant-Flavored Vodka
fill with Lemon-Lime Soda

GLASS: COLLINS
Build over ice and stir

Pineapple Splash

1 part Peach Schnapps
1 part Vodka
1 part Orange Juice
1 part Pineapple Juice

GLASS: COLLINS
Shake with ice and pour

Pink Cello

1 part Vodka
½ part Limoncello
fill with Cranberry Juice Cocktail

GLASS: COLLINS
Build over ice and stir

Pink Creamsicle®

1 part Vodka
1 part Orange Juice
fill with Cream Soda

GLASS: COLLINS
Build over ice and stir

Pink Flamingo

1 part Vodka
1 part Cointreau®
fill with Orange Juice

GLASS: COLLINS
Shake with ice and pour

Pink Pillow

2 parts Vodka
splash Grenadine
1 part Sour Mix
1 part Ginger Ale

GLASS: COLLINS
Build over ice and stir

Pink Pussycat

1½ parts Vodka
splash Grenadine
fill with Pineapple Juice

GLASS: COLLINS
Build over ice and stir

Pink Tutu

1 part Peach Schnapps
½ part Vodka
½ part Campari®
dash Powdered Sugar
fill with Grapefruit Juice

GLASS: COLLINS
Shake with ice and pour

Piss in the Snow

1 part Vodka
1 part Peppermint Schnapps
fill with Mountain Dew®

GLASS: COLLINS
Build over ice and stir

Pixy Stix®

1 part Vodka
1 part Apricot Brandy
1 part Blue Curaçao
1 part Grape Schnapps
fill with Lemonade

GLASS: COLLINS

Build over ice and stir

Platinum Liver

½ part Gin
½ part Blue Curaçao
½ part Vodka
½ part Dark Rum
½ part Tequila Silver
1 part Sour Mix
1 part Lemon-Lime Soda

GLASS: COLLINS

Build over ice and stir

Playball

1 part Spiced Rum
1 part Vodka
1 part Peach Schnapps
fill with Orange Juice

GLASS: COLLINS

Shake with ice and pour

Plutonic

1 part Vodka
1 part Light Rum
1 part Gin
1 part Tequila Reposado
splash Grenadine
fill with Milk

GLASS: COLLINS

Shake with ice and pour

Polkagris

1 part Vodka
1 part Crème de Menthe (White)
½ part Grenadine
fill with Lemon-Lime Soda

GLASS: COLLINS

Build over ice and stir

Poop

1 part Raspberry Liqueur
1 part Citrus-Flavored Vodka
fill with Lemon-Lime Soda

GLASS: COLLINS

Build over ice and stir

Popo-Naval

3 parts Peach Schnapps
1½ parts Vodka
fill with Orange Juice

GLASS: COLLINS

Build over ice and stir

Popped Cherry

1 part Vodka
1 part Cherry Liqueur
1 part Cranberry Juice Cocktail
1 part Orange Juice

GLASS: COLLINS

Build over ice and stir

Portland Poker

1 part Blackberry Liqueur
1 part Citrus-Flavored Vodka
½ part Vanilla Liqueur
1 part Mango Juice
1 part Peach Puree
1 part Club Soda

GLASS: HURRICANE

*Shake all but Club Soda with ice
and strain over ice into the glass.
Top with Club Soda.*

The Power of Milk

3 dashes Sugar
1 part Vodka
fill with Milk

GLASS: COLLINS

Build over ice and stir

Power Play

1½ parts Orange-Flavored Vodka
1 part Raspberry Liqueur
½ part Lemon Juice
fill with Orange Juice

GLASS: COLLINS

Shake with ice and pour

Premium Herbal Blend

2 parts Citrus-Flavored Vodka
½ part Grenadine
fill with Sour Mix
top with Club Soda

GLASS: COLLINS

Build over ice and stir

Psycho Citrus

1 part Vodka
1 part Tequila
½ part Crème de Menthe (White)
splash Lime Juice
splash Grand Marnier®
fill with Orange Juice

GLASS: COLLINS

Shake with ice and pour

Purple Fairy Dream

½ part Currant-Flavored Vodka
1 part Blue Curaçao
1 part Raspberry Liqueur
2 parts Coconut Cream
fill with Lemon-Lime Soda
splash Cranberry Juice Cocktail

GLASS: HURRICANE

Build over ice and stir

Purple Passion

1½ parts Vodka
dash Sugar
1 part Grape Juice (Red)
1 part Grapefruit Juice

GLASS: COLLINS

Shake with ice and pour

Purple Problem Solver

{ GLASS: COLLINS

Build over ice and stir

1 part Vodka
1 part Rum
1 part Melon Liqueur
1 part Blue Curaçao
1 part Sour Apple Schnapps
1 part Peach Schnapps
1 part Sour Mix
fill with Pineapple Juice
splash Grenadine

Purple Pussycat Juice

{ GLASS: HURRICANE

Shake with ice and pour

¾ part Tequila Reposado
¾ part Vodka
½ part Triple Sec
½ part Raspberry Liqueur
1 part Pineapple Juice
1 part Sour Mix

Purple Rain

{ GLASS: COLLINS

Build over ice and stir

1 part Vodka
1 part Gin
1 part Rum
1 part Blue Curaçao
1 part Cranberry Juice Cocktail
fill with Lemon-Lime Soda

Rainbow

{ GLASS: COLLINS

Build over ice

1¼ part Citrus-Flavored Vodka
1 part Grapefruit Juice
1 part Grape Juice (Red)

Recliner

{ GLASS: COLLINS

Shake with ice and pour

1 part Vodka
1 part Whiskey
1 part Sour Mix
1 part Cranberry Juice Cocktail
2 parts Pineapple Juice
2 parts Orange Juice
½ part Grenadine

Red Crusher

{ GLASS: HURRICANE

Shake with ice and pour

1 part Tequila Silver
1 part Vodka
1 part Strawberry Syrup
1 part Mango Juice
1 part Strawberry Juice

Red Kawasaki®

{ GLASS: COLLINS

Shake all but Club Soda with ice and strain into the glass. Top with Club Soda.

1 part Gin
1 part Rum
1 part Sloe Gin
1 part Triple Sec
1 part Vodka
fill with Sour Mix
splash Club Soda

Red Point

{ GLASS: COLLINS

Shake with ice and pour

1 part Vodka
1 part Sloe Gin
splash Kiwi Schnapps
fill with Cranberry Juice Cocktail
splash Lemon Juice

Red Racer

1 part Vodka
1 part Amaretto
1 part Southern Comfort®
1 part Sloe Gin
fill with Orange Juice

{ GLASS: COLLINS

Shake with ice and pour

Redstar

½ part Vodka
fill with Red Bull® Energy Drink

{ GLASS: COLLINS

Build over ice and stir

Reef Juice

1½ parts Dark Rum
1 part Crème de Banana
½ part Vodka
1 part Grenadine
½ part Fresh Lime Juice
fill with Pineapple Juice

{ GLASS: HURRICANE

Shake with ice and pour

Reindeer's Tear

1 part Vodka
1 part Blue Curaçao
1 part Lemon Juice

{ GLASS: COLLINS

Build over ice and stir

Return to Bekah

1 part Vodka
½ part Blue Curaçao
½ part Grape Juice (Red)
fill with Sour Mix
½ part Cranberry Juice Cocktail

{ GLASS: COLLINS

Build over ice and stir

A Ride in a Bumpy Lowrider

1 part Melon Liqueur
1 part Tequila
1 part Vodka
splash Grenadine

GLASS: COLLINS

Build over ice and stir

Rodeo Tea

1 part Citrus-Flavored Vodka
2 parts Blackberry Liqueur
½ part Powdered Sugar
½ part Lemon Juice
fill with Iced Tea

GLASS: COLLINS

Shake with ice and strain over ice

Rosebud

2 parts Citrus-Flavored Vodka
½ part Triple Sec
1 part Lime Juice
fill with Grapefruit Juice

GLASS: COLLINS

Build over ice and stir

Russian Elektric

1 part Vodka
1 part Strawberry Liqueur
fill with Red Bull® Energy Drink

GLASS: COLLINS

Build over ice and stir

Russian Sunset

1 part Vodka
1 part Triple Sec
fill with Sour Mix
splash Grenadine

GLASS: COLLINS

Build over ice

Russian Virgin Fizz

2 parts Vodka
1 part Lemon-Lime Soda
1 part Lemonade

GLASS: COLLINS

Build over ice and stir

Salem Witch

½ part Vodka
½ part Raspberry Liqueur
½ part Midori®
splash Lime Juice
splash Grenadine
1 part Sour Mix
1 part Club Soda

GLASS: COLLINS

Build over ice and stir

Salty Balls

1½ parts Vodka
1 part Midori®
2 parts Orange Juice
fill with Grapefruit Juice
pinch Salt

GLASS: COLLINS

Build over ice and stir

San Francisco

1 part Vodka
1 part Triple Sec
1 part Crème de Banana
1 part Pineapple Juice
1 part Orange Juice
¼ part Grenadine

GLASS: COLLINS

Shake with ice and pour

Sanders's Special

1 part Vodka
1 part Sour Apple Schnapps
1 part Peach Schnapps
fill with Fruit Punch

GLASS: COLLINS

Shake with ice and pour

Sans Souci

1½ parts Triple Sec
splash Vodka
splash Fresh Lime Juice
fill with Lemonade

GLASS: COLLINS

Shake with ice and pour

Santa Esmeralda

1½ parts Vodka
¼ part Kiwi Schnapps
fill with Grapefruit Juice

GLASS: COLLINS
Build over ice

Santa's Pole

1 part Peppermint Schnapps
1 part Vodka
2 splashes Grenadine
fill with Lemon-Lime Soda

GLASS: COLLINS
Build over ice

Schnapp It Up

1 part Peach Schnapps
1 part Wild Berry Schnapps
1 part Vodka
fill with Cranberry Juice Cocktail

GLASS: COLLINS
Build over ice and stir

Scottie's Popsicle®

1 part Crème de Cacao (Dark)
1 part Crème de Banana
1 part Raspberry Liqueur
splash Vodka
fill with Half and Half

GLASS: COLLINS
Shake with ice and pour

Screaming in the Dark

1½ parts Black Vodka
1 part Coffee Liqueur
½ part Brandy
½ part Bourbon
fill with Cola

GLASS: COLLINS
Build over ice and stir

Screw Up

1 part Vodka
1 part Orange Juice
1 part Lemon-Lime Soda

GLASS: COLLINS

Build over ice and stir

Screwdriver with a Twist

2 parts Vodka
1 part Lemon-Lime Soda
1 part Orange Juice

GLASS: COLLINS

Build over ice and stir

Serrera

1 part Vodka
1 part Blue Curaçao
fill with Sparkling Water

GLASS: COLLINS

Build over ice and stir

Sewer Rat

1 part Vodka
½ part Peach Schnapps
½ part Coffee Liqueur
fill with Orange Juice

GLASS: COLLINS

Build in the glass with no ice

Shamrock Juice

1 part Gin
1 part Tequila
1 part Rum
1 part Vodka
1 part Blue Curaçao
fill with Orange Juice

GLASS: HURRICANE

Build over ice and stir

Shark Tank

2 parts Vodka
1 part Grenadine
fill with Lemonade

GLASS: COLLINS

Build over ice and stir

Shattered Dreams

1 part Vodka
1½ parts Blueberry Schnapps
splash Grenadine
splash Lemon-Lime Soda
fill with Grape Juice (Red)

{ GLASS: COLLINS

Build over ice and stir

Shirley Temple of Doom

2 parts Vodka
splash Grenadine
fill with Lemon-Lime Soda

{ GLASS: COLLINS

Build over ice and stir

Shock-a-Bull

1 part Peppermint Schnapps
1 part Vodka
fill with Red Bull® Energy Drink

{ GLASS: BEER MUG

Build over ice and stir

Skittle®

1 part Vodka
1 part 99-Proof Banana Liqueur
fill with Fruit Punch

{ GLASS: COLLINS

Build over ice and stir

Sky Blue Fallout

½ part Blue Curaçao
½ part Gin
½ part Vodka
½ part Triple Sec
½ part Tequila
½ part 151-Proof Rum
1 part Sour Mix
1 part Lemon-Lime Soda

{ GLASS: HURRICANE

Build over ice and stir

Sloe Coach

1 part Vodka
1 part Southern Comfort®
1 part Sloe Gin
fill with Orange Juice

GLASS: HURRICANE

Shake with ice and strain over ice

Sludge

1 part Vodka
1 part Triple Sec
½ part Blue Curaçao
½ part Peach Schnapps
1 part Cranberry Juice Cocktail
1 part Orange Juice
splash Melon Liqueur

GLASS: COLLINS

Build over ice and stir

Smoove

1 part Vodka
1 part Peach Schnapps
fill with Lemon-Lime Soda

GLASS: COLLINS

Build over ice and stir

Something Peachie

¾ part Vodka
¾ part Peach Schnapps
¾ part Triple Sec
1 part Pineapple Juice
1 part Orange Juice

GLASS: COLLINS

Shake with ice and pour

Sonic Blaster

½ part Vodka
½ part Light Rum
½ part Banana Liqueur
1 part Pineapple Juice
1 part Orange Juice
1 part Cranberry Juice Cocktail

GLASS: COLLINS

Shake with ice and pour

Sonoma

1 part Vodka
1 part Grape Juice (Red)
fill with Mountain Dew®

> GLASS: COLLINS
> *Build over ice and stir*

South End Lemonade

1 part Rum
1 part Triple Sec
1 part Vodka
1 part Raspberry Liqueur
fill with Lemon-Lime Soda

> GLASS: COLLINS
> *Build over ice and stir*

Southern Isle

¾ part Blue Curaçao
½ part Southern Comfort®
½ part Citrus-Flavored Vodka
fill with Orange Juice

> GLASS: COLLINS
> *Build over ice and stir*

Sparkling Garden

1½ parts Citrus-Flavored Vodka
⅔ part Parfait Amour
splash Lime Juice
splash Lemon Juice
fill with Sparkling Water

> GLASS: COLLINS
> *Build over ice and stir*

Sparkling Red Driver

1 part Vodka
1 part Grapefruit Juice
1 part Ginger Ale

> GLASS: COLLINS
> *Build over ice and stir*

Sputnik

1¼ parts Vodka
1¼ parts Peach Schnapps
1 part Orange Juice
1 part Light Cream

{ GLASS: COLLINS

Build over ice and stir

Squeeze

1½ parts Citrus-Flavored Vodka
1 part Pineapple Juice
1 part Orange Juice

{ GLASS: COLLINS

Build over ice and stir

Stale Perfume

1 part Raspberry-Flavored Vodka
1 part Raspberry Liqueur
fill with Lemon-Lime Soda

{ GLASS: COLLINS

Build over ice and stir

Steady Eddie

1 part Vodka
1 part Coconut-Flavored Rum
splash Passion Fruit Liqueur
fill with Orange Juice

{ GLASS: COLLINS

Shake with ice and pour

Stiffy

1 part Vodka
1 part Pink Lemonade
fill with Mountain Dew®

{ GLASS: COLLINS

Build over ice and stir

Sting

1 part Vodka
1 part Crème de Banana
fill with Lemonade

{ GLASS: COLLINS

Shake with ice and pour

Stone Cold

1 part Vodka
1 part Peach Schnapps
2 parts Orange Juice
½ part Strawberry Syrup
fill with Lemon-Lime Soda

GLASS: COLLINS
Build over ice and stir

Strawberry Screwdriver

2 parts Vodka
1 part Strawberry Liqueur
fill with Orange Juice

GLASS: COLLINS
Shake with ice and pour

Summer Delight

½ part Orange-Flavored Vodka
¼ part Peach Schnapps
1 part Cranberry Juice Cocktail
1 part Orange Juice
¾ part Melon Liqueur

GLASS: COLLINS
Build over ice and stir

Summer Hummer

2 parts Citrus-Flavored Vodka
2 parts Lemonade
1 part Lemon-Lime Soda

GLASS: COLLINS
Build over ice and stir

Summer Smile

1 part Vodka
1 part Coconut-Flavored Liqueur
fill with Orange Juice

GLASS: COLLINS
Build over ice and stir

Sunblock

1½ parts Vodka
1 part Triple Sec
fill with Grapefruit Juice

GLASS: COLLINS
Build over ice and stir

Sunny Sam

1 part Vodka
½ part Sambuca
fill with Orange Juice

GLASS: COLLINS

Build over ice and stir

Sunset

1 part Vodka
1 part Apricot Brandy
fill with Orange Juice
splash Grenadine

GLASS: COLLINS

Build over ice

Sunset Boulevard

1½ parts Vodka
¾ part Peach Schnapps
fill with Orange Juice

GLASS: COLLINS

Build over ice and stir

Sunsplash

2 parts Orange-Flavored Vodka
½ part Cointreau®
1 part Lime Juice
1 part Cranberry Juice Cocktail
1 part Orange Juice

GLASS: COLLINS

Build over ice and stir

Sunstroke

2 parts Vodka
fill with Grapefruit Juice
splash Cointreau®

GLASS: COLLINS

Build over ice

Superjuice

1 part Vodka
1 part Gin
½ part Lime Juice
1 part Orange Juice
1 part Tonic Water

GLASS: COLLINS

Build over ice and stir

Swamp Juice

1 part Vodka
1 part Blue Curaçao
1 part Triple Sec
1 part Orange Juice
1 part Pineapple Juice

GLASS: COLLINS

Shake with ice and pour

Swedish Blue

1½ parts Vodka
½ part Blue Curaçao
fill with Pineapple Juice
splash Fresh Lime Juice

GLASS: COLLINS

Build over ice and stir

Sweet Escape

1 part Citrus-Flavored Vodka
1 part Peach Schnapps
1 part Aquavit
1 part Lime Cordial
fill with Pear Juice

GLASS: COLLINS

Build over ice and stir

Sweet Melissa

1½ parts Coconut-Flavored Rum
1½ parts Vanilla-Flavored Vodka
splash Cranberry Juice Cocktail
1 part Orange Juice
1 part Pineapple Juice

GLASS: HURRICANE

Shake with ice and strain over ice

Sweet Passoã®

1 part Vodka
1 part Passoã®
1 part Tonic Water
fill with Pineapple Juice
splash Orange Juice

GLASS: COLLINS

Build over ice and stir

Sweet Pea

2 parts Citrus-Flavored Vodka
1 part Melon Liqueur
2 parts Cream
1 part Melon Puree

GLASS: HURRICANE

Build over ice and stir

Swimming Pool

1 part Vodka
1 part Gin
1 part Rum
1 part Blue Curaçao
fill with Lemon-Lime Soda

GLASS: COLLINS

Build over ice and stir

Tahitian Tea

1 part Vodka
1 part Triple Sec
1 part Gin
1 part Rum
fill with Orange Juice

GLASS: HURRICANE

Shake with ice and strain over ice

Take the A Train

1½ parts Citrus-Flavored Vodka
½ part Vodka
1 part Grapefruit Juice
1 part Cranberry Juice Cocktail

GLASS: COLLINS

Shake with ice and pour

Takemoto Twister

1 part Vodka
1 part Sour Apple Schnapps
1 part Strawberry Liqueur
1 part Grapefruit Juice
2 parts Orange Juice

GLASS: COLLINS

Shake with ice and pour

Tangeri

1½ parts Orange-Flavored Vodka
½ part Passion Fruit Liqueur
fill with Grape Juice (Red)

{ GLASS: COLLINS

Shake with ice and pour

Templar

1 part Vodka
½ part Kiwi Schnapps
½ part Triple Sec
splash Dry Vermouth
fill with Orange Juice

{ GLASS: COLLINS

Shake with ice and pour

Thompson Tonic

1 part Peach Schnapps
1 part Spiced Rum
1 part Vodka
fill with Mountain Dew®

{ GLASS: COLLINS

Build over ice and stir

Timberwolf

1 part Light Rum
1 part Tequila
1 part Gin
1 part Vodka
1 part Crème de Noyaux
fill with Orange Juice

{ GLASS: COLLINS

Shake with ice and pour

Tolle

1 part Vodka
1 part Crème de Banana
fill with Hard Apple Cider

{ GLASS: COLLINS

Build over ice and stir

Toxic Antifreeze

1 part Vodka
1 part Triple Sec
1 part Midori®
fill with Lemonade

{ GLASS: COLLINS

Build over ice and stir

Toxic Blue-Green Algae

1 part Blue Curaçao
1 part Cointreau®
1 part Green Chartreuse®
1 part Vodka
1 part Light Rum
1 part Melon Liqueur
fill with Pineapple Juice

{ GLASS: COLLINS

Shake with ice and pour

Toxic Waste

1 part Vodka
½ part Southern Comfort®
¼ part Blue Curaçao
1 part Orange Juice
1 part Pineapple Juice

{ GLASS: COLLINS

Shake with ice and pour

Trang Tricot

1 part Vodka
1 part Pineapple Juice
½ part Crème de Banana
fill with Grape Soda

{ GLASS: COLLINS

Build over ice and stir

Transfusion

1¼ part Vodka
fill with Grape Juice (Red)

{ GLASS: COLLINS

Build over ice and stir

Trevell

1 part Coconut-Flavored Rum
1 part Vodka
fill with Lemon-Lime Soda

{ GLASS: COLLINS

Build over ice and stir

Troia

1 part Vodka
1 part Coconut-Flavored Liqueur
1 part Strawberry Syrup
fill with Lemon-Lime Soda

{ GLASS: COLLINS

Build over ice and stir

Tropic Purple Haze

1½ parts Raspberry Liqueur
½ part Vodka
½ part Triple Sec
2 parts Cranberry Juice Cocktail
1 part Pineapple Juice

{ GLASS: COLLINS

Shake with ice and pour

Tropical Leprechaun

1 part Vodka
½ part Coconut-Flavored Rum
fill with Lemon-Lime Soda
splash Melon Liqueur

{ GLASS: COLLINS

Build over ice and stir

Turbocharged

1 part Sambuca
1 part Vodka
1 part Blue Curaçao
2 parts Coconut Cream
fill with Pineapple Juice

{ GLASS: COLLINS

Build over ice and stir

Twist and Shout

1 part Vodka
1 part Peach Schnapps
1½ parts Orange Juice
fill with Cola

GLASS: COLLINS
Build over ice and stir

Twisted Breeze

1½ parts Citrus-Flavored Vodka
1½ parts Kiwi Schnapps
1 part Grapefruit Juice
1 part Cranberry Juice Cocktail

GLASS: COLLINS
Shake with ice and pour

Two Seater

⅔ part Vodka
½ part Apricot Brandy
splash Triple Sec
1 part Orange Juice
1 part Grapefruit Juice

GLASS: COLLINS
Shake with ice and pour

Umbongo

1 part Vodka
2 parts Passion Fruit Liqueur
1 part Orange Juice
1 part Passion Fruit Juice

GLASS: COLLINS
Build over ice and stir

Uncle Art

2 parts Lime Juice
1 part Vodka
dash Sugar
1 part Ginger Ale
1 part Lemon-Lime Soda

GLASS: COLLINS
Build over ice and stir

Uncle Vanya

1½ parts Vodka
½ part Blackberry Liqueur
fill with Sour Mix

GLASS: COLLINS

Build over ice and stir

The Unforgettable Fire

1 part Vodka
½ part Apricot Brandy
½ part Orange Liqueur
1 part Orange Juice
1 part Red Bull® Energy Drink

GLASS: COLLINS

Build over ice and stir

Urine Sample

2 parts Vodka
fill with Malt Liquor

GLASS: COLLINS

Build in the glass with no ice

Vanilla Rose

1½ parts Vanilla-Flavored Vodka
fill with Cola
splash Tuaca®

GLASS: COLLINS

Build over ice and stir

Vaya con Dios

2 parts Vodka
1 part Pineapple-Orange Juice
1 part Strawberry Daiquiri Mix

GLASS: PILSNER

Shake with ice and pour

Vertical Horizon

1 part Vodka
1 part Gin
1½ parts Orange Liqueur
½ part Lemon Juice
fill with Cranberry Juice Cocktail

GLASS: COLLINS

Shake with ice and strain over ice

Very Screwy Driver

1 part Vodka
½ part Tequila Silver
½ part Gin
fill with Orange Juice

GLASS: COLLINS
Build over ice and stir

Vietnam Acid Flashback

1 part Apple Liqueur
1 part 151-Proof Rum
1 part Jim Beam®
1 part Light Rum
1 part Vodka
1 part Yukon Jack®
1 part Triple Sec
splash Grenadine
fill with Orange Juice

GLASS: HURRICANE
Shake with ice and pour

Vitamin C

1½ parts Orange-Flavored Vodka
1 part Sour Mix
1 part Orange Juice

GLASS: COLLINS
Shake with ice and pour

Vlad the Impaler

2 parts Vodka
⅔ part Peach Schnapps
fill with Cranberry Juice Cocktail

GLASS: COLLINS
Shake with ice and pour

Vodka 7

2 parts Vodka
½ part Lime Juice
fill with Lemon-Lime Soda

GLASS: COLLINS
Build over ice and stir

Vodka Collins

2 parts Vodka
½ part Lemon Juice
dash Powdered Sugar
fill with Carbonated Water

GLASS: COLLINS

Shake all but Carbonated Water with ice and strain into the glass. Top with Carbonated Water.

Vodka Paralyzer

¾ part Vodka
¾ part Coffee Liqueur
2 parts Milk
fill with Cola

GLASS: COLLINS

Build over ice and stir

Vodka Smooth

1½ parts Vodka
½ part Triple Sec
fill with Orange Juice
splash Grenadine

GLASS: COLLINS

Build over ice

Vodka Storm

1 part Vodka
1 part Raspberry Liqueur
fill with Cola

GLASS: COLLINS

Build over ice and stir

Vodka with Wings

1½ parts Vodka
fill with Red Bull® Energy Drink

GLASS: COLLINS

Build over ice and stir

Vodka Yummy

2 parts Vodka
1 part Cinnamon Schnapps
fill with Apple Juice

GLASS: COLLINS

Build over ice and stir

Volcano

½ part Vodka
½ part Jim Beam®
½ part Gin
½ part Rum
½ part Tequila
1 part Orange Juice
1 part Pineapple Juice
splash Grenadine
splash Lemon-Lime Soda

GLASS: COLLINS

Build over ice and stir

Vomit Juice

1 part Cinnamon Schnapps
½ part Irish Whiskey
½ part Southern Comfort®
½ part Tequila Silver
½ part Vodka
fill with Red Bull® Energy Drink

GLASS: BEER MUG

Build over ice and stir

Voodoo Sunrise

1 part Vodka
1 part Rum
2 parts Grenadine
fill with Orange Juice

GLASS: COLLINS

Build over ice and stir

Walking Home

½ part Vodka
½ part Rum
½ part Tequila
½ part Sloe Gin
1 part Lime Juice
splash Maraschino Cherry Juice

GLASS: COLLINS

Shake with ice and pour

Water Buffalo

1½ parts Vodka
½ part Grand Marnier®
fill with Orange Juice

GLASS: COLLINS

Build over ice and stir

Watermelon Slice

½ part Grenadine
½ part Rum
½ part Gin
½ part Triple Sec
½ part Vodka
1 part Orange Juice
1 part Cranberry Juice Cocktail
1 part Melon Liqueur

GLASS: HURRICANE

Build over ice and stir

Wedding Anniversary

1 part Vodka
1 part Galliano®
1 part Campari®
fill with Orange Juice

GLASS: COLLINS

Shake with ice and strain over ice

Weightlessness

1½ parts Vodka
1 part Peach Schnapps
1 part Sour Mix
1 part Coconut Cream
1 part Cranberry Juice Cocktail

GLASS: COLLINS

Shake with ice and strain over ice

West Salem Cider

1 part Peach Brandy
1 part Vodka
fill with Apple Cider

GLASS: COLLINS

Build over ice and stir

Whale Orgasm

1 part Vodka
1 part Crème de Menthe (White)
2 parts Piña Colada Mix

GLASS: COLLINS

Shake with ice and pour

Whiting Sunset

2 parts Vodka
1 part Tequila
fill with Orange Juice
splash Grenadine

GLASS: COLLINS

Build over ice and stir

Wrong Number

1 part Gin
1 part Rum
1 part Vodka
1 part Orange Juice
1 part Pineapple Juice

GLASS: COLLINS

Build over ice and stir

Xixu

1½ parts Vodka
½ part Campari®
½ part Melon Liqueur
splash Crème de Menthe (White)
fill with Cola

GLASS: COLLINS

Build over ice and stir

Yeah Dude

1 part Vodka
1 part Southern Comfort®
splash Tabasco® Sauce
fill with Cola

GLASS: COLLINS

Build over ice and stir

Yellow Fingers

1 part Southern Comfort®
1 part Vodka
½ part Galliano®
1 part Orange Juice
1 part Lemon-Lime Soda

GLASS: COLLINS

Build over ice and stir

Yellow Screwdriver

2 parts Vodka
fill with Lemonade

GLASS: COLLINS

Build over ice and stir

Zyphar

2 parts Vodka
1 part Maraschino Cherry Juice
fill with Mountain Dew®

GLASS: COLLINS

Build over ice and stir

TASTY TASTY TASTY TASTY TASTY
TASTY TASTY TASTY TASTY TASTY

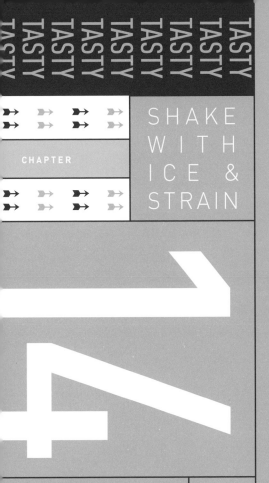

SHAKE WITH ICE & STRAIN

CHAPTER

14

SHORT DRINKS

THESE ALTITUDINALLY CHALLENGED DRINKS
DON'T FIT INTO ANY OTHER MARKETABLE
CATEGORY.

DRINK UP!

77 Sunset Strip

½ part Vodka
½ part Gin
½ part Spiced Rum
½ part Triple Sec
1½ parts Pineapple Juice
½ part Grenadine

GLASS: HIGHBALL

Build over ice and stir

Absolero Liqueur

¾ part Melon Liqueur
¾ part Absolut® Citron Vodka
¾ part Absolut® Kurant Vodka
1 Egg White
¼ part Fresh Lime Juice

GLASS: HIGHBALL

Build over ice and stir

Absolut® Heaven

1½ parts Absolut® Orange-Flavored Vodka
fill with Pineapple Juice
splash Cranberry Juice Cocktail

GLASS: HIGHBALL

Build over ice and stir

Absolut® Mixer

1 part Absolut® Citron Vodka
1 part Absolut® Peppar Vodka
1 part Absolut® Kurant Vodka
1 part Absolut® Vodka
fill with Orange Juice

GLASS: HIGHBALL

Build over ice and stir

Absolut® Stress

1 part Absolut® Vodka
1 part Coconut-Flavored Rum
1 part Peach Schnapps
splash Cranberry Juice Cocktail
splash Orange Juice

GLASS: HIGHBALL

Build over ice and stir

Absolut® Trouble

1½ parts Absolut® Citrus-Flavored Vodka
1 part Grand Marnier®
1 part Orange Juice
½ part Grenadine

GLASS: HIGHBALL

Build over ice and stir

Absolut® Vacation

1 part Absolut® Vodka
1 part Cranberry Juice Cocktail
1 part Orange Juice
1 part Pineapple Juice

GLASS: OLD-FASHIONED

Shake with ice and strain over ice

Airborne Lemon Drop

1¼ parts Vodka
¾ part Chambord®
¾ part 151-Proof Rum
1 Lemon Wedge
dash Sugar

GLASS: OLD-FASHIONED

Shake with ice and strain over ice

Albysjön

2 parts Vodka
1 part Orange Fanta® Soda
½ part Lemon-Lime Soda
½ part Kiwi Concentrate

GLASS: HIGHBALL

Build over ice and stir

The Alderman

1 part Citrus-Flavored Vodka
½ part Strawberry Liqueur
½ part Lemon Juice
1½ parts Apple Juice
⅔ part Sparkling Water

GLASS: OLD-FASHIONED

Shake with ice and strain over ice

Alex Chi-Chi

2 parts Vodka
1 part Cointreau®
1 part Coconut Cream
2 parts Pineapple Juice

{ GLASS: WHITE WINE

Shake with ice and strain over ice

Alexander the Great

1½ parts Vodka
½ part Crème de Cacao (White)
½ part Coffee Liqueur
½ part Cream

{ GLASS: HIGHBALL

Shake with ice and strain over ice

Algae

½ part Vodka
½ part Melon Liqueur
½ part Raspberry Liqueur
½ part Blue Curaçao
2 parts Sour Mix
fill with Lemon-Lime Soda

{ GLASS: HIGHBALL

Shake with ice and strain over ice

Alien Slime

1 part Vodka
2 parts Blue Curaçao
3 parts Orange Juice

{ GLASS: HIGHBALL

Shake with ice and strain over ice

Alligator Tongue

1 part Vodka
1½ parts Melon Liqueur
2 parts Pineapple Juice
½ part Lemon-Lime Soda
¼ part Fresh Lime Juice

{ GLASS: OLD-FASHIONED

Shake with ice and strain over ice

Almond Schwarzenegger

2 parts Blavod® Black Vodka
1 part Amaretto

GLASS: OLD-FASHIONED

Shake with ice and strain over ice

Almost a Virgin

²/₃ part Raspberry Liqueur
²/₃ part Amaretto
1½ parts Currant-Flavored Vodka
splash Pineapple Juice
splash Cranberry Juice Cocktail

GLASS: HIGHBALL

Build over ice and stir

Aloha Screwdriver

1 part Vodka
1 part Orange Juice
2 parts Pineapple Juice

GLASS: HIGHBALL

Build over ice and stir

Amaretto '57 Chevy

1 part Vodka
1 part Amaretto
1 part Cherry Juice
1 part Lemonade
1 part Orange Juice

GLASS: HIGHBALL

Build over ice and stir

Amaretto '57 T-Bird

1 part Vodka
1 part Amaretto
1 part Cherry Juice
1 part Sour Mix
1 part Pineapple Juice

GLASS: HIGHBALL

Build over ice and stir

Amaretto Pucker

1 part Vodka
1 part Amaretto
1 part Cherry Juice
fill with Grapefruit Juice

GLASS: HIGHBALL

Build over ice and stir

Amaretto Pussycat

1 part Vodka
1 part Amaretto
1 part Cherry Juice
fill with Pineapple Juice

GLASS: HIGHBALL

Build over ice and stir

Amaretto Russian Tea

1 part Vodka
1 part Amaretto
1 part Sour Mix
fill with Cola

GLASS: HIGHBALL

Build over ice and stir

Amaretto Slinger

1 part Vodka
1 part Amaretto
1 part Sour Mix
fill with Orange Juice

GLASS: HIGHBALL

Build over ice and stir

Amaretto Smooth Sailing

1 part Vodka
1 part Amaretto
1 part Sour Mix
1 part Cranberry Juice Cocktail
1 part Orange Juice

GLASS: HIGHBALL

Build over ice and stir

Amaretto Vodka Hawaiian

1 part Vodka
1 part Amaretto
1 part Sour Mix
1 part Lemon-Lime Soda
fill with Pineapple Juice

GLASS: HIGHBALL
Build over ice and stir

Amaretto Vodka Punch

1 part Vodka
1 part Amaretto
1 part Cherry Juice
1 part Orange Juice
1 part Pineapple Juice

GLASS: HIGHBALL
Build over ice and stir

Amaretto White Italian

1 part Vodka
1 part Amaretto
fill with Cream

GLASS: HIGHBALL
Build over ice and stir

Ambijaxtrious

1 part Vodka
1 part Tequila
1 part Coffee Liqueur
fill with Milk
splash Grenadine

GLASS: OLD-FASHIONED
Build over ice and stir

Amsterdam Surprise

½ part Goldschläger®
½ part Amaretto
½ part Vodka
½ part Southern Comfort®
3 parts Pineapple Juice

GLASS: HIGHBALL
Build over ice and stir

Amy's Ambrosia

½ part Currant-Flavored Vodka
1 part Melon Liqueur
1 part Strawberry Liqueur
fill with Cranberry Juice Cocktail

GLASS: HIGHBALL

Build over ice and stir

Andy's Blend

2 parts Vodka
1 part Orange Juice
1 part Pineapple Juice

GLASS: HIGHBALL

Build over ice and stir

Angie's Dildo

1 part Vodka
2 parts Triple Sec
dash Sugar

GLASS: OLD-FASHIONED

Shake with ice and pour

Antifreeze

1 part Vodka
½ part Blue Curaçao
½ part Crème de Banana
fill with Orange Juice

GLASS: HIGHBALL

Shake with ice and pour

Anvil

2 parts Vodka
2 parts Coconut Cream
3 parts Pineapple Juice

GLASS: HIGHBALL

Build over ice and stir

Apfel Orange

1 part Apple Brandy
½ part Vodka
1 part Orange Juice
1 part Lemon-Lime Soda

GLASS: HIGHBALL

Build over ice and stir

Apfelkuchen

1 part Vodka
fill with Apple Juice
splash Grenadine

GLASS: HIGHBALL
Build over ice and stir

Apple Delight

1 part Vodka
1 part Peach Schnapps
1 part Melon Liqueur
½ part Crème de Banana

GLASS: OLD-FASHIONED
Shake with ice and pour

Apple Eden

1½ parts Vodka
3 parts Apple Juice

GLASS: HIGHBALL
Shake with ice and pour

Apple Pucker

1 part Vodka
1 part Sour Apple Schnapps
1 part Cherry Juice
fill with Grapefruit Juice

GLASS: HIGHBALL
Shake with ice and pour

Apple Pussycat

1 part Vodka
1 part Sour Apple Schnapps
1 part Cherry Juice
fill with Pineapple Juice

GLASS: HIGHBALL
Shake with ice and pour

Apple Screwdriver

1 part Vodka
1 part Sour Apple Schnapps
fill with Orange Juice

GLASS: HIGHBALL
Build over ice and stir

Apricot Lemondrop

1 part Vodka
1 part Apricot Brandy
fill with Lemonade

GLASS: WHISKEY SOUR

Shake with ice and pour

Apricot Screwdriver

1 part Vodka
1 part Apricot Brandy
fill with Orange Juice

GLASS: HIGHBALL

Build over ice and stir

Aqua

1 part Vodka
1 part Irish Cream Liqueur
1 part Blue Curaçao
fill with Lemon-Lime Soda

GLASS: HIGHBALL

Build over ice and stir

Arkansas Razorback

1 part Rum
1 part Vodka
1 part Amaretto
1 part Coffee Liqueur

GLASS: OLD-FASHIONED

Shake with ice and strain over ice

Arturro's Death

1 part Rum
1 part Tequila
1 part Sweet Vermouth
1 part Vodka
1 part Blue Curaçao
splash Grenadine

GLASS: HIGHBALL

Shake with ice and strain

Aruba Ariba

¾ part Rum
¾ part Vodka
½ part Grand Marnier®
splash Grenadine
splash Orange Juice
splash Pineapple Juice
splash Grapefruit Juice

GLASS: HIGHBALL

Shake with ice and pour

A-Team

1 part Vodka
1 part Brandy
1 part Lime Juice
2 parts Sour Mix
fill with Fruit Punch

GLASS: HIGHBALL

Shake with ice and pour

Atlantic Sun

1 part Vodka
1 part Southern Comfort®
1 part Grenadine
2 parts Sour Mix
splash Club Soda

GLASS: HIGHBALL

Shake all but Club Soda with ice and strain into the glass. Top with Club Soda.

Atlas

2 parts Vodka
1 part Blue Curaçao
splash Orange Juice
fill with Cranberry Juice Cocktail

GLASS: HIGHBALL

Shake with ice and strain over ice

Atomic Body Slam

1 part Gin
1 part Vodka
1 part Blackberry Brandy
1 part Light Rum
2 parts Strawberry Fruit Drink

GLASS: HIGHBALL

Build over ice and stir

B-53

1 part Coffee Liqueur
1 part Irish Cream Liqueur
1 part Grand Marnier®
1 part Vodka

GLASS: OLD-FASHIONED

Layer in the glass with no ice

B-69

1 part Grand Marnier®
1 part Coffee Liqueur
1 part Irish Cream Liqueur
1 part Amaretto
1 part Vodka

GLASS: WHISKEY SOUR

Layer over ice. Drink through a straw.

Backseat Boogie

½ part Gin
½ part Vodka
1 part Cranberry Juice Cocktail
1 part Ginger Ale

GLASS: HIGHBALL

Build over ice and stir

Baehr Chunky Monkey

½ part Apricot Brandy
½ part Blue Curaçao
1 part Vodka
2 parts Blueberry Schnapps

GLASS: HIGHBALL

Build over ice and stir

Bahamut Gold

²/₃ part Vodka
splash Peppermint Liqueur
1 part Goldschläger®

GLASS: HIGHBALL
Build over ice and stir

Balalaika

2 parts Vodka
1 part Triple Sec

GLASS: OLD-FASHIONED
Shake with ice and stir

Banana Apple Pie

1 part Vodka
1 part Banana Liqueur
fill with Apple Juice

GLASS: HIGHBALL
Build over ice and stir

Banana Breeze

1 part Vodka
1 part Banana Liqueur
1 part Pineapple Juice
1 part Cranberry Juice Cocktail

GLASS: HIGHBALL
Build over ice and stir

Banana Pop

1 part Vodka
1 part Cherry Juice
1 part Banana Juice
fill with Orange Juice

GLASS: HIGHBALL
Build over ice and stir

Banana Pudding

1 part Banana Liqueur
1 part Crème de Cacao (White)
3 parts Milk
1 part Tia Maria®
1 part Vodka

GLASS: HIGHBALL

Shake with ice and strain

Banana Rainstorm

1 part Vodka
1 part Blue Curaçao
2 parts Lemon-Lime Soda
1 part Pineapple Juice

GLASS: HIGHBALL

Build over ice and stir

Bananagrove

1 part Vodka
1 part Crème de Banana
1 part Orange Juice

GLASS: HIGHBALL

Shake with ice and strain

Bartender's Delight

1 part Orange-Flavored Vodka
1 part Dry Vermouth
1 part Dubonnet® Blonde
1 part Dry Sherry

GLASS: HIGHBALL

*Shake with ice and strain
over ice*

Battering Ram

1 part Vodka
1 part Tequila
fill with Red Bull® Energy Drink

GLASS: HIGHBALL

Build over ice and stir

Bay Breeze

1½ parts Vodka
fill with Grapefruit Juice
splash Cranberry Juice Cocktail

GLASS: OLD-FASHIONED

Shake with ice and pour

Beam Me Up

1 part Vodka
1 part Peach Schnapps
1 part Cherry Juice
fill with Lemon-Lime Soda

GLASS: HIGHBALL

Build over ice and stir

Beam Me Up Scotty (Smooth 'n' Painless)

1 part Whiskey
½ part Vodka
½ part Amaretto
½ part Crème de Banana
splash Southern Comfort®

GLASS: OLD-FASHIONED

Build over ice and stir

Belgian Blue

1 part Vodka
½ part Coconut-Flavored Liqueur
½ part Blue Curaçao
fill with Lemon-Lime Soda

GLASS: HIGHBALL

Build over ice and stir

Bellas Noches De Mai

1 part Vodka
½ part Parfait Amour
½ part Maraschino Liqueur

GLASS: HIGHBALL

Shake with ice and strain over ice

Bend Me Over

1 part Amaretto
1 part Vodka
1 part Sour Mix
4 parts Orange Juice

GLASS: HIGHBALL

Build over ice and stir

Beth and Jen's Sleigh Ride

1 part Vodka
1 part Lemon-Lime Soda
1 part Cranberry Juice Cocktail

GLASS: HIGHBALL

Build over ice and stir

Betsy Clear

1 part Vodka
1 part Peach Schnapps
fill with Lemon-Lime Soda

GLASS: HIGHBALL

Build over ice and stir

Big Bang Boom

1 part Vodka
1 part Crème de Banana
1 part Melon Liqueur
1 part Pineapple Juice
1 part Orange Juice
½ part Grenadine

GLASS: OLD-FASHIONED

Shake with ice and strain

Big Dog

1½ parts Vodka
1 part Coffee Liqueur
fill with Milk
splash Cola

GLASS: HIGHBALL

Build over ice and stir

Big Fat One

1 part Vodka
1 part Triple Sec
1 part Melon Liqueur
splash Orange Juice

GLASS: OLD-FASHIONED

Shake with ice and pour

Big Red Chevy

1 part Vodka
1 part Sour Mix
1 part Strawberry Soda
splash Orange Juice

GLASS: HIGHBALL
Build over ice and stir

Bijoux

1 part Vodka
1 part Melon Liqueur
splash Triple Sec
splash Lemon Juice
splash Pineapple Juice

GLASS: HIGHBALL
Shake with ice and strain

The Bionic Drink

2 parts Vodka
fill with Grapefruit Juice
splash Lemon Juice

GLASS: HIGHBALL
Build over ice and stir

Bison

1 part Vodka
splash Blue Curaçao
splash Campari®
splash Sweet Vermouth

GLASS: HIGHBALL
Shake with ice and strain

Bitter Pill

1 part Vodka
1 part Jack Daniel's®
splash Lemon Juice
fill with Cola

GLASS: HIGHBALL
Build over ice and stir

Bittersweet Italian

1½ parts Vodka
1 part Amaretto
1 part Grapefruit Juice
½ part Lemon Juice
dash Sugar
fill with Pineapple Juice

GLASS: OLD-FASHIONED

Shake with ice and strain

Black Cherry

1 part Vodka
1 part Raspberry Liqueur
1 part Irish Cream Liqueur
1 part Coffee Liqueur
1 part Half and Half
splash Cola

GLASS: HIGHBALL

Shake with ice and pour

Black Lagoon

1 part Citrus-Flavored Vodka
1 part Blackberry Liqueur
fill with Orange Juice
splash Cranberry Juice Cocktail

GLASS: HIGHBALL

Build over ice and stir

Black of Night

1 part Vodka
1 part Wild Berry Schnapps
2 parts Lemonade
1 part Cola

GLASS: HIGHBALL

Build over ice and stir

Black Opal

½ part Gin
½ part Rum
½ part Vodka
½ part Triple Sec
2 parts Sour Mix

GLASS: HIGHBALL

Build over ice and stir

Black Russian

1½ parts Vodka
1 part Coffee Liqueur

GLASS: OLD-FASHIONED

Build over ice and stir

Blackberry Breeze

1 part Vodka
1 part Blackberry Liqueur
1 part Pineapple Juice
1 part Cranberry Juice Cocktail

GLASS: HIGHBALL

Shake with ice and pour

Blackberry Chill

1 part Vodka
2 parts Blackberry Juice
2 parts Lemonade
1 part Pineapple Juice

GLASS: HIGHBALL

Shake with ice and pour

Blackberry Lifesaver

1½ parts Vodka
1 part Blackberry Liqueur
fill with Orange Juice

GLASS: HIGHBALL

Build over ice and stir

Blackberry Pussycat

1 part Vodka
1 part Blackberry Liqueur
1 part Cherry Juice
fill with Pineapple Juice

GLASS: HIGHBALL

Shake with ice and pour

Blindside

2 parts Vodka
2 parts Orange Juice
2 parts Grapefruit Juice
1 part Strawberry Syrup

GLASS: HIGHBALL

Build over ice and stir

Blonde Bombshell

1 part Vodka
1 part Brandy
½ part Sour Apple Schnapps
½ part Peach Schnapps

GLASS: HIGHBALL

Shake with ice and pour

Bloody Biker

2 parts Vodka
5 parts Spicy Vegetable Juice Blend
splash Worchestershire Sauce
splash Hot Sauce
1 Lime Wedge
splash Olive Brine

GLASS: OLD-FASHIONED

Shake with ice and pour

Bloody Bitch

2 parts Grapefruit Juice
1 part Vodka
1 part Grenadine

GLASS: HIGHBALL

Shake with ice and pour

Bloody Mary

1 part Vodka
1 part Sherry
splash Worcestershire Sauce
dash Salt
splash Tabasco® Sauce
dash Pepper
1 Celery Stalk
1 Lime Wedge

GLASS: HIGHBALL

Build over ice and stir. There are many different variations on the Bloody Mary. This is the basic recipe that you can adjust to your taste.

Bloody Sunday

1 part Tropical Punch Schnapps
1 part Grenadine
1 part Piña Colada Mix
1½ parts Vodka

GLASS: HIGHBALL

Shake with ice and pour

Bloody Temple

2 parts Vodka
1 part Grenadine
1 part Lemon-Lime Soda

GLASS: HIGHBALL

Build over ice and stir

Blue Ball

1 part Blue Curaçao
1 part Coconut-Flavored Rum
1 part Raspberry-Flavored Vodka

GLASS: OLD-FASHIONED

Build over ice and stir

Blue Bike

1 part Vodka
½ part Light Rum
1 part Blue Curaçao
½ part Triple Sec
½ part Sour Mix

GLASS: HIGHBALL

Shake with ice and pour

Blue Eye

1½ parts Vodka
1 part Battery® Energy Drink
1 part Sour Mix
splash Blue Curaçao

GLASS: HIGHBALL

Shake with ice and strain over ice

Blue Lagoon

1 part Vodka
1 part Blue Curaçao
fill with Lemonade
1 Maraschino Cherry

GLASS: HIGHBALL

Build over ice and stir

Blue Mango

1 part Blue Curaçao
1 part Vodka
1 part Mango Nectar
fill with Orange Juice

{ GLASS: HIGHBALL

Build over ice and stir

Blue Monkey

1 part Orange-Flavored Vodka
1 part Banana Liqueur
1 part Cream
splash Blue Curaçao

{ GLASS: HIGHBALL

Shake with ice and strain over ice

Blue Mountain

1½ parts Añejo Rum
½ part Tia Maria®
½ part Vodka
1 part Orange Juice
splash Lemon Juice

{ GLASS: OLD-FASHIONED

Shake with ice and strain over ice

Blue Poison

1 part Tequila Silver
1 part Vodka
1 part Blue Curaçao
fill with Lemonade

{ GLASS: HIGHBALL

Build over ice and stir

Blue Russian

1 part Blue Curaçao
1 part Vodka
fill with Cream

{ GLASS: OLD-FASHIONED

Shake with ice and pour

Blueberry Pucker

1 part Vodka
1 part Blueberry Schnapps
1 part Cherry Juice
fill with Grapefruit Juice

GLASS: HIGHBALL

Build over ice and stir

Blue-Woo

1 part Vodka
1 part Blueberry Schnapps
fill with Cranberry Juice Cocktail

GLASS: HIGHBALL

Build over ice and stir

Blushing Bride

1 part Vodka
2 parts Cranberry Juice Cocktail
3 parts Orange Juice
2 parts Lemon-Lime Soda

GLASS: HIGHBALL

Build over ice and stir

Bonfire

2/3 part Apricot Brandy
splash Sweet Vermouth
splash Benedictine®
splash Orange-Flavored Vodka

GLASS: HIGHBALL

Shake with ice and pour

Boogy Woogy

2 parts Blue Curaçao
2/3 part Orange-Flavored Vodka
fill with Lemon-Lime Soda

GLASS: HIGHBALL

Build over ice and stir

Boston Tea Party

½ part Vodka
½ part Scotch
½ part Dry Vermouth
½ part Triple Sec
½ part Rum
½ part Gin
½ part Tequila
1 part Orange Juice
1 part Cola
splash Sour Mix

GLASS: HIGHBALL

Build over ice and stir

Bottom Rose

1 part Vodka
splash Apricot Brandy
splash Sweet Vermouth

GLASS: HIGHBALL

Build over ice and stir

Brass Monkey

1 part Vodka
1 part Light Rum
fill with Orange Juice

GLASS: HIGHBALL

Shake with ice and pour

Brave Bull

1½ parts Tequila
1 part Coffee-Flavored Vodka
1 Lemon Twist

GLASS: OLD-FASHIONED

Layer over ice

Breeze

1 part Vodka
½ part Blue Curaçao
½ part Crème de Menthe (Green)

GLASS: OLD-FASHIONED

Shake with ice and pour

Broadway

½ part Vodka
½ part Apricot Brandy
1 part Mango Juice

GLASS: HIGHBALL
Shake with ice and strain

Broken Heart

1 part Vodka
1 part Raspberry Liqueur
fill with Orange Juice
splash Grenadine

GLASS: HIGHBALL
Shake with ice and pour

Brown Russian

1 part Chocolate Liqueur
2 parts Vodka

GLASS: OLD-FASHIONED
Layer over ice

Bull Shot

1½ parts Vodka
fill with Chilled Beef Bouillion
splash Worcestershire Sauce
dash Salt
dash Pepper

GLASS: OLD-FASHIONED
Shake with ice and pour

Bullfrog

1 part Vodka
1 part Margarita Mix
fill with Lemon-Lime Soda

GLASS: HIGHBALL
Build over ice and stir

Caipiroska

2 parts Vodka
1 part freshly squeezed Lime
2 dashes Sugar

GLASS: OLD-FASHIONED
Layer over ice

Californian

1 part Vodka
1 part Orange Juice
1 part Grapefruit Juice

GLASS: HIGHBALL
Build over ice and stir

Calypso Kool-Aid®

1 part Vodka
1 part Raspberry Liqueur
1 part Cherry Juice
2 parts Lemonade
1 part Pineapple Juice

GLASS: HIGHBALL
Build over ice and stir

Cape Grape

1½ parts Vodka
1 part Cranberry Liqueur
fill with Grapefruit Juice

GLASS: HIGHBALL
Build over ice and stir

Caribbean Bliss

1 part Vodka
1 part Tequila
fill with Orange Juice

GLASS: HIGHBALL
Build over ice and stir

Carmalita

1 part Vodka
1 part Coffee
1 part Frangelico®

GLASS: OLD-FASHIONED
Shake with ice and pour

Casablanca

1 part Vodka
½ part Southern Comfort®
½ part Amaretto
¾ part Orange Juice
splash Grenadine

GLASS: HIGHBALL
Shake with ice and pour

Caucasian

2 parts Vodka
1½ parts Coffee Liqueur
splash Cream

GLASS: OLD-FASHIONED

Shake with ice and strain

Celtic Comrade

1 part Coffee Liqueur
1 part Drambuie®
1 part Irish Cream Liqueur
1 part Vodka

GLASS: HIGHBALL

*Shake with ice and strain
over ice*

Chattanooga

1½ parts Vodka
½ part Apricot Brandy
½ part Fresh Lime Juice
fill with Pineapple Juice

GLASS: OLD-FASHIONED

*Shake with ice and strain
over ice*

Cheap Sunglasses

1 part Vodka
1 part Cranberry Juice Cocktail
1 part Lemon-Lime Soda

GLASS: OLD-FASHIONED

Build over ice and stir

Cherry Breeze

1 part Vodka
1 part Cherry Liqueur
1 part Pineapple Juice
1 part Cranberry Juice Cocktail

GLASS: HIGHBALL

*Shake with ice and strain
over ice*

Cherry Pucker

1 part Vodka
1 part Cherry Liqueur
1 part Cherry Juice
fill with Grapefruit Juice

GLASS: HIGHBALL

Build over ice and stir

Chocolate-Covered Banana

1 part Vodka
1 part Crème de Cacao (Dark)
1 part Crème de Banana
1 part Cream

GLASS: HIGHBALL

Shake with ice and pour

Cinnamon Pussycat

1 part Vodka
1 part Cinnamon Schnapps
1 part Cherry Juice
fill with Pineapple Juice

GLASS: HIGHBALL

Build over ice and stir

City Lights

1 part Vodka
1 part Raspberry Liqueur
1 part Cherry Juice
fill with Lemonade

GLASS: HIGHBALL

Build over ice and stir

Clamdigger

1 part Vodka
½ part Clamato®
splash Worchestershire Sauce
dash Salt
dash Pepper
1 Lime Wedge

GLASS: HIGHBALL

Shake with ice and pour

Clockwork Orange

2 parts Vodka
2 parts Orange Juice
1½ parts Peach Schnapps
splash Campari®

GLASS: HIGHBALL

Shake with ice and strain over ice

Clueless

2 parts Vodka
1 part Orange Juice
1 part Strawberry Juice
fill with Lemon-Lime Soda

GLASS: HIGHBALL

Build over ice and stir

Coastline

1 part Blue Curaçao
1 part Vodka
fill with Pineapple Juice
splash Lemon-Lime Soda

GLASS: HIGHBALL

Build over ice and stir

Cocaine Lady

½ part Vodka
½ part Amaretto
½ part Coffee Liqueur
1 part Cream
fill with Cola

GLASS: HIGHBALL

Build over ice and stir

Cocaine Shooter

1½ parts Vodka
¾ part Raspberry Liqueur
½ part Southern Comfort®
1 part Orange Juice
1 part Cranberry Juice Cocktail

GLASS: OLD-FASHIONED

Shake with ice and strain

Coconut Apple Pie

1 part Vodka
1 part Coconut-Flavored Rum
fill with Apple Juice

GLASS: HIGHBALL

Shake with ice and pour

Cold Fusion

1 part Vodka
1 part Triple Sec
½ part Melon Liqueur
1½ parts Sour Mix
½ part Fresh Lime Juice

GLASS: HIGHBALL

Shake with ice and strain over ice

Colorado Kool-Aid®

1 part Vodka
1 part Southern Comfort®
½ part Sloe Gin
1 part Amaretto
1 part Orange Juice
2 parts Cranberry Juice Cocktail
splash Lemon-Lime Soda

GLASS: HIGHBALL

Build over ice and stir

Cool Jerk

1 part Vodka
1 part Amaretto
2 parts Orange Juice
1 part Lemon-Lime Soda

GLASS: HIGHBALL

Build over ice and stir

Cool Running

1 part Vodka
1 part Blue Curaçao
fill with Lemonade
splash Cola

GLASS: HIGHBALL

Build over ice and stir

Cool Summer

1 part Vodka
1 part Peach Schnapps
1 part Cherry Juice
1 part Lemonade
1 part Orange Juice

GLASS: HIGHBALL
Build over ice and stir

Cordial Daisy

1 part Vodka
1 part Cherry Liqueur
1 part Lemonade
1 part Club Soda

GLASS: HIGHBALL
Build over ice and stir

The Cornell

1 part Vodka
½ part Watermelon Schnapps
½ part Sour Mix

GLASS: HIGHBALL
Shake with ice and strain over ice

Crack Whore

1 part Vodka
1 part Triple Sec
fill with Orange Soda

GLASS: HIGHBALL
Build over ice and stir

Cranberry Lemondrop

1 part Vodka
1 part Triple Sec
1 part Lemonade
1 part Cranberry Juice Cocktail

GLASS: HIGHBALL
Shake with ice and pour

Cran-Collins

1½ parts Vodka
2 parts Cranberry Juice Cocktail
2 parts Collins Mix

GLASS: OLD-FASHIONED
Shake with ice and strain over ice

Cranilla Dew

1 part Vanilla-Flavored Vodka
1 part Cranberry Juice Cocktail
1 part Mountain Dew®

GLASS: HIGHBALL

Build over ice and stir

Crazy Orgasm

1 part Vodka
1 part Triple Sec
1 part Cranberry Juice Cocktail
1 part Orange Juice

GLASS: HIGHBALL

Shake with ice and pour

Creamy Mimi

1 part Vodka
1 part Sweet Vermouth
2 splashes Crème de Cacao (White)
2 splashes Triple Sec

GLASS: HIGHBALL

Shake with ice and pour

Creeping Death

1 part Vodka
1 part Extra Dry Vermouth
dash Salt
fill with Orange Juice

GLASS: HIGHBALL

Shake with ice and pour

Crème d'Amour

1 part Vodka
1 part Crème de Banana
splash Cherry Brandy
1 part Pineapple Juice
splash Cream

GLASS: HIGHBALL

Shake with ice and pour

Critical Mass

1 part Vodka
1 part Blue Curaçao
1 part Cherry Juice
fill with Lemonade

GLASS: HIGHBALL

Build over ice and stir

The Crown Cherry

1½ parts Crown Royal® Whiskey
1 part Cherry Brandy
½ part Cherry Vodka
fill with Cherry Cola

GLASS: HIGHBALL

Build over ice and stir

Cry No More

1 part Vodka
1 part Cherry Brandy
1½ parts Orange Juice
fill with Lemon-Lime Soda

GLASS: HIGHBALL

Build over ice and stir

Crypto Nugget

¾ part Sour Apple Schnapps
½ part Vodka
¼ part Blue Curaçao
¼ part Sweetened Lime Juice

GLASS: WHISKEY SOUR

Shake with ice and pour

Crystal de Amour

1½ parts Vodka
½ part Parfait Amour

GLASS: HIGHBALL

Build over ice and stir

Danini

2 parts Vodka
1 part Lime Cordial
fill with Cola

GLASS: HIGHBALL

Build over ice and stir

Danish Kiss

1½ parts Vanilla-Flavored Vodka
½ part Amaretto
2 parts Orange Juice
fill with Red Bull® Energy Drink

{ GLASS: OLD-FASHIONED
Build over ice and stir

Danish Slammer

1½ parts Vodka
1½ parts Kirschwasser
1 part Aquavit

{ GLASS: OLD-FASHIONED
Shake with ice and strain

Dark Eyes

1 part Vodka
¼ part Blackberry Brandy
splash Sweetened Lime Juice

{ GLASS: BRANDY SNIFTER
Shake with ice and strain

Daytona 501

1½ parts Dark Rum
½ part Vodka
½ part Triple Sec
2 parts Orange Juice

{ GLASS: HIGHBALL
Shake with ice and pour

Dead Bitches

1 part Vodka
1 part Canadian Mist®
1 part Jack Daniel's®
1 part Coffee Liqueur

{ GLASS: HIGHBALL
Shake with ice and pour

Deep Pearl Diver

1 part Vodka
1 part Melon Liqueur
1 part Coconut-Flavored Rum
fill with Cream

{ GLASS: HIGHBALL
Shake with ice and pour

Denver Bulldog

1 part Vodka
1 part Coffee Liqueur
2/3 part Cream
1/3 part Lemon-Lime Soda

GLASS: HIGHBALL

Shake with ice and pour

Desert Shield

1½ parts Vodka
½ part Cranberry Liqueur
fill with Cranberry Juice Cocktail

GLASS: HIGHBALL

Shake with ice and pour

Devotion

1 part Watermelon Schnapps
1 part Apple-Flavored Vodka
fill with Lemon-Lime Soda

GLASS: HIGHBALL

Build over ice and stir

Dictator

1 part Vodka
2/3 part Cherry Brandy
splash Apricot Brandy

GLASS: HIGHBALL

Build over ice and stir

Dirty Ashtray

½ part Gin
½ part Vodka
½ part Light Rum
½ part Tequila
½ part Blue Curaçao
½ part Grenadine
1½ parts Pineapple Juice
2 parts Sour Mix

GLASS: HIGHBALL

Shake with ice and pour

Dirty Bastard

1½ parts Vodka
½ part Blackberry Brandy
splash Lime Juice

GLASS: HIGHBALL
Shake with ice and strain

Dirty Girl Scout

1 part Irish Cream Liqueur
1 part Coffee Liqueur
1 part Vodka
splash Crème de Menthe (Green)

GLASS: HIGHBALL
Shake with ice and pour

Dirty Momma

1 part Coffee Liqueur
1 part Brandy
1 part Vodka
fill with Milk

GLASS: HIGHBALL
Build over ice and stir

Dizzy Blue

1 part Vodka
1 part Lemon-Lime Soda
½ part Blue Curaçao
½ part Kiwi Schnapps
½ part Lychee Liqueur

GLASS: HIGHBALL
Build over ice and stir

Dog House Dew

3 parts Vodka
fill with Mountain Dew®
3 splashes Lemon Juice

GLASS: HIGHBALL
Build over ice and stir

Dollar Bill

1 part Vodka
1 part Melon Liqueur
½ part Lime Cordial

GLASS: OLD-FASHIONED
Shake with ice and pour

Drag Queen

½ part Triple Sec
1 part Vodka
dash Angostura® Bitters
dash Salt

GLASS: HIGHBALL

Shake with ice and pour

Dragon Breath

2 parts Vodka
1 part Ouzo
½ part Jägermeister®

GLASS: HIGHBALL

Shake with ice and pour

Dragon Slayer

½ part Vodka
½ part Coconut-Flavored Rum
¾ part Blueberry Schnapps
¼ part Blue Curaçao
1 part Pineapple Juice
1 part Orange Juice
fill with Lemon-Lime Soda
splash Grenadine

GLASS: WHISKEY SOUR

Shake with ice and pour

Dreamsicle®

1 part Vodka
1 part Cherry Juice
1 part Orange Juice
1 part Pineapple Juice
splash Cream

GLASS: HIGHBALL

Shake with ice and pour

Drink of the Gods

2 parts Vodka
1 part Blueberry Schnapps
1 part Pineapple Juice

GLASS: HIGHBALL

Shake with ice and pour

Drunken Monkey's Lunch

1 part Banana Liqueur
1 part Coffee Liqueur
1 part Vodka
fill with Milk

GLASS: OLD-FASHIONED

Build over ice and stir

Dry Hump

1 part Vodka
1 part Coffee Liqueur
1 part Amaretto

GLASS: HIGHBALL

Shake with ice and pour

Easter Bunny

1½ parts Crème de Cacao (Dark)
½ part Vodka
splash Chocolate Syrup
splash Cherry Brandy

GLASS: OLD-FASHIONED

*Shake with ice and strain
over ice*

Edison

1 part Strawberry Liqueur
1 part Vodka
1 part Grand Marnier®
splash Grapefruit Juice
fill with Lemon-Lime Soda

GLASS: HIGHBALL

Build over ice and stir

The Eel Skin

1 part Coconut-Flavored Rum
½ part Citrus-Flavored Vodka
2 parts Pineapple Juice
½ part Smirnoff® Citrus Twist
1 part Midori®

GLASS: OLD-FASHIONED

Shake with ice and strain

The Egret

2 parts Vodka
2 parts Apple Juice
1 part Cola

GLASS: HIGHBALL
Build over ice and stir

Eight-Inch Tongue

1 part Southern Comfort®
1 part Vodka
1 part Peach Schnapps
1 part Brandy
1 part Amaretto
fill with Cranberry Juice Cocktail

GLASS: HIGHBALL
Shake with ice and pour

Electric Dreams

1 part Vodka
1 part Amaretto
1 part Lemonade
1 part Orange Juice

GLASS: HIGHBALL
Shake with ice and pour

Electric Jam

1¼ parts Vodka
½ part Blue Curaçao
2 parts Sour Mix
2 parts Lemon-Lime Soda

GLASS: HIGHBALL
Shake with ice and pour

Elmo

1 part Southern Comfort®
1 part Amaretto
1 part Vodka

GLASS: HIGHBALL
Shake with ice and pour

Endless Summer

1 part Vodka
1 part Peach Schnapps
1 part Strawberry Daiquiri Mix
2 parts Lemonade
1 part Orange Juice

GLASS: HIGHBALL

Shake with ice and pour

Fairy Godmother

1 part Amaretto
1 part Vodka

GLASS: HIGHBALL

Build over ice and stir

Fantasia

1¼ parts Orange-Flavored Vodka
¾ part Peach Schnapps
1 Lemon Twist
fill with Orange Soda

GLASS: HIGHBALL

Build over ice and stir

Fat Hooker

1 part Vodka
½ part Peach Schnapps
½ part Coconut-Flavored Rum
fill with Orange Juice

GLASS: HIGHBALL

Build over ice and stir

Fat Kid on the Rocks

1 part Goldschläger®
1 part Tequila
1 part Vodka
1 part Water

GLASS: HIGHBALL

Shake with ice and pour

Federation

1 part Vodka
1½ parts Peach Schnapps
2 parts Cranberry Juice Cocktail
fill with Lemon-Lime Soda

GLASS: HIGHBALL

Build over ice and stir

Fickle Pickle

¾ part Vodka
¾ part Melon Liqueur
¼ part Crown Royal® Whiskey
½ part Triple Sec
splash Sour Mix

GLASS: HIGHBALL

*Shake with ice and strain
over ice*

Fireball Glory

1 part Cinnamon Schnapps
1 part Vodka
3 parts Cranberry Juice Cocktail

GLASS: HIGHBALL

Shake with ice and pour

Firefly

1¼ parts Vodka
2 parts Grapefruit Juice
splash Grenadine

GLASS: HIGHBALL

Build over ice and stir

Flying Fortress

1 part Brandy
¾ part Vodka
½ part Absinthe
½ part Triple Sec

GLASS: WHITE WINE

Shake with ice and pour

Foxhaven Surprise

1½ parts Vodka
1 part Gin
¼ part Grenadine
2 parts Orange Juice

{ GLASS: HIGHBALL

Shake with ice and strain

French Sailor

1 part Cointreau®
1 part Vodka
1 Sugar Cube

{ GLASS: HIGHBALL

Build over ice and stir

Friday Harbor

1 part Vodka
1 part Peach Schnapps
1 part Cranberry Juice Cocktail
1 part Grapefruit Juice

{ GLASS: HIGHBALL

Build over ice and stir

Froot Loop®

½ part Vodka
½ part Cherry Brandy
1 part Apple Brandy
1 part Orange Juice

{ GLASS: OLD-FASHIONED

Shake with ice and pour

Fruit Grenade

1 part Blackberry Liqueur
½ part Light Rum
1 part Orange-Flavored Vodka
½ part Sour Mix
fill with Cranberry Juice Cocktail

{ GLASS: HIGHBALL

Build over ice and stir

The Full Monty

1 part Vodka
½ part Pisang Ambon® Liqueur
½ part Passoa®
fill with Orange Juice
splash Grenadine

GLASS: HIGHBALL
Build over ice and stir

Fury

1 part Vodka
1 part Spiced Rum
splash Sour Mix
2 parts Orange Juice

GLASS: WHISKEY SOUR
Build over ice and stir

Fuzzy Balls

½ part Peach Schnapps
½ part Vodka
½ part Melon Liqueur
1½ parts Grapefruit Juice
1½ parts Cranberry Juice Cocktail

GLASS: OLD-FASHIONED
Build over ice and stir

Fuzzy Navel

1 part Vodka
1 part Peach Schnapps
fill with Orange Juice

GLASS: HIGHBALL
Build over ice and stir

Fuzzy Peach

1 part Vodka
1 part Peach Schnapps
fill with Grapefruit Juice
splash Grenadine

GLASS: OLD-FASHIONED
Shake with ice and pour

Gadzooks

1 part Vodka
1 part Raspberry Liqueur
1 part Cherry Juice
2 parts Lemonade
1 part Cola

GLASS: HIGHBALL

Build over ice and stir

Gangbuster Punch

1½ parts Vodka
1½ parts Peach Schnapps
1 part Cranberry Juice Cocktail
splash Lemon-Lime Soda

GLASS: HIGHBALL

Shake with ice and pour

Geezer!

1 part Citrus-Flavored Vodka
1 part Triple Sec
½ part Lime Juice

GLASS: WHISKEY SOUR

Shake with ice and strain over ice

Gene Splice

1 part Vodka
½ part Triple Sec
½ part Raspberry Liqueur
2 parts Pineapple Juice
¼ part Lime Juice

GLASS: HIGHBALL

Shake with ice and pour

Get Laid

1 part Vodka
¾ part Raspberry Liqueur
fill with Pineapple Juice
splash Cranberry Juice Cocktail

GLASS: HIGHBALL

Build over ice and stir

Ghost

2 parts Vanilla-Flavored Vodka
1 part Jack Daniel's®
fill with Cream Soda

GLASS: HIGHBALL

Build over ice and stir

Godmother

3 parts Vodka
1 part Amaretto

GLASS: HIGHBALL

Shake with ice and pour

Gooseberry Jam

1 part Vodka
1 part Southern Comfort®
2 parts Blue Curaçao
fill with Orange Juice

GLASS: HIGHBALL

Build over ice and stir

Grainne

1 part Vodka
1 part Maraschino Liqueur
1 part Crème de Banana
splash Lemon Juice
splash Orange Juice

GLASS: HIGHBALL

Shake with ice and strain over ice

Grape Expectations

1 part Melon Liqueur
1 part Vodka
1 part Grape Juice (Red)
1 part Lemon-Lime Soda

GLASS: HIGHBALL

Build over ice and stir

Grape Rainstorm

1 part Vodka
1 part Blue Curaçao
1 part Pineapple Juice
1 part Lemon-Lime Soda

GLASS: HIGHBALL

Build over ice and stir

Grateful Dead

½ part Gin
½ part Vodka
½ part Triple Sec
½ part Rum
2 parts Sour Mix
1 part Raspberry Liqueur

GLASS: HIGHBALL

Shake with ice and pour

Greek Passion

2 parts Vodka
⅔ part Vanilla Liqueur
⅔ part Passion Fruit Liqueur
splash Triple Sec
fill with Orange Juice

GLASS: HIGHBALL

Build over ice and stir

Green Babe

1½ parts Citrus-Flavored Rum
1½ parts Vodka
1 part Melon Liqueur
fill with Cranberry Juice Cocktail
splash Sour Mix

GLASS: HIGHBALL

Build over ice and stir

Green Cow

1 part Vodka
1 part Pisang Ambon® Liqueur
½ part Milk
fill with Lemon-Lime Soda

GLASS: OLD-FASHIONED

Build over ice and stir

Green Delight

1 part Vodka
1 part Pisang Ambon® Liqueur
1 part Lemon-Lime Soda
1 part Orange Juice

GLASS: HIGHBALL
Build over ice and stir

Green Demon

1 part Vodka
1 part Rum
1 part Melon Liqueur
fill with Lemonade
1 Maraschino Cherry

GLASS: HIGHBALL
Build over ice and stir

Green-Eyed Lady

1 part Vodka
1 part Melon Liqueur
1 part Lemonade
1 part Lemon-Lime Soda

GLASS: HIGHBALL
Build over ice and stir

Green Hornet

1½ parts Vodka
½ part Sweetened Lime Juice
splash Crème de Menthe (Green)

GLASS: HIGHBALL
Shake with ice and strain

Green Killer

1 part Vodka
1 part Crème de Banana
1 part Blue Curaçao
fill with Orange Juice

GLASS: RED WINE
Shake with ice and pour

Green Sea

1 part Crème de Menthe (Green)
1 part Vodka
1 part Dry Vermouth

GLASS: OLD-FASHIONED
*Shake with ice and strain
over ice*

Green Slime

2 parts Vodka
1 part Limeade
1 part Orange Juice

GLASS: HIGHBALL

Build over ice and stir

Gremlin Fixer

1 part Vodka
1 part Dry Vermouth
1 part Apricot Brandy
1 part Pisang Ambon® Liqueur
fill with Pineapple Juice

GLASS: OLD-FASHIONED

Build over ice and stir

G-Strings

1 part 151-Proof Rum
1 part Vodka
1 part Grenadine
1 part Pineapple Juice

GLASS: HIGHBALL

*Shake with ice and strain
over ice*

GTV

1 part Gin
1 part Tequila
1 part Vodka

GLASS: WHISKEY SOUR

Shake with ice and pour

Guatacarazo

1 part Dark Rum
½ part Vodka
¼ part Crème de Banana
¼ part Pineapple Juice
splash Lemon Juice

GLASS: OLD-FASHIONED

*Shake with ice and strain
over ice*

Hairy Happy Trail

1 part Vodka
1 part RedRum®
½ part Limoncello
½ part Lime Juice
fill with Orange Juice

GLASS: HIGHBALL

Build over ice and stir

Hairy Navel

1 part Vodka
1 part Peach Schnapps
fill with Orange Juice

GLASS: HIGHBALL

Build over ice and stir

Halloween

2 parts Vodka
1 part Scotch
fill with Orange Juice

GLASS: HIGHBALL

Shake with ice and strain over ice

Harbor Lights

1 part Vodka
2 parts Peach Nectar
2 parts Lemonade
1 part Cranberry Juice Cocktail

GLASS: HIGHBALL

Shake with ice and pour

Harlequin Frappé

1 part Vodka
1 part Crème de Cacao (Dark)
1 part Triple Sec

GLASS: OLD-FASHIONED

Build over ice and stir

Harvey Cowpuncher

1 part Vodka
½ part Galliano®
fill with Milk

GLASS: HIGHBALL

Build over ice and stir

Hawaiian Volcano

1 part Amaretto
1 part Southern Comfort®
½ part Vodka
2 parts Orange Juice
1 part Pineapple Juice
1 Maraschino Cherry

GLASS: HIGHBALL

Build over ice and stir

Headspin

1 part Vodka
1 part Crème de Banana
1 part Apricot Brandy
fill with Orange Juice

GLASS: OLD-FASHIONED

Shake with ice and pour

Hell Raiser

1 part Jack Daniel's®
1 part Tequila
1 part Vodka

GLASS: HIGHBALL

Shake with ice and strain over ice

High Roller

1½ parts Vodka
¾ part Grand Marnier®
fill with Orange Juice
splash Grenadine

GLASS: HIGHBALL

Build over ice

Hollywood

1½ parts Vodka
1½ parts Raspberry Liqueur
1 part Triple Sec
splash Sweetened Lime Juice

GLASS: HIGHBALL

Shake with ice and strain over ice

Hoo Doo

1 part Southern Comfort®
1 part Vodka
½ part Orange Juice
½ part Lime Juice
splash Peppermint Schnapps
splash Lemon-Lime Soda

GLASS: OLD-FASHIONED

Shake with ice and strain over ice

Hop Frog

2 parts Vodka
1 part Crème de Menthe (Green)
1 part Dry Vermouth

GLASS: OLD-FASHIONED

Shake with ice and strain over ice

Horny Toad

2 parts Vodka
½ part Triple Sec
fill with Lemonade

GLASS: HIGHBALL

Shake with ice and strain over ice

Hot Summer Breeze

1 part Vodka
1 part Orange Juice
1 part Ginger Ale

GLASS: HIGHBALL

Build over ice and stir

Hula Hoop

1 part Vodka
1 part Peach Schnapps
1 part Lemonade
1 part Orange Juice
1 part Cranberry Juice Cocktail

GLASS: HIGHBALL

Shake with ice and pour

Hulkster

1 part Vodka
1 part Melon Liqueur
1 part Kiwi Schnapps
fill with Lemon-Lime Soda

GLASS: HIGHBALL

Build over ice and stir

Ice Blue Aqua Velva®

¾ part Vodka
¾ part Gin
½ part Blue Curaçao
fill with Lemon-Lime Soda

GLASS: OLD-FASHIONED

Build over ice and stir

Ice Breaker

1 part Peppermint Schnapps
1 part Vodka

GLASS: HIGHBALL

Shake with ice and pour

Incredible Hulk®

2 parts Melon Liqueur
1 part Vodka
fill with Mountain Dew®

GLASS: HIGHBALL

Build over ice and stir

Indian Summer

1 part Vodka
1 part Coffee Liqueur
fill with Pineapple Juice

GLASS: HIGHBALL

Shake with ice and strain over ice

Irish Curdling Cow

1 part Irish Cream Liqueur
1 part Vodka
1 part Irish Whiskey
fill with Orange Juice

GLASS: HIGHBALL

Build over ice and stir

Irish Russian

1 part Vodka
1 part Coffee Liqueur
splash Cola
fill with Guinness® Stout

GLASS: HIGHBALL

Build in the glass with no ice

Iron Butterfly

1 part Vodka
1 part Coffee Liqueur
1 part Irish Cream Liqueur

GLASS: HIGHBALL

Shake with ice and strain

Iron Curtain

2 parts Vodka
½ part Apricot Brandy

GLASS: HIGHBALL

Shake with ice and strain over ice

Italian Ice

1 part Vodka
1 part Blue Curaçao
1 part Raspberry Liqueur
1 part Sour Mix
fill with Lemon-Lime Soda

GLASS: WHISKEY SOUR

Build over ice

Jackhammer

1½ parts Vodka
fill with Pineapple Juice

GLASS: HIGHBALL

Build over ice and stir

Jacobs Haze

1 part Jägermeister®
1 part Currant-Flavored Vodka
fill with Red Bull® Energy Drink

GLASS: HIGHBALL

Build over ice and stir

Jaffa Frost

1 part Vodka
1 part Crème de Cacao (Dark)
1 part Triple Sec

GLASS: HIGHBALL

Shake with ice and strain over ice

Jaguar

1 part Vodka
1 part Crème de Banana
fill with Lemon-Lime Soda

GLASS: HIGHBALL

Build over ice and stir

Jamaican Mountain Bike

1 part Vodka
1 part Melon Liqueur
1 part Crème de Banana
1 part Coconut-Flavored Rum
fill with Cream

GLASS: HIGHBALL

Shake with ice and strain over ice

Jazzy Green

1 part Citrus-Flavored Vodka
1 part Blue Curaçao
1 part Peach Schnapps
1 part Orange Juice
1 part Pineapple Juice

GLASS: HIGHBALL

Shake with ice and pour

Jericho's Breeze

1 part Vodka
¾ part Blue Curaçao
2½ parts Sour Mix
splash Lemon-Lime Soda
splash Orange Juice

GLASS: HIGHBALL

Build over ice and stir

Jersey Shore Cherry Lemonade

1½ parts Vodka
1¼ parts Sour Mix
dash Sugar
fill with Lemon-Lime Soda
splash Grenadine

GLASS: HIGHBALL

Build over ice and stir

Jitterbug

2 parts Gin
1½ parts Vodka
3 splashes Grenadine
splash Lime Juice
dash Sugar
3 splashes Simple Syrup
fill with Seltzer Water

GLASS: HIGHBALL

Build over ice and stir

Juice Juice

1 part Vodka
1 part Triple Sec
1 part Grape Juice (Red)
1 part Orange Juice
1 part Cranberry Juice Cocktail

GLASS: HIGHBALL

Build over ice and stir

Juicy Fruit Remix

½ part Banana Liqueur
½ part Peach Schnapps
½ part Vodka
½ part Cranberry Juice Cocktail
1 part Lemonade
1½ parts Orange Juice

GLASS: HIGHBALL

Shake with ice and pour

Just Like Romeo

1 part Vodka
1 part Raspberry Liqueur
1 part Strawberry Daiquiri Mix
2 parts Lemonade
1 part Orange Juice

GLASS: HIGHBALL

Build over ice and stir

Kansas City Ice Water

¾ part Gin
¾ part Vodka
½ part Lime Juice
fill with Lemon-Lime Soda

GLASS: HIGHBALL

Build over ice and stir

Karen's Melons

1½ parts Melon Liqueur
1 part Vodka
fill with Lemon-Lime Soda

GLASS: HIGHBALL

Build over ice and stir

Karma Chameleon

1 part Vodka
1 part Peach Schnapps
fill with Lemon-Lime Soda
splash Grenadine

GLASS: HIGHBALL

Build over ice and stir

Key West Lemonade

1 part Vodka
1 part Sour Mix
splash Lemon-Lime Soda
splash Cranberry Juice Cocktail

GLASS: OLD-FASHIONED

Build over ice and stir

Kiwi Pussycat

1 part Vodka
1 part Kiwi Schnapps
1 part Cherry Juice
fill with Pineapple Juice

GLASS: HIGHBALL

Build over ice and stir

Kiwi Screwdriver

1 part Vodka
1 part Kiwi Schnapps
fill with Orange Juice

GLASS: HIGHBALL

Build over ice and stir

Klingon Battlejuice

2 parts Vodka
1 part Lemon Juice
splash Orange Juice

GLASS: OLD-FASHIONED

Build over ice and stir

Kokomo

1 part Vodka
1 part Triple Sec
1 part Margarita Mix
1 part Orange Juice
1 part Cranberry Juice Cocktail

GLASS: HIGHBALL

Shake with ice and pour

Kosak's Milk

1 part Vodka
1 part Coffee Liqueur
fill with Milk

GLASS: HIGHBALL

Shake with ice and pour

K-Otic

1½ parts Vodka
1½ parts Grand Marnier®
1 part Lemon Juice

GLASS: HIGHBALL

Shake with ice and strain over ice

Krypto Kami

1 part Currant-Flavored Vodka
1 part Melon Liqueur
1 part Peach Schnapps
1 part Pineapple Juice
1 part Sour Mix

GLASS: HIGHBALL

Shake with ice and strain over ice

Kryptonite

1 part Vodka
½ part Melon Liqueur
fill with Pineapple Juice

GLASS: HIGHBALL

Shake with ice and strain over ice

Kurant Affair

1 part Currant-Flavored Vodka
1 part Orange Juice
1 part Cranberry Juice Cocktail

GLASS: WHISKEY SOUR

Shake with ice and strain over ice

La Bamba

1 part Vodka
1 part Frangelico®
fill with Orange Juice

GLASS: HIGHBALL

Shake with ice and strain over ice

Lacy Blue

1 part Vodka
1 part Blue Curaçao
1 part Cream
1 part Orange Juice
1 part Pineapple Juice

GLASS: HIGHBALL

Shake with ice and strain over ice

Lemon Loop

2 parts Citrus-Flavored Vodka
½ part Melon Liqueur
½ part Kiwi Schnapps
2 parts Sour Mix
2 parts Lemon-Lime Soda
splash Lemon Juice
dash Sugar

GLASS: HIGHBALL
Build over ice and stir

Lemonado Denado

1 part Citrus-Flavored Vodka
1 part Bacardi® Limón Rum
splash Grenadine
fill with Lemon-Lime Soda
splash Sour Mix

GLASS: HIGHBALL
Build over ice and stir

Lethal Weapon Shooter

1 part Vodka
½ part Peach Schnapps
splash Lime Cordial

GLASS: OLD-FASHIONED
Build over ice and stir

Lick Me Silly

1 part Blue Curaçao
1 part Cointreau®
1 part Gin
1 part Vodka
1 part Melon Liqueur
fill with Lemonade

GLASS: HIGHBALL
Shake with ice and pour

Lightning Lemonade

1 part Citrus-Flavored Vodka
1 part Triple Sec
fill with Lemonade
splash Sour Mix

GLASS: HIGHBALL
Build over ice and stir

Lollapalooza

1 part Vodka
1 part Triple Sec
1 part Lemonade
1 part Cola

GLASS: HIGHBALL

Build over ice and stir

Love Junk

1 part Vodka
¾ part Peach Schnapps
¾ part Melon Liqueur
fill with Apple Juice

GLASS: OLD-FASHIONED

Build over ice and stir

Love Potion Number 9

1 part Vodka
1 part Raspberry Liqueur
1 part Lemonade
1 part Orange Juice
1 part Cranberry Juice Cocktail

GLASS: HIGHBALL

Shake with ice and pour

Lucky Lemon

1 part Vodka
fill with Lemon-Lime Soda
splash Lemonade

GLASS: OLD-FASHIONED

Build over ice and stir

Ludwig and the Gang

1 part Añejo Rum
1 part Vodka
½ part Amaretto
½ part Southern Comfort®
dash Bitters

GLASS: OLD-FASHIONED

Shake with ice and strain

Lulu

1 part Vodka
1 part Light Rum
1 part Peach Schnapps
1 part Triple Sec
1 part Sour Mix

GLASS: HIGHBALL

Shake with ice and strain over ice. Garnish with a Maraschino Cherry.

Mad Hatter

1 part Vodka
1 part Peach Schnapps
2 parts Lemonade
1 part Cola

GLASS: HIGHBALL

Shake with ice and pour

Madras

1½ parts Vodka
4 parts Cranberry Juice Cocktail
1 part Orange Juice

GLASS: HIGHBALL

Shake with ice and pour

Magpie

1 part Cream
½ part Crème de Cacao (White)
1 part Melon Liqueur
1 part Vodka

GLASS: HIGHBALL

Shake with ice and strain

Malawi

1 part Vodka
½ part Coconut-Flavored Liqueur
½ part Passoã®
fill with Pineapple Juice

GLASS: HIGHBALL

Build over ice and stir

Man

²/₃ part Vodka
splash Grenadine
1½ part Mandarine Napoléon® Liqueur
²/₃ part Lemon Juice

GLASS: HIGHBALL

Build over ice and stir

Man Overboard

2 parts Vodka
½ part Melon Liqueur
1 part Raspberry Liqueur
fill with Pineapple Juice

GLASS: HIGHBALL

Shake with ice and strain over ice

March Hare

1 part Vodka
1 part Wild Berry Schnapps
2 parts Lemonade
1 part Cola

GLASS: HIGHBALL

Build over ice and stir

March Madness

1 part Peach Schnapps
1½ parts Vodka
1 part Triple Sec
fill with Gatorade®

GLASS: HIGHBALL

Build over ice and stir

Maserati®

1 part Citrus-Flavored Vodka
1 part Cranberry Juice Cocktail
fill with Lemon-Lime Soda

GLASS: HIGHBALL

Build over ice and stir

Masked Mirror

1 part Citrus-Flavored Vodka
1 part Blackberry Liqueur
2 parts Cranberry Juice Cocktail
2 parts Sour Mix
fill with Lemon-Lime Soda

GLASS: HIGHBALL

Build over ice and stir

Matisse

2½ parts Orange-Flavored Vodka
splash Raspberry Liqueur

GLASS: HIGHBALL

Shake with ice and strain over ice

Mattapoo Shooter

2 parts Vodka
1 part Melon Liqueur
1 part Grapefruit Juice
1 part Pineapple Juice

GLASS: OLD-FASHIONED

Shake with ice and strain

Mean Green Lovemaking Machine

1 part Vodka
1 part Melon Liqueur
1 part Blue Curaçao
fill with Orange Juice

GLASS: HIGHBALL

Shake with ice and pour

Mega Mixer

2 parts Vodka
1 part Cranberry Juice Cocktail
2 parts Lemonade

GLASS: HIGHBALL

Build over ice and stir

Melon Ball

1 part Vodka
1 part Melon Liqueur
fill with Pineapple Juice

GLASS: HIGHBALL

Shake with ice and strain over ice

Melon Citron

1 part Citrus-Flavored Vodka
¾ part Melon Liqueur
splash Raspberry Liqueur
1 part Grapefruit Juice

GLASS: OLD-FASHIONED

Shake with ice and strain over ice

Melon Snowball

¾ part Melon Liqueur
¾ part Citrus-Flavored Vodka
½ part Pineapple Juice
¼ part Cream

GLASS: OLD-FASHIONED

Shake with ice and strain over ice

Midnight

1 part Black Sambuca
1 part Vodka

GLASS: BRANDY SNIFTER

Build over ice

A Midsummer Night's Dream

2 parts Vodka
1 part Kirschwasser
½ part Strawberry Liqueur
2 parts Strawberry Puree

GLASS: HIGHBALL

Shake with ice and strain over ice

Mir

1 part Vodka
1 part Jack Daniel's®
fill with Cola

GLASS: HIGHBALL

Build over ice and stir

Moat Float

1 part Vodka
1 part Amaretto
fill with Cola

GLASS: WHITE WINE

Build over ice and stir

Monterey Bay

1 part Vodka
1 part Melon Liqueur
1 part Cherry Juice
1 part Banana Juice
fill with Orange Juice

GLASS: HIGHBALL

Shake with ice and pour

Moon River

1 part Vodka
1 part Blue Curaçao
²/₃ part Lemon Juice
fill with Grape Juice (White)

GLASS: HIGHBALL

Shake with ice and pour

Morango

1 part Vodka
1 part Strawberry Daiquiri Mix
1 part Lemonade
1 part Orange Juice
1 part Cranberry Juice Cocktail
1 part Wild Berry Schnapps

GLASS: HIGHBALL

Build over ice and stir

More Orgasms

1 part Irish Cream Liqueur
1 part Vodka
1 part Coconut-Flavored Rum

GLASS: HIGHBALL

Shake with ice and pour

Moscow Dawn

2 parts Vodka
1 part Crème de Menthe (White)
¼ part Triple Sec

GLASS: WHITE WINE

Shake with ice and strain

Mother

1 part Vodka
1 part Gin
1 part Sour Mix
1 part Grenadine

GLASS: HIGHBALL

Shake with ice and strain over ice

Mountain Cider High

1 part Vodka
1 part Apple Cider
1 part Mountain Dew®

GLASS: BEER MUG

Build over ice and stir

Mud Puddle

1 part Vanilla-Flavored Vodka
²/₃ part Coffee Liqueur
½ part Irish Cream Liqueur
1 part Cream

GLASS: HIGHBALL

Shake with ice and strain over ice

Mud Slide

2 parts Vodka
2 parts Coffee Liqueur
2 parts Irish Cream Liqueur

GLASS: HIGHBALL

Shake with ice and pour

Mustang Sally

1 part Vodka
1 part Strawberry Liqueur
1 part Raspberry Liqueur
fill with Lemonade

GLASS: HIGHBALL

Shake with ice and pour

Mutual Orgasm

2 parts Amaretto
1 part Crème de Cacao (White)
1 part Vodka
fill with Half and Half

GLASS: HIGHBALL

Shake with ice and pour

MVP

1 part Melon Liqueur
1 part Coconut-Flavored Rum
1 part Vodka
1 part Pineapple Juice

GLASS: HIGHBALL

Shake with ice and strain

Mystical Marquee

1 part Jack Daniel's®
1 part Peach Schnapps
1 part Vodka
fill with Lemon Juice

GLASS: HIGHBALL

Shake with ice and strain over ice

Nail Puller

2 parts Coffee Liqueur
1 part Vodka
fill with Dr Pepper®

GLASS: HIGHBALL

Build over ice and stir

National Aquarium

½ part Rum
½ part Vodka
½ part Gin
½ part Blue Curaçao
2 parts Sour Mix
fill with Lemon-Lime Soda

GLASS: HIGHBALL

Build over ice and stir

Navsky at Noon

1 part Vodka
1 part Blackberry Liqueur
1 part Orange Juice
½ part Lime Juice
splash Grenadine
fill with Sour Mix

GLASS: HIGHBALL

Shake with ice and strain over ice

Nazzy Baby

1 part Coconut-Flavored Rum
1 part Peach Schnapps
1 part Vodka
splash Lemon Juice
fill with Orange Juice

GLASS: HIGHBALL

Shake with ice and pour

Newport Punch

1 part Amaretto
1 part Peach Schnapps
1 part Southern Comfort®
1 part Ketel One® Vodka
splash Cranberry Juice Cocktail
splash Orange Juice

GLASS: HIGHBALL

Build over ice and stir

Nilla® Wafer

2 parts Vodka
2 parts Cream
½ part Vanilla Liqueur
½ dash Brown Sugar

GLASS: HIGHBALL

Shake with ice and strain over ice

Ninety-Nine Palms

1 part Vodka
1 part Peach Schnapps
1 part Piña Colada Mix
1 part Lemonade
1 part Pineapple Juice

GLASS: HIGHBALL

Shake with ice and pour

Noche de Phoof

1 part Vodka
½ part Light Rum
½ part Crown Royal® Whiskey
1 part Pineapple Juice
1 part Cranberry Juice Cocktail
splash Melon Liqueur

GLASS: HIGHBALL

Shake with ice and strain over ice

Nokia

1 part Blackberry Liqueur
½ part Vodka
1½ parts Milk
1 Egg Yolk

GLASS: CHAMPAGNE FLUTE
Shake with ice and strain

Nothing Is Eternal

1½ parts Orange-Flavored Vodka
½ part Apricot Brandy
½ part Lemon Juice
fill with Orange Juice
dash Bitters

GLASS: HIGHBALL
Build over ice and stir

Notre Dame Pick-Me-Up

1 part Vodka
1 part Light Rum
1 part Triple Sec
fill with Orange Juice
dash Powdered Sugar

GLASS: HIGHBALL
Build over ice and stir

Notte a Mosca

1½ parts Vodka
½ part Campari®
splash Blue Curaçao

GLASS: HIGHBALL
Shake with ice and strain over ice

Nuclear Screwdriver

1 part Vodka
1 part Grand Marnier®
fill with Orange Juice

GLASS: HIGHBALL
Build over ice and stir

Null and Void

1 part Vodka
½ part Wild Berry Schnapps
½ part Peach Schnapps
splash Southern Comfort®
fill with Fruit Punch

GLASS: HIGHBALL

Shake with ice and pour

Nutcracker

1 part Vodka
1 part Coffee Liqueur
1 part Irish Cream Liqueur
1 part Amaretto

GLASS: HIGHBALL

Shake with ice and strain over ice

Nutty Belgian

1 part Chocolate Liqueur
1 part Frangelico®
½ part Vodka

GLASS: OLD-FASHIONED

Shake with ice and strain over ice

Nutty Russian

1 part Vodka
1 part Frangelico®
1 part Coffee Liqueur

GLASS: HIGHBALL

Shake with ice and strain over ice

October Sky

1 part Vodka
½ part Wild Berry Schnapps
2 parts Lemonade
1 part Orange Juice

GLASS: HIGHBALL

Shake with ice and pour

Octopus in the Water

1 part Vodka
1 part Blue Curaçao
1 part Lemonade
1 part Margarita Mix
1 part Wild Berry Schnapps

GLASS: HIGHBALL
Build over ice and stir

Odwits

1½ parts Mescal
1½ parts Vodka
1 part Southern Comfort®
splash Galliano®
fill with Orange Juice

GLASS: HIGHBALL
Shake with ice and pour

Oil Spill

1 part Vodka
1 part Blue Curaçao
1 part Irish Cream Liqueur
fill with Cola

GLASS: HIGHBALL
Build over ice and stir

Okinawa Special

1 part Coconut-Flavored Rum
1 part Light Rum
1 part Vodka
1 part Orange Juice
1 part Pineapple Juice

GLASS: HIGHBALL
Shake with ice and pour

Old Dirty Surprise

1 part Vodka
½ part Bacardi® Limón Rum
½ part Melon Liqueur
fill with Pineapple Juice

GLASS: HIGHBALL
Shake with ice and strain over ice

Old Hag's Cackle

1 part Vodka
1 part Raspberry Liqueur
1 part Lemonade
1 part Cola

GLASS: HIGHBALL

Build over ice and stir

Old Pirate

1½ parts Vodka
1 part Coconut-Flavored Rum
1 part Irish Cream Liqueur
½ part Orange Juice
½ part Pineapple Juice
½ part Mango Juice

GLASS: OLD-FASHIONED

Shake with ice and pour

Old Spice®

1 part Gin
1 part Vodka
1 part Applejack

GLASS: WHISKEY SOUR

Shake with ice and strain over ice

Ooh-La-La

1 part Vodka
1 part Cherry Juice
1 part Piña Colada Mix
2 parts Lemonade
1 part Cola

GLASS: HIGHBALL

Build over ice and stir

Orange Bliss

1½ parts Orange-Flavored Vodka
1 part Grand Marnier®
fill with Orange Juice

GLASS: OLD-FASHIONED

Shake with ice and strain over ice

Orange Clockwork

1½ parts Orange-Flavored Vodka
½ part Triple Sec
½ part Orange Juice
¼ part Fresh Lime Juice

GLASS: OLD-FASHIONED

Shake with ice and strain over ice

Orange Smartie®

1 part Vodka
1 part Coffee Liqueur
1 part Triple Sec
fill with Orange Juice

GLASS: HIGHBALL

Shake with ice and pour

Orange Surprise

1 part Vodka
1 part Peach Schnapps
2 parts Sour Mix
fill with Lemon-Lime Soda

GLASS: HIGHBALL

Build over ice and stir

Orange Whip

1 part Rum
1 part Vodka
1 part Cream
fill with Orange Juice

GLASS: HIGHBALL

Shake with ice and strain over ice

Orchid

1 part Vodka
1 part Peach Schnapps
1 part Cherry Juice
1 part Lemonade
1 part Orange Juice
1 part Cranberry Juice Cocktail

GLASS: HIGHBALL

Shake with ice and pour

Orlando Sun

1 part Light Rum
½ part Vodka
½ part Grand Marnier®
1 part Orange Juice
¼ part Lemon Juice

{ GLASS: HIGHBALL

Shake with ice and strain over ice

Out of the Blue

½ part Vodka
½ part Blueberry Schnapps
½ part Blue Curaçao
1 part Club Soda
splash Sour Mix

{ GLASS: HIGHBALL

Build over ice and stir

Outrigger

1 part Peach Brandy
1 part Vodka
1 part Pineapple Juice
splash Lime Juice

{ GLASS: OLD-FASHIONED

Shake with ice and strain over ice

Oxymoron

1 part Vodka
½ part Lemon Juice
splash Honey

{ GLASS: OLD-FASHIONED

Shake with ice and strain over ice

P.T.O.

1½ parts Dark Rum
½ part Vodka
½ part Triple Sec
fill with Orange Juice

{ GLASS: HIGHBALL

Shake with ice and strain over ice

Pacific Blue

1 part Crème de Banana
1 part Blue Curaçao
splash Vodka
splash Coconut-Flavored Liqueur

GLASS: HIGHBALL

Build over ice and stir

Paisano

1 part Vodka
1 part Frangelico®
fill with Milk

GLASS: HIGHBALL

Shake with ice and pour

Pajama Jackhammer

1 part Vodka
1 part Blue Curaçao
1 part Peach Schnapps
fill with Pineapple Juice

GLASS: HIGHBALL

Shake with ice and strain over ice

Palisades Park

1 part Vodka
1 part Peach Schnapps
1 part Banana Juice
2 parts Lemonade
1 part Orange Juice

GLASS: HIGHBALL

Shake with ice and pour

Paradise Bliss

1½ parts Vodka
1½ parts Coconut-Flavored Rum
1 part Cranberry Juice Cocktail
1 part Pineapple Juice

GLASS: HIGHBALL

Shake with ice and pour

Parrot

1 part Vodka
1 part Gin
3 splashes Tabasco® Sauce

GLASS: OLD-FASHIONED

Shake with ice and strain over ice

Partly Cloudy

1 part Vodka
1 part Blue Curaçao
1 part Piña Colada Mix
fill with Lemonade

GLASS: HIGHBALL

Shake with ice and pour

Passion Cup

2 parts Vodka
2 parts Orange Juice
1 part Passion Fruit Juice
½ part Pineapple Juice
½ part Coconut Cream

GLASS: WHITE WINE

Shake with ice and strain over ice

Pavlova

1 part Vodka
½ part Crème de Cacao (White)
½ part Cream

GLASS: OLD-FASHIONED

Shake with ice and strain over ice

Peach Crush

1 part Vodka
1 part Peach Schnapps
1½ parts Sour Mix

GLASS: OLD-FASHIONED

Shake with ice and strain over ice

Peacher

⅔ part Peach Schnapps
⅔ part Citrus-Flavored Vodka
1 part Lemon-Lime Soda
1 part Club Soda

GLASS: HIGHBALL

Build over ice and stir

Pee Wee's Beamer

¾ part Vodka
¾ part Coconut-Flavored Rum
½ part Orange Juice

GLASS: OLD-FASHIONED

Shake with ice and strain over ice

Pentecostal

1 part Vodka
1 part Bourbon
fill with Lemon-Lime Soda

GLASS: WHISKEY SOUR

Shake with ice and pour

Perestroika

1½ parts Vodka
1 part Vanilla Liqueur
1 part Crème de Cacao (White)

GLASS: HIGHBALL

Shake with ice and strain over ice

Persian Prince

1 part Vodka
1 part Citrus-Flavored Rum
1 part Sour Mix
1 part Orange Juice
1 part Lemon-Lime Soda

GLASS: HIGHBALL

Shake with ice and strain over ice

Petit Caprice

1 part Vodka
½ part Melon Liqueur
½ part Limoncello
½ part Lemon Juice
1½ parts Apple Juice

GLASS: HIGHBALL

Shake with ice and pour

Phillips Head Screwdriver

2 parts Vodka
1 part Orange Juice
1 part Pineapple Juice

GLASS: HIGHBALL

Shake with ice and pour

Pier 66

1 part Vodka
1 part Wild Berry Schnapps
1 part Piña Colada Mix
2 parts Lemonade
1 part Orange Juice

GLASS: HIGHBALL

Shake with ice and pour

Pierced Navel

1 part Vodka
1 part Peach Schnapps
1 part Orange Juice
1 part Cranberry Juice Cocktail

GLASS: HIGHBALL

Shake with ice and strain over ice

Pinetree Martyr

1 part Vodka
½ part Peach Schnapps
fill with Pineapple Juice

GLASS: HIGHBALL

Shake with ice and strain over ice

Pink

1 part Vodka
1 part Grenadine
fill with Milk

GLASS: HIGHBALL

Shake with ice and pour

Pink Cloud

1 part Vodka
1 part Crème de Almond
2 parts Piña Colada Mix
fill with Lemonade

GLASS: HIGHBALL

Shake with ice and pour

Pink Drink

2 parts Vodka
fill with Lemon-Lime Soda
splash Cranberry Juice Cocktail

GLASS: HIGHBALL

Build over ice and stir

Pink Elephants on Parade

2 parts Vodka
½ part Melon Liqueur
dash Sugar
fill with Pink Lemonade

GLASS: HIGHBALL

Shake with ice and strain over ice

Pink Lemonade

1½ parts Citrus-Flavored Vodka
½ part Raspberry Liqueur
fill with Sour Mix

GLASS: HIGHBALL

Shake with ice and pour

Pink Missile

2 parts Vodka
1 part Raspberry Liqueur
1 part Cranberry Juice Cocktail
1 part Ginger Ale
1 part Grapefruit Juice

GLASS: HIGHBALL

Build over ice and stir

Pink Panty Pulldown

1½ parts Vodka
1 part Sour Mix
splash Lemon-Lime Soda
splash Grenadine

GLASS: HIGHBALL

Build over ice

Pink Russian

1 part Tequila Rose®
1 part Coffee Liqueur
1 part Vodka

GLASS: HIGHBALL

Shake with ice and pour

Pirate Float

1 part Spiced Rum
1 part Root Beer Schnapps
1 part Vanilla-Flavored Vodka
1 part Cream

GLASS: HIGHBALL

Shake with ice and pour

Pluto

1 part Vodka
1 part Peach Schnapps
1 part Lime Cordial
½ part Blue Curaçao

GLASS: OLD-FASHIONED

Shake with ice and strain over ice

Plutonium Q 26 Space Modulator

1 part Vodka
1 part Cherry Juice
1 part Lemonade
1 part Orange Juice
1 part Cola

GLASS: HIGHBALL

Build over ice and stir

Poison Sumac

2 parts Vodka
1 part Blue Curaçao
1 part Orange Juice

GLASS: HIGHBALL

Shake with ice and strain over ice

Polar Bear

1 part Vodka
1 part Triple Sec
1 part Maraschino Liqueur
1 scoop Vanilla Ice Cream
1 Egg White

GLASS: HIGHBALL

Shake with ice and pour

Polish Red Hair

1 part Vodka
½ part Amaretto
½ part Lime Cordial
splash Grenadine
fill with Cola

GLASS: OLD-FASHIONED

Build over ice and stir

Porky Bone

1 part Vodka
½ part Maple Syrup
1 part Cinnamon Schnapps
2 parts Coffee Liqueur

GLASS: HIGHBALL

Stir gently with ice

Prince of Norway

¾ part Vodka
¾ part Apricot Brandy
¼ part Lime Juice
fill with Lemon-Lime Soda

GLASS: HIGHBALL

Build over ice and stir

Purple Chevy

1 part Vodka
1 part Cherry Juice
1 part Wild Berry Schnapps
1 part Sour Mix
2 parts Orange Juice

GLASS: HIGHBALL

Shake with ice and pour

Purple Dinosaur

1 part Vodka
1 part Blue Curaçao
1 part Wild Berry Schnapps
1 part Orange Juice
1 part Cranberry Juice Cocktail

GLASS: HIGHBALL

Shake with ice and strain over ice

Purple Moon

1 part Vodka
1 part Blue Curaçao
1 part Cherry Juice
1 part Lemonade
1 part Cranberry Juice Cocktail

GLASS: HIGHBALL

Shake with ice and strain over ice

Purple Nurple

1 part Vodka
1 part Grape Juice (Red)
2 parts Wild Berry Schnapps

GLASS: HIGHBALL

Shake with ice and strain over ice

Purple Passion Tea

¼ part Vodka
¼ part Rum
¼ part Gin
½ part Blackberry Liqueur
1 part Sour Mix
1 part Lemon-Lime Soda

GLASS: HIGHBALL

Build over ice and stir

Purple Pussycat

1 part Vodka
1 part Cherry Juice
1 part Wild Berry Schnapps
fill with Pineapple Juice

GLASS: HIGHBALL

Shake with ice and strain over ice

Purple Rose of Cairo

1 part Citrus-Flavored Vodka
1 part Raspberry Liqueur
fill with Cranberry Juice Cocktail

GLASS: HIGHBALL

Shake with ice and strain over ice

Purple Russian

2 parts Vodka
2 parts Raspberry Liqueur
1 part Cream

GLASS: HIGHBALL

Shake with ice and strain over ice

Push Up

2 parts Vodka
splash Grenadine
1 part Lemon-Lime Soda
1 part Orange Juice

GLASS: HIGHBALL

Build over ice and stir

Pushkin

1 part Crème de Cacao (White)
1 part Vodka
1 part Gin

GLASS: OLD-FASHIONED

Shake with ice and strain over ice

Quashbuckler

2 parts Vodka
1 part Gin
1 part Orange Juice
1 part Strawberry Juice

GLASS: HIGHBALL

Shake with ice and strain over ice

Ragin' Cajun

1 part Tequila Silver
1 part Vodka
dash Cayenne Pepper
dash Salt

GLASS: OLD-FASHIONED

Shake with ice and strain over ice

Raging Ratoga

1 part Melon Liqueur
1 part Amaretto
1 part Cranberry-Flavored Vodka
fill with Pineapple Juice

GLASS: HIGHBALL

Build over ice and stir

Rainstorm

1 part Vodka
1 part Blue Curaçao
2 parts Lemonade
1 part Cola

GLASS: HIGHBALL

Shake with ice and strain over ice

Rainy Day Marley

1 part Vodka
1 part Triple Sec
1 part Coconut-Flavored Rum
fill with Orange Juice

GLASS: HIGHBALL

Build over ice and stir

Raspberry Breeze

1 part Vodka
2 parts Raspberry Liqueur
1 part Pineapple Juice
1 part Cranberry Juice Cocktail

GLASS: HIGHBALL
Shake with ice and pour

Red Baby

1 part Southern Comfort®
1 part Vodka
1 part Amaretto
½ part Grenadine
1 part Orange Juice
1 part Lemon Juice

GLASS: HIGHBALL
Shake with ice and pour

Red Baron

1½ parts Vodka
fill with Orange Juice
splash Grenadine

GLASS: HIGHBALL
Build over ice

Red Devil

1 part Vodka
1 part Southern Comfort®
1 part Triple Sec
1 part Banana Liqueur
1 part Sloe Gin
splash Lime Juice
fill with Orange Juice

GLASS: HIGHBALL
Shake with ice and pour

Red Rage

1 part Jägermeister®
1 part Vodka
fill with Red Bull® Energy Drink

GLASS: HIGHBALL
Shake with ice and pour

Red Rasputin

2 parts Vodka
1 part Grenadine
fill with Cola

GLASS: HIGHBALL

Build over ice and stir

Redhead on the Moon

½ part Vodka
½ part Melon Liqueur
½ part Sour Apple Schnapps
1 part Sour Mix
splash Cranberry Juice Cocktail
fill with Lemon-Lime Soda

GLASS: HIGHBALL

Build over ice and stir

Rest in Peace

1 part Jack Daniel's®
½ part Vodka
½ part Tequila
½ part Jim Beam®

GLASS: HIGHBALL

Shake with ice and strain over ice

Rigor Mortis

1½ parts Vodka
¾ part Amaretto
1 part Pineapple Juice
1 part Orange Juice

GLASS: OLD-FASHIONED

Shake with ice and strain over ice

Roadrunner

1 part Vodka
½ part Amaretto
½ part Coconut Cream

GLASS: CHAMPAGNE FLUTE

Shake with ice and strain over ice

Roller

1½ parts Vodka
splash Amaretto
splash Melon Liqueur
fill with Cranberry Juice Cocktail

GLASS: HIGHBALL

Shake with ice and pour

Rolling Green Elixer

1½ parts Peach Schnapps
1 part Blue Curaçao
½ part Vodka
fill with Cranberry Juice Cocktail

GLASS: HIGHBALL

Build over ice and stir

Roxanne

¾ part Vodka
¾ part Peach Schnapps
½ part Amaretto
½ part Orange Juice
½ part Cranberry Juice Cocktail

GLASS: OLD-FASHIONED

Shake with ice and strain over ice

Rubenstein's Revenge

1 part Vodka
1 part Cranberry Juice Cocktail
1 part Gin
1 part Orange Juice
1 part Tonic Water

GLASS: HIGHBALL

Shake with ice and strain over ice

Russian Chameleon

1 part Blue Curaçao
2 parts Vodka
fill with Orange Juice

GLASS: HIGHBALL

Build over ice and stir

Russian Cream

2 parts Vodka
1 part Coffee Liqueur
1 part Irish Cream Liqueur

GLASS: OLD-FASHIONED

Shake with ice and pour

Russian Jack

1 part Vodka
1 part Jack Daniel's®
fill with Sour Mix

GLASS: HIGHBALL

Shake with ice and pour

Russian Quaalude

1 part Vodka
1 part Irish Cream Liqueur
1 part Frangelico®

GLASS: HIGHBALL

Shake with ice and strain over ice

Russian Quartet

1 part Vodka
1 part Peppermint Schnapps
1 part Coffee Liqueur
1 part Irish Cream Liqueur
1 part Amaretto
1 part Half and Half

GLASS: OLD-FASHIONED

Shake with ice and strain over ice

Russian Turkey

1 part Vodka
1 part Cranberry Juice Cocktail

GLASS: OLD-FASHIONED

Shake with ice and strain over ice

Salisbury Special

1 part Vodka
1 part Raspberry Liqueur
1 part Cola
1 part Orange Juice

GLASS: CORDIAL

Build over ice and stir

Sambario

1 part Vodka
½ part Apricot Brandy
½ part Dry Vermouth

GLASS: HIGHBALL

Build over ice and stir

San Diego Silver Bullet

1 part Vodka
1 part Sambuca

GLASS: OLD-FASHIONED

Shake with ice and strain over ice

San Francisco Driver

1 part Vodka
1 part Sour Mix
1 part Orange Juice

GLASS: HIGHBALL

Shake with ice and pour

Saratoga Swim

1 part Citrus-Flavored Vodka
1 part Peach Schnapps
½ part Passion Fruit Liqueur
1 part Sour Mix
fill with Orange Juice

GLASS: HIGHBALL

Build over ice and stir

Saronnada

1½ parts Vodka
1½ parts Pineapple Juice
¾ part Amaretto
¾ part Coconut Cream

GLASS: WHITE WINE

Shake with ice and strain over ice

Saturn's Rings

1 part Vodka
1 part Raspberry Liqueur
1 part Lemon-Lime Soda
1 part Orange Juice
1 part Cranberry Juice Cocktail

GLASS: HIGHBALL

Shake with ice and pour

Screamin' Blue

1 part Gin
1 part Vodka
1 part Light Rum
1 part Triple Sec
1 part Banana Liqueur
1 part Blue Curaçao
1 part Pineapple Juice
1 part Sour Mix

GLASS: HIGHBALL

Shake with ice and strain over ice

Screamin' Coyote

1 part Crème de Menthe (White)
1 part Goldschläger®
1 part Absolut® Peppar Vodka
splash Tabasco® Sauce

GLASS: OLD-FASHIONED

Shake with ice and strain over ice

Screaming Blue Monkey

¾ part Vodka
1 part Blue Curaçao
1 part Banana Liqueur
fill with Sour Mix

GLASS: HIGHBALL

Shake with ice and strain over ice

Screwdriver

2 parts Vodka
fill with Orange Juice

GLASS: HIGHBALL

Build over ice and stir

Screwdriver Boricua

2 parts Vodka
1 part Orange Juice
1 part Cranberry Juice Cocktail

GLASS: HIGHBALL

Build over ice and stir

Screwlimer

2 parts Vodka
splash Lime Juice
fill with Orange Juice

GLASS: HIGHBALL

Build over ice and stir

Sea Breeze

1½ parts Vodka
3 parts Cranberry Juice Cocktail
1 part Grapefruit Juice

GLASS: HIGHBALL

Build over ice and stir

Sea Horses

⅔ part Blue Curaçao
splash Irish Cream Liqueur
1 part Orange-Flavored Vodka

{ GLASS: HIGHBALL

*Shake with ice and strain
over ice*

Sea Turtle

1 part Melon Liqueur
1 part Vodka
2 parts Pineapple Juice
splash Grenadine

{ GLASS: OLD-FASHIONED

*Shake with ice and strain
over ice*

Secret Blue

1½ parts Vodka
½ part Lime
dash Sugar
splash Blue Curaçao

{ GLASS: HIGHBALL

*Shake with ice and strain
over ice*

Seesaw

1 part Vodka
1 part Light Rum
½ part Dark Rum
2 parts Cranberry Juice Cocktail
2 parts Orange Juice
dash Bitters

{ GLASS: HIGHBALL

Build over ice and stir

Serena

1 part Vodka
½ part Strawberry-Flavored Vodka
½ part Dry Vermouth
½ part Pineapple Juice
½ part Blue Curaçao
splash Lemon Juice

{ GLASS: HIGHBALL

Shake with ice and pour

Serendipity

1 part Vodka
½ part Grand Marnier®
½ part Amaretto
½ part Triple Sec
¼ part Grenadine
fill with Orange Juice

GLASS: HIGHBALL

Shake with ice and pour

Seven Deadly Sins

1 part Vodka
½ part Sour Apple Schnapps
½ part Raspberry Liqueur
½ part Watermelon Schnapps
1 part Orange Juice
1 part Sour Mix
1 part Papaya Juice

GLASS: OLD-FASHIONED

Shake with ice and pour

Shalom

1½ parts Vodka
1 part Madeira
splash Orange Juice

GLASS: HIGHBALL

Shake with ice and pour

Shark in the Water

1 part Vodka
1 part Blue Curaçao
fill with Lemonade
splash Strawberry Daiquiri Mix

GLASS: OLD-FASHIONED

Shake with ice and strain over ice

Shogun

1 part Citrus-Flavored Vodka
1 part Grand Marnier®
1 part Sweetened Lime Juice

GLASS: BRANDY SNIFTER

Build in the glass with no ice

Short-Sighted

1 part Vodka
1½ parts Dry Vermouth
⅔ part Calvados Apple Brandy
½ part Triple Sec

GLASS: HIGHBALL

Shake with ice and strain over ice

Shotgun

1 part Citrus-Flavored Vodka
1 part Grand Marnier®
1 part Lime Juice

GLASS: BRANDY SNIFTER

Shake with ice and strain over ice

Siberian Sleighride

1¼ parts Vodka
¾ part Crème de Cacao (White)
½ part Crème de Cacao (Dark)
3 parts Light Cream

GLASS: HIGHBALL

Shake with ice and strain over ice

Silverado

1½ parts Vodka
1½ parts Campari®
1 part Orange Juice

GLASS: OLD-FASHIONED

Shake with ice and strain over ice

Sino Soviet Split

2 parts Vodka
1 part Amaretto
fill with Milk

GLASS: OLD-FASHIONED

Build over ice and stir

Sir Francis

1 part Raspberry-Flavored Vodka
1 part Peach-Flavored Vodka
1 part Vanilla-Flavored Vodka
fill with Lemonade
1 part Grenadine

GLASS: HIGHBALL

Build over ice and stir

Ski Slope

1 part Vodka
1 part Amaretto
½ part Jack Daniel's®
½ part Southern Comfort®
½ part Sloe Gin

GLASS: HIGHBALL

Shake with ice and pour

Skylab

1 part Vodka
½ part Peach Schnapps
splash Blue Curaçao
1 part Pineapple Juice
1 part Orange Juice
1 part Lemon-Lime Soda

GLASS: HIGHBALL

Build over ice and stir

Slacker's Slammer

1 part Vodka
1 part Root Beer Schnapps
fill with Root Beer
1 scoop Ice Cream

GLASS: HIGHBALL

Build over ice

Slapshot

1 part Vodka
splash Banana Liqueur
splash Pineapple Juice
fill with Orange Juice

GLASS: HIGHBALL

Build over ice and stir

Sled Ride

1½ parts Vodka
1½ parts Sloe Gin
½ part Sour Apple Schnapps
fill with Lemon-Lime Soda

GLASS: HIGHBALL

Build over ice and stir

Slime

2 parts Vodka
1 part Cream
1 part Melon Liqueur

GLASS: OLD-FASHIONED

Shake with ice and strain over ice

Sloehand

1½ parts Sloe Gin
1 part Vodka
1½ parts Orange Juice
½ part Lemon Juice
2 splashes Grenadine

GLASS: HIGHBALL

Shake with ice and strain over ice

Smashed Pumpkin

1 part Vodka
1 part Orange Juice
1 part Cranberry Ginger Ale

GLASS: HIGHBALL

Shake with ice and pour

Smith & Wesson®

½ part Coffee Liqueur
½ part Vodka
fill with Cola

GLASS: HIGHBALL

Build over ice and stir. Top with Cream

Smooth Sailing

1½ parts Vodka
1½ parts Triple Sec
½ part Cherry Brandy
1 part Orange Juice
1 part Cranberry Juice Cocktail

GLASS: HIGHBALL

Build over ice and stir

Smoothberry

1 part Vodka
1 part Strawberry Liqueur
1 part Pear Juice
fill with Lemonade

GLASS: HIGHBALL

Build over ice and stir

Smurf®

1 part Vodka
1 part Orange Juice
2 splashes Grenadine
splash Strawberry Daiquiri Mix
fill with Lemon-Lime Soda

GLASS: HIGHBALL

Build over ice and stir

Snow White

2 parts Southern Comfort®
1 part Vodka
1 part Pineapple Juice
½ part Orange Juice

GLASS: HIGHBALL

Shake with ice and strain over ice

Socket Wrench

2½ parts Vodka
fill with Apple Juice

GLASS: HIGHBALL

Shake with ice and pour

Soda Cracker

2 parts Vodka
1 part Frangelico®

GLASS: OLD-FASHIONED

Build over ice and stir

Sonora Sunset

1 part Melon Liqueur
1 part Amaretto
1 part Vodka
4 parts Orange Juice
2 parts Cranberry Juice Cocktail

GLASS: HIGHBALL

Build over ice

Soup

1 part Vodka
1 part Coconut-Flavored Rum
1 part Cointreau®
1 part Peach Schnapps
fill with Red Bull® Energy Drink

GLASS: HIGHBALL

Build over ice and stir

Sour Kiss

1 part Vodka
1 part Sour Apple Schnapps
fill with Sour Mix

{ GLASS: HIGHBALL

Build over ice and stir

South Pacific

1 part Vodka
2 parts Brandy
3 parts Pineapple Juice
splash Grenadine

{ GLASS: HIGHBALL

Shake with ice and strain over ice

Soviet Holiday

2 parts Vodka
½ part Coconut-Flavored Rum
¼ part Tequila Rose®
fill with Fruit Punch

{ GLASS: HIGHBALL

Build over ice and stir

Special K®

1 part Vodka
½ part Blue Curaçao
½ part Triple Sec
dash Sugar
fill with Lemonade

{ GLASS: HIGHBALL

Shake with ice and pour

Spice and Ice

1 part Citrus-Flavored Vodka
1 part Goldschläger®
fill with Dr Pepper®

{ GLASS: HIGHBALL

Build over ice and stir

Spicy Tiger

1½ parts Peach Schnapps
1½ parts Vodka
2 parts Lemon-Lime Soda
1 part Cranberry Juice Cocktail
1 part Orange Juice

GLASS: HIGHBALL

Build over ice and stir

Spiky Cactus

1 part Blue Curaçao
1 part Vodka
1 part Triple Sec
fill with Mountain Dew®

GLASS: HIGHBALL

Build over ice and stir

Spinster's Delight

1 part Vodka
1 part Brandy
1 part Crème de Cacao (White)
1 part Cream

GLASS: HIGHBALL

Shake with ice and strain over ice

Spooky Juice

1 part Vodka
2 splashes Blue Curaçao
splash Grenadine
fill with Orange Juice

GLASS: HIGHBALL

Build over ice and stir

Spymaster

1½ parts Vodka
½ part Crème de Banana
½ part Lemon Juice
1 Egg White

GLASS: OLD-FASHIONED

Shake with ice and strain over ice

St. Louis Blues

1 part Vodka
1 part Blue Curaçao
1 part Lemonade
1 part Lemon-Lime Soda

GLASS: HIGHBALL

Build over ice and stir

St. Paul Punch

2 parts Melon Liqueur
1 part Vodka
1 part Lime Juice
fill with Lemonade

GLASS: HIGHBALL

Build over ice and stir

St. Peter

1 part Vodka
1 part Coffee Liqueur

GLASS: OLD-FASHIONED

Shake with ice and strain over ice

St. Valentine's Day

2/3 part Peach Schnapps
2/3 part Citrus-Flavored Vodka
1 part Cream

GLASS: HIGHBALL

Shake with ice and strain over ice

Starry Starry Night

1 part Vodka
1 part Wild Berry Schnapps
fill with Lemon-Lime Soda

GLASS: HIGHBALL

Build over ice and stir

Storm at Sea

1 part Vodka
1 part Apricot Brandy
½ part Melon Liqueur
1 part Sour Mix
1 part Orange Juice

GLASS: HIGHBALL

Build over ice and stir

Stormtrooper

1 part Vodka
1 part Coconut-Flavored Rum
fill with Milk

GLASS: HIGHBALL
Build over ice and stir

Strawberry Assassin

1 part Vodka
fill with Cranberry Juice Cocktail
1 scoop Ice Cream

GLASS: HIGHBALL
Shake with ice and pour

Strawberry Pussycat

1 part Vodka
1 part Strawberry Liqueur
1 part Cherry Juice
fill with Pineapple Juice

GLASS: HIGHBALL
Shake with ice and pour

Stress Ball

1 part Vodka
½ part Rum
¼ part Galliano®
¼ part Irish Cream Liqueur
fill with Orange Juice

GLASS: HIGHBALL
Shake with ice and pour

Stubbly Beaver

1 part Vodka
1 part Irish Cream Liqueur
splash Butterscotch Schnapps
fill with Milk

GLASS: HIGHBALL
Build over ice and stir

Sucker Punch

2 parts Vodka
1 part Sour Apple Schnapps
splash Cranberry Juice Cocktail
fill with Lemon-Lime Soda

GLASS: HIGHBALL
Build over ice and stir

Sugar Reef

1½ parts Orange-Flavored Vodka
½ part Triple Sec
1 part Pineapple Juice
1 part Cranberry Juice Cocktail
1 part Orange Juice
splash Lime Juice

GLASS: HIGHBALL

Shake with ice and strain over ice

Summer Bahia Baby

1 part Vodka
1 part Pisang Ambon® Liqueur
½ part Triple Sec
fill with Pineapple Juice

GLASS: OLD-FASHIONED

Shake with ice and strain over ice

Summer in the City

1 part Vodka
1 part Cherry Juice
1 part Lemonade
1 part Iced Tea

GLASS: HIGHBALL

Build over ice and stir

Summer of 69

1 part Vodka
1 part Strawberry Liqueur
1 part Lemonade
1 part Cola

GLASS: HIGHBALL

Build over ice and stir

Summer Share

1 part Light Rum
1 part Vodka
½ part Tequila
splash Apricot Brandy
1 part Cranberry Juice Cocktail
1 part Orange Juice
fill with Lemon-Lime Soda

GLASS: HIGHBALL

Build over ice and stir

Sundance

1 part Apricot Brandy
1 part Vodka
splash Passion Fruit Nectar
splash Lemon Juice
fill with Pineapple Juice

GLASS: HIGHBALL

Shake with ice and pour

Sundown

1 part Vodka
1 part Apricot Brandy
fill with Pineapple Juice

GLASS: OLD-FASHIONED

Build over ice and stir

Superman

1 part Scotch
1 part Vodka
1 part Gin
1 part Grenadine
splash Orange Juice

GLASS: OLD-FASHIONED

*Shake with ice and strain
over ice*

Supersonic Sunshine

1 part Coconut-Flavored Rum
1 part Vodka
fill Chocolate Milk
1 Orange Slice

GLASS: HIGHBALL

Shake with ice and pour

Swedish Bear

¾ part Vodka
½ part Crème de Cacao (Dark)
fill with Heavy Cream

GLASS: OLD-FASHIONED

Shake with ice and pour

Swedish Pinkie

1 part Currant-Flavored Vodka
1 part Cranberry Juice Cocktail
1 part Sour Mix

GLASS: CHAMPAGNE FLUTE

Shake with ice and pour

Sweet Caroline

1 part Vodka
1 part Strawberry Liqueur
1 part Peach Schnapps
1 part Lemonade
2 parts Lemon-Lime Soda

GLASS: HIGHBALL
Build over ice and stir

Sweet City

1 part Vodka
1 part Apricot Brandy
1 part Sweet Vermouth

GLASS: HIGHBALL
Build over ice and stir

Sweet Death

1 part Coconut-Flavored Rum
1 part 151-Proof Rum
1 part Vodka
1 part Sour Mix
1 part Cranberry Juice Cocktail

GLASS: HIGHBALL
Shake with ice and pour

Tainted Cherry

1 part Vodka
1 part Cherry Brandy
fill with Orange Juice

GLASS: HIGHBALL
Shake with ice and strain over ice

Tanahgoyang

1 part Vodka
½ part Pisang Ambon® Liqueur
½ part Coconut-Flavored Liqueur
1 part Lemon Juice
fill with Orange Juice

GLASS: HIGHBALL
Shake with ice and strain over ice

Tango & Cash

½ part Crème de Cassis
1 part Vanilla-Flavored Vodka
⅔ part Lemon Juice
2 parts Raspberry-Flavored Seltzer

GLASS: HIGHBALL

Stir gently with ice

Tawny Russian

1 part Amaretto
1 part Vodka

GLASS: HIGHBALL

Build over ice and stir

Temptress

1 part Vodka
1 part Grenadine

GLASS: HIGHBALL

Shake with ice and strain over ice

Tennessee Tea

1 part Vodka
1 part Rum
1 part Gin
1 part Triple Sec
1 part Jack Daniel's®
fill with Sour Mix
splash Orange Juice
splash Cola

GLASS: HIGHBALL

Shake with ice and strain over ice

Texas Cool-Aid

1 part Vodka
1 part Midori®
1 part Crème de Noyaux
splash Cranberry Juice Cocktail

GLASS: HIGHBALL

Shake with ice and pour

Think Tank

½ part Vodka
1 part Coffee Liqueur
1 part Cream
fill with Carbonated Water

GLASS: HIGHBALL

Build over ice and stir

Three Fifths

2 parts Vodka
1½ parts Grape Soda
1½ parts Club Soda

GLASS: OLD-FASHIONED

Build over ice and stir

Threesome

1½ parts Vodka
1 part Amaretto
splash Sour Mix
splash Blue Curaçao
splash Grenadine

GLASS: HIGHBALL

Shake all but Blue Curaçao and Grenadine with ice. Place the Blue Curaçao in the glass, fill the glass with ice, and strain the shaken mixture into the glass. Top with Grenadine.

Thunder King

1 part Citrus-Flavored Vodka
1 part Whiskey
½ part Coffee Liqueur
fill with Milk

GLASS: WHISKEY SOUR

Shake with ice and pour

Tidal Wave

1 part Vodka
1 part Blue Curaçao
2 parts Margarita Mix
1 part Lemon-Lime Soda

GLASS: HIGHBALL

Shake with ice and pour

Tie-Dyed

1 part Blueberry Schnapps
1 part Raspberry-Flavored Vodka
1 part Cranberry Juice Cocktail
1 part Orange Juice
1 part Lemon-Lime Soda

GLASS: HIGHBALL

Build over ice and stir

Tiffany's

1½ parts Vodka
⅔ part Crème de Cassis

GLASS: HIGHBALL

Build over ice and stir

Toast the Ghost

1 part Vodka
1 part Coconut-Flavored Liqueur
1 part Amaretto
1 part Irish Cream Liqueur
fill with Milk

GLASS: HIGHBALL

Shake with ice and strain over ice

Tokyo Tea

½ part Vodka
½ part Rum
½ part Triple Sec
½ part Gin
1 part Melon Liqueur
fill with Sour Mix

GLASS: HIGHBALL

Shake with ice and pour

Tomahawk

1 part Vodka
½ part Crème de Cacao (White)
½ part Triple Sec
2 splashes Lime Juice
1 part Cream

GLASS: HIGHBALL

Shake with ice and strain over ice

Tomakazi

¾ part Vodka
¾ part Gin
½ part Lime Cordial
splash Sour Mix
splash Cola

GLASS: HIGHBALL

Build over ice and stir

Top o' the Morning

1 part Vodka
1 part Triple Sec
¼ part Tequila
1 part Orange Juice
1 part Cranberry Juice Cocktail

GLASS: HIGHBALL

Shake with ice and strain over ice

Tremor

1 part Midori®
1 part Spiced Rum
1 part Vodka
1 part Crème de Noyaux
fill with Orange Juice

GLASS: HIGHBALL

Shake with ice and pour

Triple Jump

1½ parts Vodka
½ part Triple Sec
½ part Apricot Brandy
½ part Strawberry Liqueur
fill with Orange Juice

GLASS: OLD-FASHIONED

Build over ice and stir

Triple Pleasure

1 part Vodka
1 part Tequila
1 part Yukon Jack®
1 part Cranberry Juice Cocktail
1 part Orange Juice
1 part Pineapple Juice

GLASS: HIGHBALL

Build over ice and stir

Tropical Daydream

1 part Vodka
1 part Peach Schnapps
½ part Amaretto
1 part Cranberry Juice Cocktail
1 part Orange Juice

GLASS: HIGHBALL

Build over ice and stir

Tropical Itch

1 part Light Rum
1 part Dark Rum
1 part Vodka
1 part Grand Marnier®
1 part Lemon Juice
fill with Mango Nectar

GLASS: HIGHBALL

Shake with ice and pour

Tropical LifeSaver®

¾ part Midori®
¾ part Coconut-Flavored Rum
½ part Citrus-Flavored Vodka
2 parts Pineapple Juice
1 part Sour Mix
splash Lemon-Lime Soda

GLASS: HIGHBALL

Build over ice and stir

Tropical Rainstorm

1 part Vodka
1 part Blue Curaçao
2 parts Lemon-Lime Soda
1 part Pineapple Juice

GLASS: HIGHBALL

Build over ice and stir

Tropical Sunset

1 part Vodka
1 part Cherry Juice
1 part Wild Berry Schnapps
fill with Orange Juice

GLASS: HIGHBALL

Build over ice and stir

Tumbleweed

1 part Vodka
1 part Peach Schnapps
1 part Raspberry Liqueur
2 parts Lemonade
1 part Cola

GLASS: HIGHBALL

Build over ice and stir

Twilight Zone

1 part Vodka
1 part Blue Curaçao
splash Lemon Juice

GLASS: HIGHBALL

Shake with ice and strain over ice

Twister

1 part Triple Sec
1 part Vodka
fill with Orange Juice
splash Grenadine

GLASS: HIGHBALL

Build over ice

Umbrella Man Special

1 part Vodka
1 part Coffee Liqueur
1 part Irish Cream Liqueur
1 part Grand Marnier®
1 part Drambuie®

GLASS: HIGHBALL

Shake with ice and strain over ice

Usual Suspect

1 part Cream
splash Vodka
splash Crème de Banana

GLASS: OLD-FASHIONED

Shake with ice and strain over ice

V8® Ceasar's

1 part Vodka
1 part V8® Vegetable Juice Blend
1 part Clamato® Juice
¼ part Worcestershire® Sauce
dash Salt
dash Pepper
splash Lime Juice

GLASS: HIGHBALL

Shake with ice and pour

V8® Mary

1 part Vodka
fill with V8® Vegetable Juice Blend
¼ part Worcestershire® Sauce
dash Salt
dash Pepper
splash Lime Juice

GLASS: HIGHBALL

Shake with ice and pour

Valentine

2 parts Banana Liqueur
1 part Vodka
fill with Cranberry Juice Cocktail

GLASS: RED WINE

Shake with ice and strain

Vampire's Kiss

2 parts Vodka
½ part Dry Gin
½ part Dry Vermouth
½ part Tequila
dash Salt

GLASS: OLD-FASHIONED

Shake with ice and strain over ice

Vaughn Purple Haze

2 parts Vodka
1½ parts Raspberry Liqueur
fill with Cranberry Juice Cocktail

GLASS: HIGHBALL

Build over ice and stir

VCG

1 part Vodka
fill with Cranberry Juice Cocktail
splash Grenadine

GLASS: OLD-FASHIONED
Build over ice and stir

Velociraptor

1½ parts Vodka
splash Chicken Broth
3 splashes Tabasco® Sauce

GLASS: HIGHBALL
Shake with ice and strain over ice

Ventura Highway

1 part Vodka
2 parts Raspberry Liqueur
1 part Lemonade
1 part Orange Juice

GLASS: HIGHBALL
Shake with ice and strain over ice

Victoria's Secret®

1 part Currant-Flavored Vodka
1½ parts Sweet Vermouth
¼ part Sour Mix

GLASS: OLD-FASHIONED
Shake with ice and strain

Vincow Somba

1 part Vodka
1 part Triple Sec
1 part Pineapple Juice

GLASS: HIGHBALL
Build over ice and stir

Virgo

1 part Vodka
1 part Wild Berry Schnapps
2 parts Lemonade
1 part Cola

GLASS: HIGHBALL
Build over ice and stir

Vodka Boatman

1 part Vodka
1 part Cherry Brandy
fill with Orange Juice

GLASS: HIGHBALL

Build over ice and stir

Vodka Dog

1 part Vodka
fill with Grapefruit Juice

GLASS: HIGHBALL

Build over ice and stir

Vodka Red Bull®

2½ parts Vodka
fill with Red Bull® Energy Drink

GLASS: HIGHBALL

Build over ice and stir

Vodka Salty Dog

1½ parts Vodka
fill with Grapefruit Juice
dash Salt

GLASS: HIGHBALL

Shake with ice and pour

Vodka Screw-Up

1 part Vodka
1 part Lemon-Lime Soda
1 part Orange Juice

GLASS: HIGHBALL

Build over ice and stir

Vodka Sour

2 parts Vodka
½ part Lemon Juice
dash Sugar

GLASS: OLD-FASHIONED

Shake with ice and strain over ice

Vodka Sourball

1½ parts Lemon-Flavored Vodka
½ part Triple Sec
½ part Pineapple Juice

GLASS: OLD-FASHIONED

Shake with ice and strain over ice

Vodka Sunrise

1 part Vodka
fill with Orange Juice
splash Grenadine

{ GLASS: HIGHBALL

Build over ice

Vodka Sunset

1½ parts Vodka
fill with Grapefruit Juice
2 splashes Grenadine

{ GLASS: HIGHBALL

Build over ice

Vodka Volcano

2 parts Vodka
1 part Grapefruit Juice
splash Grenadine

{ GLASS: HIGHBALL

Build over ice

Waffle Dripper

1½ parts Vodka
1 part Butterscotch Schnapps
fill with Orange Juice

{ GLASS: HIGHBALL

Shake with ice and strain

Wake-Up Call

1 part Jack Daniel's®
1 part Vodka
½ part Lemon Juice

{ GLASS: OLD-FASHIONED

Shake with ice and strain

A Walk on the Moon

2 parts Blackberry Liqueur
1 part Vodka
3 parts Cola
3 parts Milk

{ GLASS: HIGHBALL

Shake with ice and strain over ice

Warm Summer Rain

1½ parts Vodka
½ part Coconut-Flavored Liqueur
fill with Pineapple Juice
splash Orange Juice

GLASS: HIGHBALL

Shake with ice and strain over ice

Wave Breaker

1 part Vodka
1 part Coconut Cream
splash Fresh Lime Juice

GLASS: OLD-FASHIONED

Shake with ice and strain over ice

Wedding Day

1 part Gin
½ part Vodka
1 part Jägermeister®
fill with Apple Cider

GLASS: HIGHBALL

Build over ice and stir

West Indies Russian

1 part Vodka
1 part Rum
1 part Coffee Liqueur
fill with Cola

GLASS: HIGHBALL

Build over ice and stir

Whippet

1 part Vodka
fill with Orange Juice
splash Raspberry Liqueur

GLASS: HIGHBALL

Build over ice

Whirly Bird

1 part Pineapple Juice
1 part Melon Liqueur
1 part Southern Comfort®
1 part Citrus-Flavored Vodka

GLASS: OLD-FASHIONED

Shake with ice and strain over ice

White Chocolate

1 part Vanilla-Flavored Vodka
2 parts Crème de Cacao (White)

GLASS: BRANDY SNIFTER

Shake with ice and strain over ice

White Russian

1 part Vodka
1 part Coffee Liqueur
fill with Light Cream

GLASS: OLD-FASHIONED

Build over ice and stir

White Stinger

2 parts Vodka
¾ part Crème de Cacao (White)

GLASS: OLD-FASHIONED

Shake with ice and strain over ice

Windex®

2 parts Vodka
1 part Light Rum
½ part Blue Curaçao
½ part Lime Juice

GLASS: HIGHBALL

Shake with ice and strain over ice

Witch's Brew

1 part Vodka
1 part Raspberry Liqueur
1 part Cranberry Juice Cocktail
1 part Sour Mix

GLASS: HIGHBALL

Build over ice and stir

Wolf

1 part Blue Curaçao
½ part Crème de Menthe (White)
½ part Vodka
fill with Lemon-Lime Soda

GLASS: OLD-FASHIONED

Build over ice and stir

Wolfsbane

2 parts Vodka
1½ parts Cherry Brandy
½ part Cream
1 Egg White

GLASS: HIGHBALL

Shake with ice and strain over ice

Woman in Blue

1 part Vodka
1 part Crème de Cacao (White)
1 part Frangelico®
splash Blue Curaçao

GLASS: HIGHBALL

Shake with ice and strain over ice

Woo Woo

1 part Vodka
1 part Peach Schnapps
fill with Cranberry Juice Cocktail

GLASS: HIGHBALL

Shake with ice and strain over ice

Wookiee

1 part Rum
½ part Vodka
½ part Tequila
½ part Vermouth
1 part Orange Juice
1 part Cola

GLASS: HIGHBALL

Build over ice and stir

Woolly Navel

¾ part Peach Schnapps
1½ parts Vodka
fill with Orange Juice

GLASS: HIGHBALL

Build over ice and stir

Yankee Dutch

1 part Cherry Brandy
1 part Triple Sec
1 part Vodka
1 part Jim Beam®

GLASS: HIGHBALL

Shake with ice and strain over ice

Yellow Dog

1 part Vodka
1 part Coconut-Flavored Rum
1 part Mountain Dew®
1 part Pineapple Juice

GLASS: HIGHBALL

Build over ice and stir

Yellow Sock

1 part Vodka
1 part Pisang Ambon® Liqueur
fill with Orange Juice

GLASS: HIGHBALL

Build over ice and stir

Yellow Sunset

1 part Vodka
1 part Grand Marnier®
1 part Cherry Juice
fill with Pineapple Juice

GLASS: HIGHBALL

Build over ice

Yup-Yupie

1½ parts Vodka
½ part Melon Liqueur
½ part Maraschino Liqueur
½ part Crème de Cassis

GLASS: HIGHBALL

Shake with ice and strain over ice

Zebra Fizz

1 part Vodka
1 part Lemonade
1 part Lemon-Lime Soda

GLASS: HIGHBALL

Build over ice and stir

Zoom Bang Boom

1 part Vodka
1 part Wild Berry Schnapps
1 part Lemonade
2 parts Lemon-Lime Soda

GLASS: HIGHBALL

Build over ice and stir

Zoom Shooter

1 part Vodka
1 part Grand Marnier®
1 part Cherry Juice
fill with Orange Juice

GLASS: HIGHBALL

Build over ice and stir

ICED TEAS

CHAPTER

SHAKE
WITH
ICE &
STRAIN

15

THE SPIKED TEA STARTED WITH THE LONG
ISLAND ICED TEA IN THE 1970s, AND RAPIDLY
GREW INTO A COLLECTION OF POTENT DRINKS
THAT COMBINED VARIOUS INGREDIENTS TO
MAKE A MUDDY BROWN COLOR. THESE DRINKS
DON'T NECESSARILY CONTAIN ANY ACTUAL TEA
(ALTHOUGH SOME DO).

DRINK UP!

3-Mile Long Island Iced Tea

1 part Gin
1 part Light Rum
1 part Tequila
1 part Vodka
1 part Triple Sec
1 part Melon Liqueur
splash Sour Mix
splash Cola

GLASS: COLLINS

Mix with ice

Bambi's Iced Tea

1 part Vodka
splash Sour Mix
1 part Cola
1 part Lemon-Lime Soda

GLASS: COLLINS

Build over ice and stir

Binghampton Iced Tea

1 part Coconut-Flavored Rum
1 part Vanilla-Flavored Vodka
1 part Gin
1 part Tequila
½ part Rum
fill with Sour Mix
splash Cola

GLASS: COLLINS

Build over ice and stir

BJ's Long Island Iced Tea

1 part Amaretto
1 part Rum
1 part Triple Sec
1 part Vodka
splash Lime Juice
fill with Cola

GLASS: HIGHBALL

Build over ice and stir

Blue Long Island Iced Tea

1 part Vodka
1 part Tequila
1 part Rum
1 part Gin
1 part Blue Curaçao

{ GLASS: COLLINS

Build over ice and stir

Boston Iced Tea

1 part Vodka
1 part Gin
1 part Rum
1 part Tia Maria®
1 part Grand Marnier®
fill with Sour Mix
splash Cola

{ GLASS: COLLINS

Build over ice and stir

California Iced Tea

½ part Gin
½ part Light Rum
½ part Tequila
½ part Vodka
½ part Triple Sec
½ part Sour Mix
1 part Orange Juice
1 part Pineapple Juice

{ GLASS: HIGHBALL

Build over ice and stir

Caribbean Iced Tea

1 part Gin
1 part Light Rum
1 part Tequila
1 part Vodka
1 part Blue Curaçao
fill with Sour Mix

{ GLASS: HURRICANE

Build over ice and stir

Carolina Iced Tea

1½ parts Southern Comfort®
1 part Spiced Rum
1 part Peach Schnapps
½ part Vodka
fill with Iced Tea

GLASS: HIGHBALL
Build over ice and stir

Dignified Iced Tea

2 parts Citrus-Flavored Vodka
fill with Iced Tea

GLASS: HIGHBALL
Build over ice and stir

Electric Iced Tea

1½ parts Rum
1½ parts Vodka
1½ parts Gin
1 part Tequila
1 part Triple Sec
splash Blue Curaçao
fill with Lemon-Lime Soda

GLASS: COLLINS
Build over ice and stir

Embassy Iced Tea

1 part Blue Curaçao
1 part Vodka
1 part Light Rum
1 part Cachaça®
fill with Lemon-Lime Soda

GLASS: COLLINS
Build over ice and stir

Ewa Beach Iced Tea

½ part Gin
½ part Tequila
½ part Spiced Rum
½ part Vodka
½ part Triple Sec
1 part Fruit Punch
1 part Pineapple Juice

GLASS: COLLINS
Build over ice and stir

Georgia Peach Iced Tea

1 part Vodka
1 part Gin
1 part Rum
1 part Peach Schnapps
fill with Sour Mix

GLASS: COLLINS

Shake with ice and pour

Iced Tea

1 part Vodka
1 part Gin
½ part Triple Sec
2 parts Sour Mix
splash Cola
1 Lemon Wedge

GLASS: COLLINS

Build over ice and stir

Iced Teaspoon

1 part Tequila Silver
1 part Vodka
1 part Triple Sec
1 part Light Rum
1 part Gin
2 parts Sour Mix
fill with Iced Tea

GLASS: COLLINS

Shake with ice and pour

Lake George Iced Tea

½ part Tequila
½ part Rum
½ part Vodka
½ part Gin
½ part Triple Sec
1 part Pineapple Juice
fill with Cola

GLASS: HIGHBALL

Shake all but Cola with ice and strain into the glass. Top with Cola.

Long Austin Iced Tea

½ part Vodka
½ part Gin
½ part Rum
½ part Triple Sec
1 part Ginger Ale
1 part Iced Tea

GLASS: HIGHBALL

Build over ice and stir

Long Beach Ice Tea

1 part Vodka
1 part Rum
1 part Gin
1 part Triple Sec
1 part Melon Liqueur
fill with Cranberry Juice Cocktail

GLASS: HIGHBALL

Build over ice and stir

Long Island Beach

1 part Vodka
1 part Rum
1 part Triple Sec
2 parts Sour Mix
1 part Cranberry Juice Cocktail

GLASS: HIGHBALL

Build over ice and stir

Long Island Blue

½ part Tequila Silver
½ part Vodka
½ part Light Rum
½ part Gin
1 part Blue Curaçao
2 parts Pineapple Juice
fill with Lemonade

GLASS: COLLINS

Build over ice and stir

Long Island Iced Tea

1 part Vodka
1 part Tequila
1 part Rum
1 part Gin
1 part Triple Sec
1½ parts Sour Mix
splash Cola
1 Lemon Wedge

GLASS: COLLINS

Mix ingredients together over ice. Pour into shaker and give one brisk shake. Pour back into glass and make sure there is a touch of fizz at the top. Garnish with Lemon Wedge.

Long Island Spiced Tea

¾ part Spiced Rum
½ part Vodka
½ part Fresh Lime Juice
½ part Gin
¼ part Triple Sec
fill with Cola

GLASS: COLLINS

Build over ice and stir

Long Iver Iced Tea

1 part Coconut-Flavored Rum
1 part Vodka
1 part Gin
1 part Tequila
1 part Triple Sec
fill with Sour Mix
splash Cola

GLASS: COLLINS

Build over ice and stir

Nuclear Iced Tea

½ part Vodka
½ part Gin
½ part Rum
½ part Triple Sec
1 part Melon Liqueur
fill with Sour Mix
splash Lemon-Lime Soda

GLASS: COLLINS

Build over ice and stir

Radioactive Long Island Iced Tea

1 part Rum
1 part Vodka
1 part Tequila
1 part Gin
1 part Triple Sec
1 part Raspberry Liqueur
1 part Melon Liqueur
fill with Pineapple Juice
splash Cola

GLASS: COLLINS

Build over ice and stir

Raspberry Long Island Iced Tea #1

½ part Gin
½ part Vodka
½ part Light Rum
½ part Tequila
2 parts Sour Mix
2 parts Cola
½ part Raspberry Liqueur
1 Lemon Wedge

GLASS: HIGHBALL

Build over ice and stir. Float Raspberry Liqueur on top and garnish with Lemon Wedge.

Raspberry Long Island Iced Tea #2

1 part Vodka
1 part Rum
1 part Tequila
1 part Gin
1 part Triple Sec
1 part Chambord®
fill with Sour Mix
splash Cola

GLASS: COLLINS

Shake with ice and pour

A Real Iced Tea

¾ part Vodka
¾ part Gin
¾ part Rum
¾ part Tequila
½ part Triple Sec
splash Cranberry Juice Cocktail
splash Sour Mix
splash Cola

GLASS: HIGHBALL

Build over ice and stir

Russian Iced Tea

1 part Vodka
fill with Iced Tea

GLASS: HIGHBALL

Build over ice and stir

Sidney Iced Tea

½ part Cointreau®
½ part Gin
½ part Rum
½ part Vodka
1 part Peach Schnapps
fill with Cola

GLASS: COLLINS

Build over ice and stir

Southern Long Island Tea

1 part Gin
1 part Tequila Silver
1 part Vodka
1 part Light Rum
1 part Triple Sec
fill with Orange Juice
splash Cola

GLASS: HIGHBALL

Shake with ice and pour

Three Mile Island Iced Tea

1 part Gin
1 part Rye Whiskey
1 part Tequila
1 part Triple Sec
1 part Vodka
fill with Cola

GLASS: COLLINS

Build over ice and stir

Tokyo Iced Tea

½ part Gin
½ part Rum
½ part Vodka
½ part Tequila Silver
½ part Triple Sec
½ part Melon Liqueur
1 part Fresh Lime Juice
fill with Lemonade

GLASS: COLLINS

Shake with ice and pour

Tropical Iced Tea

½ part Vodka
½ part Rum
½ part Gin
½ part Triple Sec
1 part Sour Mix
1 part Pineapple Juice
1 part Cranberry Juice Cocktail
½ part Grenadine

GLASS: COLLINS

Shake with ice and pour

Westwood Iced Tea

1 part Vanilla-Flavored Vodka
½ part Tequila
½ part Gin
½ part Light Rum
½ part Goldschläger®
½ part 151-Proof Rum
fill with Sour Mix
splash Cola

GLASS: BEER MUG

Build over ice and stir

CHAPTER

SHAKE
WITH
ICE &
STRAIN

16

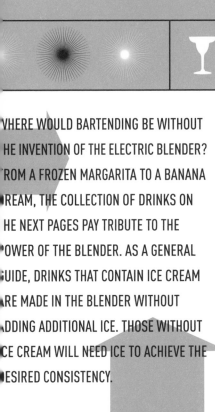

BLENDED
& FROZEN DRINKS

WHERE WOULD BARTENDING BE WITHOUT
THE INVENTION OF THE ELECTRIC BLENDER?
FROM A FROZEN MARGARITA TO A BANANA
CREAM, THE COLLECTION OF DRINKS ON
THE NEXT PAGES PAY TRIBUTE TO THE
POWER OF THE BLENDER. AS A GENERAL
GUIDE, DRINKS THAT CONTAIN ICE CREAM
ARE MADE IN THE BLENDER WITHOUT
ADDING ADDITIONAL ICE. THOSE WITHOUT
ICE CREAM WILL NEED ICE TO ACHIEVE THE
DESIRED CONSISTENCY.

DRINK UP!

3rd Street Promenade

1½ parts Vanilla-Flavored Vodka
1 part Gin
1 part Tequila
1 part Triple Sec
½ part Goldschläger®
6 parts Orange Juice

GLASS: HURRICANE

Combine all ingredients in a blender with ice. Blend until smooth.

98 Beatle

1 part Vodka
1 part Peach Schnapps
1 part Grenadine
2 parts Cranberry Juice Cocktail
1 Banana

GLASS: COLLINS

Combine all ingredients in a blender with ice. Blend until smooth.

155 Belmont

1 part Dark Rum
2 parts Light Rum
1 part Vodka
1 part Orange Juice

GLASS: WHITE WINE

Combine all ingredients in a blender. Blend until smooth.

Agent Orange

1 part Vodka
1 part Gin
1 part Yukon Jack®
1 part Sour Apple Schnapps
1 part Melon Liqueur
2 parts Grenadine
6 parts Orange Juice

GLASS: HURRICANE

Combine all ingredients in a blender with ice. Blend until smooth.

Alaskan Monk

1 part Frangelico®
1 part Irish Cream Liqueur
1 part Coffee Liqueur
1 part Vodka
1 part White Chocolate Liqueur
splash Half and Half

GLASS: COUPETTE

Combine all ingredients in a blender with ice. Blend until smooth.

Alaskan Suntan

1 part Gin
1 part Rum
1 part Vodka
3 parts Orange Juice
3 parts Pineapple Juice

GLASS: COUPETTE

Combine all ingredients in a blender with ice. Blend until smooth.

Albino Baby Snowpiglet

1 part Vodka
1 part Butterscotch Schnapps
1 part Crème de Menthe (White)
2 parts Cream

GLASS: COUPETTE

Combine all ingredients in a blender with ice. Blend until smooth.

Amaretto Chi Chi

1 part Vodka
1 part Amaretto
½ part Orange Juice
2 parts Pineapple Juice
2 parts Coconut Cream

GLASS: COLLINS

Combine all ingredients in a blender with ice. Blend until smooth.

Amaretto Dreamsicle®

1 part Cream
1 part Vodka
1 part Amaretto
1 part Orange Juice
1 part Pineapple Juice

GLASS: HURRICANE

Combine all ingredients in a blender with ice. Blend until smooth.

American Leroy

1 part Coffee Liqueur
1 part Vodka
1 part Irish Cream Liqueur
1 part Crème de Cacao (White)

GLASS: HIGHBALL

Combine all ingredients in a blender with ice. Blend until smooth.

Angel in Harlem

1½ parts Vodka
1 part Peach Schnapps
splash Cranberry Juice Cocktail
3 parts Lemonade

GLASS: COUPETTE

Combine all ingredients in a blender with ice. Blend until smooth.

Anthracite

1 part Coffee Liqueur
1 part Vodka
1 scoop Coffee Ice Cream

GLASS: COUPETTE

Combine all ingredients in a blender. Blend until smooth.

Arctic Mud Slide

1 part Coffee Liqueur
1 part Irish Cream Liqueur
1 part Vodka
1 part Crème de Menthe (White)
2 scoops Ice Cream

GLASS: COUPETTE

Combine all ingredients in a blender. Blend until smooth. Top with Whipped Cream.

Atomic Smoothie

2 parts Vodka
½ part Peach Schnapps
2 scoops Ice Cream
1 part Lemon Juice
6 parts Orange Juice

GLASS: COUPETTE

Combine all ingredients in a blender. Blend until smooth.

Aurora

3 parts Vodka
3 scoops Rainbow Sherbert
1 part Orange Juice
2 parts Cranberry Juice Cocktail

{ GLASS: COLLINS

Combine all ingredients in a blender. Blend until smooth.

Baby Jane

1 part Vodka
1 part Butterscotch Schnapps
1 part Irish Cream Liqueur
1 part Grenadine
2 scoops Ice Cream

{ GLASS: COUPETTE

Combine all ingredients in a blender.Blend until smooth.

Banana Dream

1 part Vodka
1 part Banana Liqueur
3 parts Orange Juice
1 part Cream

{ GLASS: COUPETTE

Combine all ingredients in a blender with ice. Blend until smooth.

Banana Dreamsicle®

1 part Vodka
1 part Banana Liqueur
1 part Cherry Juice
1 part Orange Juice
1 part Pineapple Juice
1 part Cream

{ GLASS: HIGHBALL

Combine all ingredients in a blender with ice. Blend until smooth.

Banana's Milk

1 part Vodka
1½ parts Banana Puree
3 parts Milk

{ GLASS: COUPETTE

Combine all ingredients in a blender with ice. Blend until smooth.

Barnaby's Buffalo Blizzard

¾ part Vodka
1 part Crème de Cacao (White)
1 part Galliano®
1 scoop Vanilla Ice Cream
splash Grenadine

GLASS: COUPETTE

Combine all ingredients in a blender. Blend until smooth.

Barney® Fizz

1 part Raspberry Liqueur
1 part Amaretto
½ part Vodka
3 parts Grape Juice (Red)
1 Egg White
1 part Sugar

GLASS: COLLINS

Combine all ingredients in a blender with ice. Blend until smooth.

Bay City Bomber

½ part Vodka
½ part Rum
½ part Tequila
½ part Gin
½ part Triple Sec
1 part Orange Juice
1 part Pineapple Juice
1 part Cranberry Juice Cocktail
1 part Sour Mix
splash 151-Proof Rum

GLASS: COLLINS

Combine all ingredients in a blender with ice. Blend until smooth.

Big John's Special

1 part Vodka
½ part Gin
3 parts Grapefruit Juice
3 dashes Orange Bitters
3 dashes Maraschino Cherry Juice

GLASS: COUPETTE

Combine all ingredients in a blender with ice. Blend until smooth.

Black Forest

1 part Vodka
1 part Coffee Liqueur
1 part Blackberry Liqueur
1 scoop Chocolate Ice Cream

GLASS: COUPETTE

Combine all ingredients in a blender. Blend until smooth.

Blended Georgia Peach

¾ part Vodka
¾ part Peach Schnapps
3 parts Orange Juice
2 parts Peach Puree

GLASS: HURRICANE

Combine all ingredients in a blender with ice. Blend until smooth.

Blue Max

1 part Vodka
1 part Blue Curaçao
½ part Coconut Cream
3 parts Pineapple Juice
2 parts Cream

GLASS: HURRICANE

Combine all ingredients in a blender with ice. Blend until smooth.

Blue Whale

1 part Vodka
1 part Blue Curaçao
2 parts Sour Mix

GLASS: COUPETTE

Combine all ingredients in a blender with ice. Blend until smooth.

Blushin' Russian

1 part Coffee Liqueur
1 part Vodka
1 scoop Vanilla Ice Cream
4 Strawberries

GLASS: PARFAIT

Combine all ingredients in a blender. Blend until smooth.

Bunky Punch

1½ parts Vodka
1 part Melon Liqueur
1 part Peach Schnapps
1½ parts Cranberry Juice Cocktail
2 parts Orange Juice
½ part Grape Juice (Red)

{ GLASS: PARFAIT

Combine all ingredients in a blender with ice. Blend until smooth.

Cactus

1½ parts Vodka
1 part Melon Liqueur
1 part Coconut Cream
fill with Pineapple Juice

{ GLASS: COUPETTE

Combine all ingredients in a blender with ice. Blend until smooth.

Carol Ann

1 part Vodka
1 part Amaretto
fill with Skim Milk

{ GLASS: HURRICANE

Combine all ingredients in a blender with ice. Blend until smooth.

Chi Chi

1½ parts Vodka
1 part Coconut Cream
3 parts Pineapple Juice

{ GLASS: COUPETTE

Combine all ingredients in a blender with ice. Blend until smooth.

Chocolate Almond Kiss

1 part Crème de Cacao (Dark)
1 part Frangelico®
1 part Vodka
2 scoops Vanilla Ice Cream

{ GLASS: COUPETTE

Combine all ingredients in a blender. Blend until smooth.

Comfortably Numb

1 part Spiced Rum
1 part Vanilla-Flavored Vodka
1 part Coconut-Flavored Liqueur
²/₃ part Coconut Cream
2 parts Pineapple Juice
1 part Orange Juice

GLASS: COUPETTE

Combine all ingredients in a blender with ice. Blend until smooth.

Devil's Tail

1½ parts Light Rum
1 part Vodka
2 splashes Grenadine
2 splashes Apricot Brandy
1 part Lime Juice
1 Lemon Twist

GLASS: CHAMPAGNE FLUTE

Combine all ingredients in a blender with ice. Blend until smooth.

Dirty Dog

1 part Hennessy®
1½ parts Vodka
fill with Orange Juice
1 part Cranberry Juice Cocktail

GLASS: COUPETTE

Combine all ingredients in a blender with ice. Blend until smooth.

Donna Reed

1 part Absolut® Vodka
2 parts Cranberry Juice Cocktail
2 parts Sour Mix

GLASS: COUPETTE

Combine all ingredients in a blender with ice. Blend until smooth.

Dreamy Monkey

1 part Vodka
½ part Crème de Banana
½ part Crème de Cacao (Dark)
1 Banana
2 scoops Vanilla Ice Cream
1 part Light Cream

GLASS: PARFAIT

Combine all ingredients in a blender. Blend until smooth.

The Event Horizon

1 part Peppermint Schnapps
1 part Vodka
1 part Milk
1 scoop Chocolate Ice Cream

GLASS: HIGHBALL

Combine all ingredients in a blender. Blend until smooth.

Finnish Flash

1 part Cranberry-Flavored Vodka
½ part Crème de Menthe (White)
½ part Tequila Silver

GLASS: COUPETTE

Combine all ingredients in a blender with ice. Blend until smooth.

Flying Carpet

1 part Vodka
1 part Advocaat
1 part Crème de Banana

GLASS: HIGHBALL

Combine all ingredients in a blender with ice. Blend until smooth.

Flying Gorilla

1 part Vodka
1 part Banana Liqueur
1 part Crème de Cacao (White)
2 scoops Vanilla Ice Cream

GLASS: COUPETTE

Combine all ingredients in a blender. Blend until smooth.

Freezy Melonkiny

1½ parts Vodka
²/₃ part Kiwi Schnapps
²/₃ part Melon Liqueur
2 parts Cream

GLASS: COUPETTE

Combine all ingredients in a blender with ice. Blend until smooth.

Frozen Arctic Cream

2 parts Vodka
2 parts Vanilla Liqueur
1 part Blue Curaçao
2 parts Cream
1 scoop Vanilla Ice Cream

GLASS: COLLINS

Combine all ingredients in a blender. Blend until smooth.

Frozen Black Irish

1 part Coffee Liqueur
1 part Irish Cream Liqueur
1 part Vodka
1 scoop Chocolate Ice Cream

GLASS: COUPETTE

Combine all ingredients in a blender. Blend until smooth.

Frozen Citron Neon

1½ parts Citrus-Flavored Vodka
1 part Melon Liqueur
½ part Blue Curaçao
½ part Lime Juice
1 part Sour Mix

GLASS: PARFAIT

Combine all ingredients in a blender. with ice. Blend until smooth.

Frozen Danube

2 parts Vodka
2 parts Melon Liqueur
1 part Blue Curaçao
3 parts Grapefruit Juice
3 parts Melon Puree

GLASS: HURRICANE

Combine all ingredients in a blender with ice. Blend until smooth.

Frozen Mud Slide

1 part Vodka
1 part Coffee Liqueur
1 part Irish Cream Liqueur
2 scoops Vanilla Ice Cream

GLASS: COUPETTE

Combine all ingredients in a blender. Blend until smooth.

Fruit Booty

2 parts 151-Proof Rum
1 part Blue Curaçao
1 part Cranberry Liqueur
1 part Cranberry-Flavored Vodka
3 parts Apple-Cranberry Juice
3 parts Pineapple Juice
splash Grenadine

GLASS: HIGHBALL

Combine all ingredients in a blender with ice. Blend until smooth.

Green Weenie

1 part Jack Daniel's®
1 part Rum
1 part Tequila
1 part Vodka
fill with Margarita Mix

GLASS: COUPETTE

Combine all ingredients in a blender with ice. Blend until smooth.

Hawaiian Eye

½ part Banana Liqueur
1 part Coffee Liqueur
1 part Heavy Cream
1 Egg White
½ part Vodka
splash Pernod®

GLASS: COUPETTE

Combine all ingredients in a blender with ice. Blend until smooth.

Hi-Rise

1 part Vodka
¼ part Cointreau®
2 parts Orange Juice
1 part Sour Mix
¼ part Grenadine

GLASS: OLD-FASHIONED

Combine all ingredients in a blender with ice. Blend until smooth.

Honey Boombastic

1½ parts Vodka
1 part Crème de Cacao (Dark)
1 part Frangelico®
1½ parts Honey
1 Egg
½ part Vanilla Extract

GLASS: HURRICANE

Combine all ingredients in a blender with ice. Blend until smooth.

Horny Leprechaun

1 part Melon Liqueur
1 part Peach Schnapps
1 part Vodka
2 parts Orange Juice

GLASS: COUPETTE

Combine all ingredients in a blender with ice. Blend until smooth.

Hummer

1 part Coffee-Flavored Vodka
1 part Light Rum
2 scoops Vanilla Ice Cream

GLASS: HIGHBALL

Combine all ingredients in a blender. Blend until smooth.

Hydraulic Screwdriver

1 can Frozen Orange Juice
   Concentrate
1 part Vodka
1 part Triple Sec
1 part Water

GLASS: COUPETTE

Make the Orange Juice but instead of refilling container with water 3 times, fill with Vodka once, Triple Sec once, and water once. Mix well and serve on the rocks, or blend it with ice for a frozen drink.

Igloo Sue

2 parts Vodka
1 part Grenadine
fill with Lemonade

GLASS: HURRICANE

Combine all ingredients in a blender with ice. Blend until smooth.

Inertia Creeps

1½ parts Vodka
2 parts Strega®
⅔ part Pineapple Juice
½ part Cream

GLASS: COLLINS

Combine all ingredients in a blender with ice. Blend until smooth.

Jersey Girl

1 part Currant-Flavored Vodka
1 part Strawberry Liqueur
2 parts Pineapple Juice
1½ parts Orange Juice
1 part Strawberry Syrup

GLASS: HURRICANE

Combine all ingredients in a blender with ice. Blend until smooth.

Killer Colada

1½ parts Vanilla-Flavored Vodka
1 part Coconut-Flavored Rum
1 part Crème de Banana
fill with Cream

GLASS: HURRICANE

Combine all ingredients in a blender with ice. Blend until smooth.

Lazy Luau

2 parts Coconut-Flavored Rum
1 part Peach Schnapps
1 part Vodka
1 part Cranberry Juice Cocktail
2 parts Orange Juice
1 part Pineapple Juice
1 can Pineapple Chunks

GLASS: OLD-FASHIONED

Combine all ingredients in a blender with ice. Blend until smooth.

Lechery

1 part Vodka
½ part Apricot Brandy
½ part Mandarine Napoleon Liqueur
2 parts Lemon Sherbet
2½ parts Orange Juice

GLASS: COUPETTE

Combine all ingredients in a blender. Blend until smooth.

Limelight

½ part Blue Curaçao
¼ part Banana Liqueur
¼ part Vodka
2 parts Orange Juice
2 parts Pineapple Juice

GLASS: COUPETTE

Combine all ingredients in a blender with ice. Blend until smooth.

Little Brother

2 parts Coffee Liqueur
1 part Vodka
1 scoop Ice Cream
splash Vanilla Extract

GLASS: OLD-FASHIONED

Combine all ingredients in a blender. Blend until smooth.

Love Birds

1½ parts Vodka
2 parts Lemon Juice
splash Dark Rum
½ part Grenadine

GLASS: OLD-FASHIONED

Combine all ingredients in a blender with ice. Blend until smooth.

Malibu Wipeout

1 part Coconut-Flavored Rum
1 part Citrus-Flavored Vodka
1 part Cranberry Juice Cocktail
1 part Pineapple Juice

GLASS: PARFAIT

Combine all ingredients in a blender with ice. Blend until smooth.

Marlin

1 part Vodka
2 parts Orange Juice
1 part Grapefruit Juice

GLASS: COLLINS

Combine all ingredients in a blender with ice. Blend until smooth.

Mud Slide (Mud Boy Recipe)

1 part Coffee Liqueur
1 part Irish Cream Liqueur
1 part Vodka
½ part Chocolate Syrup

GLASS: COUPETTE

Combine all ingredients in a blender with ice. Blend until smooth.

Neon Voodoo

1 part Vodka
1 part Apple Juice
3 parts Mountain Dew®

GLASS: COUPETTE

Combine all ingredients in a blender with ice. Blend until smooth.

Nuclear Slush

¾ part Citrus-Flavored Vodka
¾ part Bacardi® Limon Rum
½ part Melon Liqueur
½ part Blue Curaçao
fill with Sour Mix

GLASS: COUPETTE

Combine all ingredients in a blender with ice. Blend until smooth.

Orange Bonbon

1 part Crème de Cacao (White)
1 part Vodka
1 part Orange Juice
2 scoops Orange Sorbet

GLASS: WHITE WINE

Combine all ingredients in a blender. Blend until smooth.

Orange Julius

1 part Vodka
1 part Milk
1 part Orange Juice
dash Sugar
splash Vanilla Extract

GLASS: COUPETTE

Combine all ingredients in a blender with ice. Blend until smooth.

Out of Africa

2½ parts Vodka
2½ parts Safari®
1 part Pineapple Juice
1 part Grapefruit Juice
2 splashes Grenadine

GLASS: HURRICANE

Combine all ingredients in a blender with ice. Blend until smooth.

Papakea

1 part Coconut-Flavored Liqueur
1 part Vodka
fill with Pineapple Juice

GLASS: COLLINS

Combine all ingredients in a blender with ice. Blend until smooth.

Peach Tree

1½ parts Vodka
¾ part Peach Schnapps
1 part Cranberry Juice Cocktail
1 part Orange Juice

GLASS: COLLINS

Combine all ingredients in a blender with ice. Blend until smooth.

Peaches and Cream

½ part Vodka
1 part Peach Schnapps
2 parts Cream
3 Peach Slices

GLASS: RED WINE

Combine all ingredients in a blender with ice. Blend until smooth.

Plainfield Sleeper

1 part Vodka
1 part Coffee Liqueur
3 scoops Vanilla Ice Cream

GLASS: COUPETTE

Combine all ingredients in a blender. Blend until smooth.

Polyester Velvet Hammer

1 part Vodka
1 part Bourbon
1 part Raspberry Liqueur
1 scoop Ice Cream
fill with Cream

{ GLASS: HURRICANE

Combine all ingredients in a blender. Blend until smooth.

Puerto Banana

1½ parts Vodka
½ part Cream
¼ part Crème de Banana
¼ part Fresh Lime Juice
½ Banana

{ GLASS: COUPETTE

Combine all ingredients in a blender with ice. Blend until smooth.

Pure Ecstasy

1 part Coffee Liqueur
2 parts Irish Cream Liqueur
1 part Vodka

{ GLASS: COUPETTE

Combine all ingredients in a blender with ice. Blend until smooth.

Release Valve

1 part Rum
2 parts Vodka
1 part Grenadine
fill with Pineapple Juice

{ GLASS: COUPETTE

Combine all ingredients in a blender with ice. Blend until smooth.

Robin Hood

1 part Tequila Reposado
1 part Vodka
2 splashes Pisang Ambon® Liqueur
3 parts Orange Juice
2 parts Pineapple Juice

{ GLASS: COUPETTE

Combine all ingredients in a blender with ice. Blend until smooth.

Russian Coffee

1 part Vodka
1 part Coffee Liqueur
1 part Heavy Cream

{ GLASS: COUPETTE

Combine all ingredients in a blender with ice. Blend until smooth.

Russian in Exile

1 part Irish Cream Liqueur
1 part Coffee Liqueur
1 part Vodka
2 splashes Chocolate Syrup
2 scoops Vanilla Ice Cream

{ GLASS: COUPETTE

Combine all ingredients in a blender. Blend until smooth.

Sherbert Pervert

1 part Vodka
2 parts Lemon-Lime Soda
½ part Grenadine
1 scoop Orange Sorbet

{ GLASS: COUPETTE

Combine all ingredients in a blender. Blend until smooth.

Shit on a Hot Tin Roof

2 parts Vodka
3 parts Irish Cream Liqueur
1 Banana

{ GLASS: COLLINS

Combine all ingredients in a blender with ice. Blend until smooth.

Sin Industries

1½ parts Blue Curaçao
1½ parts Triple Sec
1 part Vodka
1 part Grapefruit Juice

{ GLASS: COUPETTE

Combine all ingredients in a blender with ice. Blend until smooth.

Slalom

1 part Vodka
1 part Crème de Cacao (White)
1 part Sambuca
1 part Heavy Cream

{ GLASS: COUPETTE

Combine all ingredients in a blender with ice. Blend until smooth.

Snow Way

1½ parts Vodka
1½ parts Pineapple Juice
2 scoops Vanilla Ice Cream

GLASS: WHITE WINE

Combine all ingredients in a blender. Blend until smooth.

Snowshot

3 parts Citrus-Flavored Vodka
1 scoop Lemon Sherbet
splash Lemon Juice
dash Sugar

GLASS: HIGHBALL

Combine all ingredients in a blender. Blend until smooth.

Sorbettino

1½ parts Vodka
1 part Triple Sec
½ part Cream
splash Grenadine
2 scoops Lemon Sherbet

GLASS: COUPETTE

Combine all ingredients in a blender. Blend until smooth.

Straw Hat

1 part Vodka
1 part Coconut-Flavored Rum
¼ cup Strawberries

GLASS: COUPETTE

Combine all ingredients in a blender with ice. Blend until smooth.

Strawberry Blush

2 parts Vodka
2 parts Strawberry Liqueur
1 part Strawberries
2 scoops Vanilla Ice Cream

GLASS: WHITE WINE

Combine all ingredients in a blender. Blend until smooth.

Sweet Love

²/₃ part Crème de Cacao (Dark)
²/₃ part Galliano®
²/₃ part Vanilla-Flavored Vodka
2 parts Milk
1 scoop Vanilla Ice Cream

{ GLASS: COLLINS

Combine all ingredients in a blender. Blend until smooth.

Teal Squeal

1 part Vodka
1 part Blue Curaçao
2 parts Pineapple Juice

{ GLASS: HIGHBALL

Combine all ingredients in a blender with ice. Blend until smooth.

Terrazo

1½ parts Vodka
½ part Crème de Banana
fill with Orange Juice

{ GLASS: COUPETTE

Combine all ingredients in a blender with ice. Blend until smooth.

Titanic Monkey

½ part Light Rum
½ part Vodka
1½ parts Banana Liqueur
2 parts Coconut Cream
2 parts Pineapple Juice

{ GLASS: COUPETTE

Combine all ingredients in a blender with ice. Blend until smooth.

White-Walled Tires

1½ parts Vanilla-Flavored Vodka
1½ parts Chocolate Liqueur
½ part Galliano®
1½ parts Crème de Cacao (White)
1 part Cream
splash Simple Syrup

{ GLASS: CHAMPAGNE FLUTE

Combine all ingredients in a blender with ice. Blend until smooth.

White Witch

1 part Vodka
1 part Crème de Cacao (White)
2 scoops Vanilla Ice Cream

{ GLASS: COUPETTE

Combine all ingredients in a blender. Blend until smooth.

Winter Sunshine

2 parts Rum
2 parts Vodka
fill with Orange Juice
1 Banana

{ GLASS: HURRICANE

Combine all ingredients in a blender with ice. Blend until smooth.

Yahoo

1 part Vodka
1 part Triple Sec
fill with Fruit Punch

{ GLASS: HURRICANE

Combine all ingredients in a blender with ice. Blend until smooth.

Yellow Tiger

1½ parts Vodka
2 scoops Ice Cream
2 parts Lemonade

{ GLASS: HIGHBALL

Combine all ingredients in a blender. Blend until smooth.

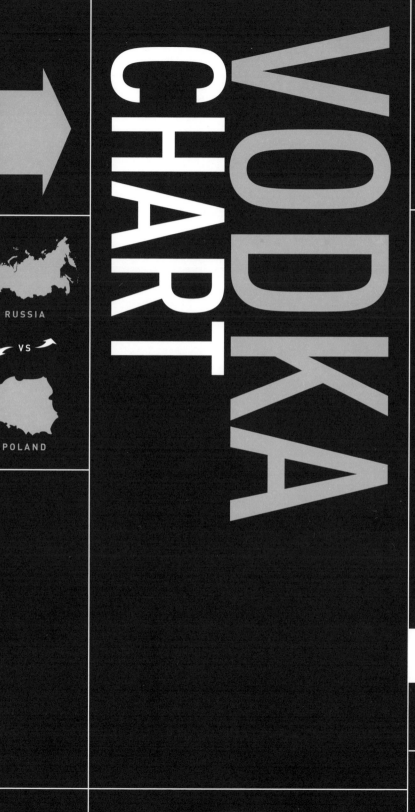

VODKA CHART

CHART

RUSSIA

vs

POLAND

CHEERS!

BRAND	SOURCE	WEB SITE
ARGENTINA		
Slitz Lemon Vodka *FLAVORS: Lemon*		
Tailov Vodka		
Vodka Nikov		
AUSTRALIA		
Boomerang Vodka	Grapes	www.boomerang-vodka.com
Bushman's Vodka	Cane	
Kirov Vodka *FLAVORS: Lemon-lime, Raspberry*		
Tasmanian Virgin Vodka	Cane	
Zhivago Vodka		
AUSTRIA		
Puriste Vodka	Grain	www.puriste.com
Vodka Monopolowa	Potatoes	www.agjab.com
BELARUS		
Akvadiv Vodka	Grain	www.akvadiv.by
Belaya Rus Lux Vodka		www.minskkristal.com/en
Charodei Vodka		
Kristall Beloj Rusi	Grain	
Kristall-100		
Leader Vodka		
Legend Vodka		
Minskaya Kristall Vodka	Grain	www.minskkristal.com/en
Old Warrior Vodka		
Vivat Vodka		
Vodka Dva Busly		
Vodka Kristall Luxe	Grain	www.minskkristal.com/en
Vodka Super Luxe		
Vodka Vodoley	Grain	www.minskkristal.com/en

BRAND	SOURCE	WEB SITE
BELGIUM		
Black Knight Vodka		
Diamond Standard Vodka	Rye	www.diamondstandardvodka.com
Hertekamp Vodka	Corn	www.bruggeman.waxinteractive6.com
Russkaya Classic Vodka		
Skorppio Vodka	Grain	www.skorppio-vodka.com
Van Hoo Vodka		
Apollo White Nights Vodka		
BELIZE		
Cane Juice Caribbean Vodka	Grain	
BRAZIL		
Amazon Rainforest Vodka	Sugar Cane	
Amazon Vodka		
Kamarada Vodka		
Keglevich Vodka	Grain	
Orloff Ice Vodka	Cereal	
Orloff Vodka	Cereal	
BULGARIA		
Balkan 176º Vodka	Grain	
Doctor's Citron Vodka		
Doctor's Silver Vodka		
Doctor's Vodka		
Peter Marras Vodka	Grain	
CANADA		
Alberta Premium Vodka		
Arctica Diluted Vodka		
Arctica Vodka		
Aurora Vodka		
Banff Ice Vodka	Grain	

BRAND	SOURCE	WEB SITE
Borealis Iceberg Vodka		
Iceberg Vodka	Corn	www.icebergvodka.net
Inferno Pepper Vodka FLAVORS: Chili peppers		
Kreskova Vodka		
Mad Monk Vodka		
Nicholas Vodka		
Pearl Vodka	Wheat	www.pearlvodka.info
Polar Ice Vodka FLAVORS: Arctic berry, Maple	Grain	
Potter's International Vodka		
Prince Igor Vodka	Grain	www.princeigorvodka.com
Seagram's Imported Vodka		
Silent Sam Vodka		
Silhouette Vodka	Grain	
CHINA		
Great Wall Vodka	Grain	
Tianhe Vodka	Corn	
Tsingtao Vodka	Grain	
COLOMBIA		
Montesskaya Vodka	Corn	
CZECH REPUBLIC		
Dvorak Vodka		
Kick Horse Vodka		
Kord Vodka	Beets	
Symphony Vodka		www.symphonyvodka.com
V Vodka	Beets	
DENMARK		
Celsius Vodka		
Danzka Vodka FLAVORS: Citrus, Cranberry, Currant, Grapefruit	Wheat	www.danzka.com

BRAND	SOURCE	WEB SITE
Denaka Vodka		
Fris Vodka Apple, Lime	Grain	www.frisvodka.com
EL SALVADOR		
Espíritu de Cana Vodka	Cane	
ESTONIA		
Asunik Vodka		www.remedia.ee
Black SEA Vodka		www.blacksea-vodka.com
Buxhoeveden Black Label Vodka	Grain	
Buxhoeveden Vodka	Grain	
Eesti Viin Vodka	Grain	
Crystal Vodka *FLAVORS: Black pepper,* *Chili pepper, Lime-lemon,* *Strawberry*		www.remedia.ee
Monopol Vodka	Grain	www.remedia.ee
Mor Vodka	Potatoes	
Platinum Lemon Vodka		
Platinum Vodka		
Poolik Vodka		
Reval Classic Vodka		
Stön Vodka *FLAVORS: Berry, Citron*	Wheat	www.remedia.ee
Tall Blond Estonian Vodka		
Tartu Vodka		
TURI Vodka	Rye	
Viru Vodka	Grain	
Viru Valge Vodka	Grain	
Volganaya Vodka	Grain	
FINLAND		
Dracula Vodka	Grain	www.scandicdistilleries.ro

BRAND	SOURCE	WEB SITE
Finlandia Vodka *FLAVORS: Cranberry, Lime, Grapefruit, Mango, Wild berries*	Wheat	www.finlandia.com
Formula Warm Up		www.zandora.fi
Koskenkorva Vodka	Grain	
Mikuloff Black Label	Grain	www.scandicdistilleries.ro
Mikuloff Blue Label	Grain	www.scandicdistilleries.ro
Scandic Blue	Grain	www.scandicdistilleries.ro
Scandic Supreme	Grain	www.scandicdistilleries.ro
FRANCE		
Alba Lupa Vodka	Grain	
Alps Vodka		
Boris Yeltsin Vodka		
Ciroc Snap Frost Vodka	Grapes	www.cirocvodka.com
Citadelle Vodka *FLAVORS: Apple, Raspberry*	Wheat	www.citadellevodka.com
Grey Goose Vodka *FLAVORS: Citron, Orange, Vanilla*	Wheat	www.greygoosevodka.com
Kremlinskaia Vodka		
Maxim's Vodka	Wheat	www.maxims-de-paris.com
NUAGE Vodka	Cereal	www.nuage-vodka.com
GEORGIA		
Crystal Ushba Vodka	Grain	
Gomi Vodka *FLAVORS: Honey, Lemon, Mint, Pepper, Tarragon*	Wheat, Grapes	www.gomi.ge
Kalakuri Black Label Vodka	Wheat	
Kalakuri White Label Vodka	Wheat	
Rustavi Vodka		
Shevardnadze Vodka		

BRAND	SOURCE	WEB SITE
GERMANY		
Arazoff Vodka		www.nuga.de
Baltic Potato Vodka	Potatoes	
Beethoven's Choice Vodka		
Beethoven's Fifth Vodka		
Beuing's No 40 Vodka		
Boris Jelzin Vodka		www.nuga.de
Caviar 5-Years Wodka		www.caviarwodka.com
Caviar Wodka		www.caviarwodka.com
Debroff Vodka		www.nuga.de
F Vodka	Wheat	
Kleiner Feigling Vodka		www.feigling.com
Gorbatschow Wodka		www.wodka.de
Karl Marx Vodka		
Nugaroff Vodka		www.nuga.de
Petrikov Vodka		www.nuga.de
Petrov Vodka *FLAVORS: Currant, Lemon*		www.nuga.de
Puschkin Black Sun Vodka		www.vodka.de
Puschkin Red Vodka		www.vodka.de
Puschkin Time Warp Vodka		www.vodka.de
Puschkin Vodka		www.vodka.de
Rasputin Vodka		
Rebroff Vodka		www.nuga.de
Rimanto Potato Vodka	Potatoes	
Wodka Gorroff		www.nuga.de
Wodka Na Sdorowje		www.nuga.de
GREECE		
Serkova Vodka		

BRAND	SOURCE	WEB SITE
HOLLAND		
Bong Vodka	Grain	www.bongvodka.com
HUNGARY		
Hungarian Diamond Vodka	Grain	
Kecskemeti Paprika Vodka		
Siberian Tiger Blood Vodka		
Vasa Vodka	Grain	
ICELAND		
Elduris Icelandic Vodka	Grain	
Icy Vodka	Grain	
Polstar Vodka *FLAVORS: Citron, Cranberry, Cucumber, Pepper*	Grain	
Reyka	Wheat	www.reykavodka.com
INDIA		
Alexandrov Vodka	Grain	www.southseasdistilleries.com
Alexei Vodka	Grain	www.southseasdistilleries.com
Amber Distilleries Limited Vodka	Grain	www.amberliquors.com
Be High Vodka	Grain	www.pinecask.com
Contessa Vodka		www.radicokhaitan.com
Karmazov Vodka		
Red Riband Premium Vodka		
White Magic Crystal Vodka		
White Magic Lemone Vodka		
White Magic Pepperone Vodka		
White Magic Tangerine Vodka		
White Mischief Vodka		www.unitedspirits.in
IRELAND		
Boru Trinity Vodka		www.boruirishvodka.com
Boru Vodka *FLAVORS: Citrus, Orange*		www.boruirishvodka.com

BRAND	SOURCE	WEB SITE
Celtic Irish Vodka	Grain	
Huzzar Vodka	Grain	www.irishdistillers.ie
Pat's Poteen Vodka	Grain	
ISRAEL		
Arkan Vodka *FLAVORS: Blueberry, Lemon, Melon, Orange, Peach, Pineapple, Strawberry*		www.mavua.com/barkan/arkan.htm
Bielaya Golavka Askalon B.G. Vodka	Grain	
Carmel Vodka	Molasses	
ITALY		
Keglevich Vodka		
Russian Diplomat Vodka		
Vodka Stopka		
Keglevich Vodka *FLAVORS: Apple, Berry mix, Blueberry, Green tea, Lemon, Licorice, Mango and maracuja, Melon, Mint, Peach, Strawberry, Strawberry and cream*	Grain	www.stock-spa.it/en/home
Mezzaluna Vodka	Grain	
Tajga Vodka *FLAVORS: Lemon, Licorice, Melon, Peach, Strawberry*		
Vodka Suhoi		
JAMAICA		
Kedem Vodka	Cane	
Ostrov Vodka		
JAPAN		
Suntory Vodka		
JORDAN		
Adamoff Vodka *FLAVORS: Citron, Currant, Chili*		

BRAND	SOURCE	WEB SITE
Penguin Cristall Vodka	Grain	
White Tiger Vodka		
KAZAKHSTAN		
Adil Premium Vodka		
Adil Vodka		
Almaty Aragy Vodka		
Altayskaya Vodka	Rye	
Astana Vodka		
Astanalyk Vodka		
Asyl-Su Vodka		
Aydabol Vodka		
Berkut Vodka	Grain	
Cedar Vodka		
Crag Vodka		
Golden Domes Vodka		
Kazakhstan Vodka	Grain	
Sunkar Vodka		
Surprise Vodka		
Taiga Vodka		
Taraz Vodka FLAVORS: Citron, Currant	Grain	
LATVIA		
Czarskaya Kristal Vodka	Grain	
Golden Vodka		
Kristal Dzidrais Vodka		
Latvijas Dzidrais Vodka		
Monopols Vodka		
Rigalia Baltic Vodka		
Rigas Originalais Vodka		
White Diamond Vodka	Wheat, Rye	www.vodkabrands.com

BRAND	SOURCE	WEB SITE
Zelta Vodka	Grain	
LITHUANIA		
Baalta Vodka		
Lithuanian Original Vodka	Grain	
Lithuanian Vodka		www.stawskidistributing.com
Stumbro Kosher Vodka		
LUXEMBOURG		
Black Death Vodka	Beets	
MEXICO		
Oso Negro Vodka *FLAVORS: Lemon*		
Villa Lobos Platinum Vodka (Without Worm)	Grain	
Villa Lobos Vodka (With Worm)	Grain	
Vodka Petrova	Grain	licoresveracruz.com/ing_vodka_petrova.htm
MOLDOVA		
Bogatyrskaya Vodka	Wheat	
Chinggis Khan Vodka		
Kvint de Lux Vodka	Wheat	www.eng.kvint.biz/catalog/vodka
Kvint Osobaya Vodka	Wheat	www.eng.kvint.biz/catalog/vodka
Moskovskaya Vodka (Moldova)	Wheat	www.moskovskaya.de
Pokrovskaya Vodka	Wheat	
Russkaya Vodka (Moldova)	Wheat	
Slavyanskaya Vodka	Rye	
Stolichnaya Vodka (Moldova)	Wheat	
Triumph Vodka	Wheat	
Zadorinka Vodka	Grain	www.eng.kvint.biz
MONGOLIA		
Genghis Khan Vodka		

BRAND	SOURCE	WEB SITE
NETHERLANDS		
Amsterdam Republic Vodka	Grain	www.amsterdamrepublic.com
Bolskaya Vodka		
Boomsma Vodka		
Cardinal Ultimate Vodka	Beets	
Cosmos Vodka		
Effen Black Cherry Vodka		
Effen Vodka *FLAVORS: Black cherry, Raspberry*	Wheat	
Ketel One Citroen Vodka	Grain	
Ketel One Vodka *FLAVORS: Citron*	Wheat	www.ketelone.com
Olifant Citron Vodka *FLAVORS: Citron*	Grain	
Olifant Vodka	Grain	
Ursus Black Currant Vodka	Grain	
Ursus Classic Vodka *FLAVORS: Black currant*	Grain	
Ursus Roter Vodka	Grain	
Van Gogh Vodka *FLAVORS: Apple, Banana,* *Black cherry, Blueberry,* *Chocolate, Citron, Coconut,* *Espresso, Mango, Melon, Mojito,* *Orange, Pineapple, Pomegranate,* *Raspberry, Vanilla*	Grain	www.vangoghvodka.com
VOX Vodka *FLAVORS: Apple, Raspberry*	Grain	www.voxvodka.com
NEW ZEALAND		
42 Below Vodka *FLAVORS: Feijoa (not available in* *USA), Honey, Kiwi, Passionfruit* *(not available in USA)*		www.42below.com
Roaring Forties Vodka		www.roaringforties.co.nz

BRAND	SOURCE	WEB SITE
NORWAY		
Christiania Vodka		www.christianiavodka.com
Hammer Lime Vodka		
Hammer Vodka Lime		
Vikingfjord Vodka	Potatoes	www.vikingfjord.com
POLAND		
Abstynent Wodka	Grain	
Alchemia Polish Vodka Chocolate, Ginger, Wild cherry	Grain	www.alchemiavodka.com
Altvater Vodka	Grain	
Balsam Zoladkowy		
Baltic Vodka	Potatoes	
Belvedere Vodka	Rye	www.belvedere-vodka.com
Biata Zimna Nord Vodka		
Black Death Vodka		
Chopin Vodka	Potatoes	www.chopinvodka.com.pl
Columbus Vodka	Grain	www.columbusvodka.com
Gvori Vodka	Rye	
Jazz Vodka	Grain	www.wodki.gda.pl
Kozi Vodka	Wheat	www.kozivodka.com
Miodowka Vodka		
Pan Tadeusz Vodka		
Potocki Vodka	Rye	www.potockivodka.com
Starka Vodka	Grain	www.polmos.szczecin.pl
Wisniowka Vodka		
Wodka Zoladkowa Gorzka		
Zubrovka Vodka	Potatoes	
PORTUGAL		
Prince of Shuya Vodka		

BRAND	SOURCE	WEB SITE
ROMANIA		
Blue Sea Vodka		
RUSSIA		
Altai Vodka	Wheat	www.altaivodka.com
Cristall Vodka *FLAVORS: Lemon twist*		www.cristall.com
Imperia Vodka	Wheat	www.russianstandardvodka.com
Jewel of Russia Vodka *FLAVORS: Berry, Wild bilberry*	Grain	www.jewelofrussia.com
Korski Vodka		
Kremlyovskaya Chocolate Vodka	Grain	
Kubanskaya Vodka	Grain	
Moskovskaya Osobaya	Grain	
Priviet Vodka	Grain	
Red Army Vodka	Grain	www.redarmyvodka.com
Russian Standard	Wheat	www.russianstandardvodka.com
Sputnik	Grain	www.sputnikvodka.com
Star of Russia Vodka	Grain	
Stolichnaya Vodka *FLAVORS: Blackberry, Blueberry, Citrus, Cranberry, Orange, Peach, Raspberry, Strawberry, Vanilla*	Grain	www.stoli.com
Stolichnaya Elit Vodka	Grain	www.stoli.com
Tambovsky Volk Vodka		
White Gold		
Youri Dolgoruki Vodka		
Zolotaya Khokhloma Vodka		
Zyr Vodka	Grain	www.zyrvodka.com
SLOVAKIA		
Double Cross Vodka	Wheat	www.doublecrossvodka.com
Nicolaus Vodka *FLAVORS: Cherry, Citron, Peach, Vanilla sugar*		www.goodvibrations.sk

BRAND	SOURCE	WEB SITE
SOUTH AFRICA		
Cape to Rio Vodka	Cane	
Savanna Royal Cane Vodka	Cane	
SPAIN		
Katutxi Vodka		
Zarkiew Vodka	Cereal	
Absolut Vodka *FLAVORS: Citron, Currant, Mandarin orange, Mango, Peach, Pear, Pepper, Raspberry, Ruby red grapefruit, Vanilla*	Grain	www.absolut.com
SWEDEN		
Absolut 100 Vodka	Grain	www.absolut.com
Blood Horn Vodka *FLAVORS: Lemon-lime, Raspberry*		
Brannvin Vodka		
Cariel Vanilla Vodka	Wheat	
Level Vodka	Wheat	www.levelvodka.com
Precis Vodka		www.precisvodka.com
Stockholm Kristall Vodka	Grain	
Sundsvall Vodka		
Svensk Vodka *FLAVORS: Apple, Lemon, Wild strawberry, Vanilla*		www.svenskvodka.se
Svensk Vodka Smultron		www.svenskvodka.se
Thor's Hammer Vodka	Wheat	www.thorshammervodka.com
SWITZERLAND		
Xellent Vodka	Rye	www.xellent.com
TRINIDAD AND TOBAGO		
Grandmaster Vodka	Molasses	
Molotoff Vodka		

BRAND	SOURCE	WEB SITE
UKRAINE		
Admiral Vodka (Ukraine)	Grain	
Arktika Vodka		
Boyar Vodka	Grain	
First Guild Vodka and Pepper	Grain	
Goldenbarr Chocolate Vodka		
Hetman Vodka	Wheat	
Khortytsa Vodka *FLAVORS: Blueberry, Caviar, Cherry, Chocolate mint, Lemon, Pepper*	Wheat	www.khortytsa.com
Kiev Star Vodka	Grain	
Kievskaya Rus Vodka		
Kievskaya Ubileynaya Vodka		
Kozak Vodka	Grain	
Lvivska Vodka	Wheat	
Nemiroff Vodka	Wheat	
Nemirovskaya Vodka	Grain	
Soomskaya Horobynova Vodka	Grain	
Taras Elegia Vodka	Wheat	
Zarskaya Datscha		
UNITED KINDGOM		
1860 Imperial Vodka		
Armadale Vodka		
Blackwood Shetland Vodka		
Blavod Vodka		
Borzoi Vodka		
Brecon Premium Vodka		

BRAND	SOURCE	WEB SITE
Burnett's Vodka *FLAVORS: Blueberry, Cherry, Citrus, Coconut, Cranberry, Espresso, Grape, Lime, Mango, Orange, Peach, Pink grapefruit, Pomegranate, Raspberry, Sour apple, Strawberry, Sweet tea, Vanilla, Watermelon*		www.burnettsvodka.com
Burrough's English Vodka	Grain	
Co-Op Citrus Vodka		
Cristalnaya Vodka		www.cristalnaya.com
KGB Vodka		
King Robert II Vodka	Grain	www.ianmacleod.com
Kinsey Dry Vodka		www.inverhouse.com
Moskova Vodka		
Red Square Vodka Apple, Wild berry		www.halewood-int.com
Three Olives Vodka *FLAVORS: Berry, Cherry, Chocolate, Citrus, Espresso, Grape, Mango, Orange, Raspberry,Pomegranate, Root beer, Vanilla, Watermelon*		www.threeolives.com
Tsaravitch Vodka		
Valt Vodka	Barley	www.valtvodka.com
Vampyre Vodka		
Virgin Vodka	Grain	
Tanqueray Sterling Vodka	Grain	www.tanqueray.com
UNITED STATES		
1.0.1 (One-O-One) Ultra Premium Vodka	Grain	www.101vodka.com
Ambur Starka Vodka		
American Corn Tradition (ACT) Vodka	Corn	
Barton Vodka	Grain	www.bartonbrands.com/bartonvodka.html

BRAND	SOURCE	WEB SITE
Black Diamond Vodka		
Blue Ice Vodka	Potatoes	www.blueicevodka.com
Blue Ice Organic Wheat Vodka	Wheat	www.blueicevodka.com
Core Vodka	Apples	www.harvestspirits.com
Death's Door Vodka	Wheat	www.deathsdoorspirits.com
Five O'Clock Vodka		
Frost Vodka		
Hangar 1 Vodka FLAVORS: Citron, Kaffir lime, Mandarin orange, Pear, Raspberry		www.hangarone.com
Hawkeye Vodka		
Karkov Pepper Vodka		
Kimnoff Vodka		
LiV Vodka	Potatoes	www.lispirits.com
Mustang Vodka	Grain	www.spirits24h.com
Prairie Vodka	Corn	www.prairievodka.com
Prestige Vodka		
Smirnoff Vodka FLAVORS: Apple, Black cherry, Blueberry, Citrus, Cranberry, Lime, Orange, Raspberry, Strawberry Vanilla, Watermelon	Grain	www.smirnoff.com
Stalingrad Silver Label Vodka		
Taaka Supreme Vodka		
Teton Glacier Potato Vodka	Potatoes	www.glaciervodka.com
Tito's Handmade Vodka	Corn	www.titos-vodka.com
UV Blue Vodka FLAVORS: Apple, Cherry, Citrus, Grape, Lemonade, Raspberry, Vanilla	Corn	www.uvvodka.com
UZBEKISTAN		
Tashkent Vodka		

GENERAL INDEX

Index of Drink Recipes